# technical analysis 2011/2

# Formu

D1581489

This was a season in which many new technical features emerged, but more than anything else it marked the return of Pirelli to Formula 1, the great protagonist in determining the outcome of the world championship. As a result of the Italian tyre manufacturer's contribution, the spectacle of the sport was given a quick and extremely effective boost and often, thanks especially to the tyres, the cards were shuffled in respect of the real technical values in the field.

They benefitted a show; otherwise the already marked domination of Red Bull would have been almost total, such was the supremacy of the RB7. The success of the reigning world championship team was still incredible with 12 victories, 11 of them by Sebastian Vettel and one by Mark Webber, with no fewer than 18 pole positions scored by the young German out of a possible 19, shattering Nigel Mansell's record of 14 poles in the 1992 season. The only pole Red Bull didn't get went to Lewis Hamilton at the GP of Korea, a result that stopped the world champion's designer Adrian Newey and his team from making a clean sweep. The lead over McLaren, who were second in the constructors' championship was, once again, abyssal: 153 points, despite the Woking team's six victories, three for each driver. There is absolutely no doubt that the RB7 is the best car to have competed in Formula 1 in the recent history of the sport, being not only competitive but also extremely reliable.

"With Bridgestone tyres we would have won at least another two races", said a smiling Newey with an underlying element of irony. "Vettel had often won while maintaining the lowest possible racing rhythm to contain the degradation of the tyres". It is no coincidence that the two events the Red Bull magician was referring to were Canada and Hungary, won by Jenson Button, the driver who best understood how to administer his tyres during a race, helped by McLaren as the team seemed to have the most 'gentle' car in its treatment of the Pirellis.

Despite a ban on refuelling during the race, pit stops for tyre changes during the season went up to 1,111, of which 22 were drive through penalties and four stop-and-goes'. Spectacle was also ensured by the introduction of the adjustable rear wing flap (DRS) in place of the one on the front wing, which had not produced positive results during the 2009 season as it increased excessively the chance of overtaking – more than double compared to 2010 – even if the values on the track seemed to have changed too radically in some cases. The decisions made in that area were interesting, especially at the start of the season, with various ratios between the main wing chord and that of the flap and the management systems, and an obvious tendency to conform to that which seemed the best compromise, a reduced chord flap to give a better equilibrium during the race.

### NEW SOLUTIONS
The 2011 was yet another extremely interesting season from the technical point of view, after the avalanche of new features that appeared in 2010. Renault distinguished itself during the pre-championship period and stupefied everyone by making the exhausts exit from the initial part of the sidepods to energise the air flow under the car and feed the diffuser, increasing its efficiency. It was a major advance in the area of exhaust blow, a sector in which the French constructor was also prominent way back in 1983.

The Renault RE30 entered for the Monaco GP boasted the new technique of exhausts that blew directly into the diffuser's side channels. At the time, there were protests, requests to ban this new Jean Claude Migeot development, but then, with the approval of the Federation, all teams adopted that technology, which became a general tendency of turbo-charged cars.

Lotus Renault also moved in the same direction with bold new elements seen in pre-season testing but, after a blast of glory in the early races, the feature showed itself to be severely limiting, so much so that the team carried out a test at the GP of Germany with traditional exhausts fitted to Nick Heidfeld's car. Still, Lotus Renault should be applauded for having tried to take a completely new path.

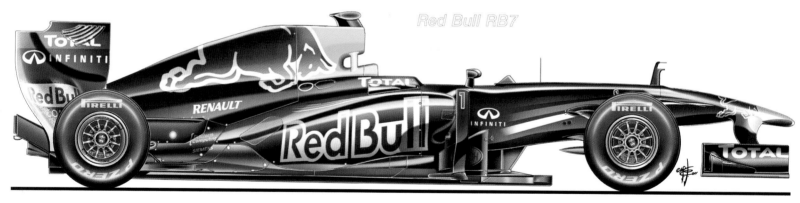

Red Bull RB7

McLaren MP4-26

Williams' choice was a courageous one, with a miniaturised gearbox and inclined drive shafts that nobody had previously dared to use. It was a solution that clashed with the considerable bulk of the Cosworth engine. Result: the worst season in the team's history.

### RETURN TO THE PAST
Some of the new developments that stupefied at the start of the season were nothing more than a modern version of those adopted in the past. Never had so much of this been going on as during the 2011 season. To tell the truth, there was a preview of this two years earlier, when that magician Adrian Newey dusted off the pull rod suspension for the RB5's rear end, a layout which had been abandoned over 20 years ago – and one that was used by eight of the 12 teams in the world championship in 2011.
Newey did it again last year and this time he brought back the lateral blow of the exhausts, which appeared so demurely in 1985 on the Renault RE50.
Exhaust blow became the main theme of 2011. Because of the British magician, teams went from lateral blow to one directed into the side channels. A technique which, when combined with the great work carried out by Renault on engine management to ensure blow even under deceleration, greatly com-

pensated for the loss of downforce caused by the abolition of double diffusers.
The two biggest surprises that can be seen by looking at the car from a distance came from McLaren and Toro Rosso, who fielded cars that were very different from the others. The former presented an MP4-26 with 'pods that were very high at the sides and low in the centre, which very much recalled the Benetton B185 and the Ferrari F310. It was a design that enabled the generation of a good passage of air in the upper part of the side-pods to make the beam wing work better, which would have had to act in unison with a new solution for the exhausts called Octopus. But McLaren's new features in the exhaust area transformed the period of the three pre-season test sessions into a sort of nightmare for the group directed by Paddy Lowe.
The other surprise was Toro Rosso with its double floor reinterpreted in a modern way by Giorgio Ascanelli, very much like the disastrous Ferrari F92 project of 1992.
The car from Faenza, Italy, brandished side-pods raised in such a way as to create a second venturi channel with an energised air flow to make the diffuser work better. A technique that was successful on the track despite the inevitable raising of the centre of gravity associated with the more complex installation of the radiators and all their accessories.

### CONSERVATIVE FERRARI
It is difficult to imagine a Formula 1 season without Ferrari among the top liners.
But the 2011 world championship experienced the harsh reality determined by an F150 Italia that was too conservative, so much so as to not worry their great rivals Red Bull and McLaren. Correlation problems between the wind tunnel and the data gathered at the track led to also using the Toyota wind tunnel, but in the end the disappointing result of the GP of Spain, with Fernando Alonso starting so well but finishing fifth and lapped, meant Aldo Costa eventually left and Pat Fry, ex-McLaren, became the new technical head of the Maranello team. But there was no turnaround in the development of the car, as had been the case in 2010.
That year, the F10 was not very competitive in the beginning, but it got better race by race to become Red Bull's main rival.
The F150 seemed an obsolete car from the outset as far as design goes, almost as if it was taken for granted that it was impossible to recover the downforce lost after the double diffusers were been banned. It was practically the only car – forgetting the three minors – not to move to the pull rod rear suspension layout, dragging Sauber down with it as Maranello was committed not only to provide Ferrari engines but also the gearbox designed

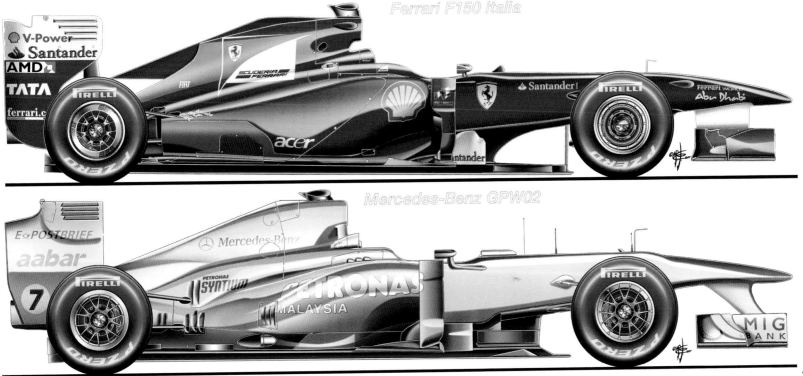

Ferrari F150 italia

Mercedes-Benz GPW02

for the push rod layout. The victory at Silverstone was due to a series of favourable circumstances: the best adaptation to the partial ban of hot blow under deceleration, the opportunity of bringing the tyres to optimum operating temperatures because the circuit has such long curves, the new rear suspension and the mistakes made when changing tyres on the Red Bull and McLaren.

## THE DEFEAT OF MERCEDES-BENZ

Coming fourth almost 200 points behind third placed Ferrari, but especially never once getting onto the podium were difficult results to swallow after the Stuttgart company's second negative season. The GPW02 project was much penalised by the decision to adopt a shorter wheelbase, the shortest of all the cars competing for the 2011 F1 world championship. The basis for that decision was the opportunity of having a diffuser zone that lost no efficiency but, evidently, the great contribution of the exhausts' direct blow had not been taken into account, which allowed the perfect control of a much more vast, and therefore more 'powerful', surface. Then the choice of a shorter fuel tank and the installation of the radiators on two levels had their negative effect on the height of the centre of gravity, especially penalising the car when it had full fuel tanks. The integration of the KERS and DRS was effective, but the most positive note struck by the team was by testing a front F-Duct in Japan, obviously for the 2012 season, which was strangely underestimated by the opposition. The expansion of the technical staff is worth noting, with the arrival of Bob Bell (ex-Renault), Geoff Willis

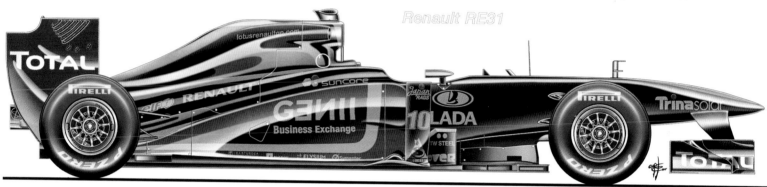

Renault RE31

Force India VJM04

Sauber C30

Toro Rosso STR06

(ex-HRT and Red Bull) and Aldo Costa (ex-Ferrari).

## FORCE INDIA AND SAUBER
While Force India took a bow for having produced a 'good' car partially due to the supply of a complete package – engine, gearbox and KERS identical to its 'cousin' McLaren, with an almost constant development taking place during the season –Sauber fell off during the course of the season. The cause was its limited budget and the decision not to adopt exhaust blow into the diffuser. The team then

suffered the cancellation of the 10 points – perhaps excessive – won by the two drivers at the opening race in Australia for the irregularity of its beam wing flap, which was not that determinate, an episode illustrated at the end of the new regulations chapter.

## THE MINOR TEAMS
As expected, Lotus was the best of the minor teams in their 'separate' championship. It was the only ones with pull rod rear suspension and to have conducted a certain amount of development during the season,

with the help of the Casumaro wind tunnel. HRT had the satisfaction of finishing ahead of Virgin, the last team in the championship, despite its extremely limited budget.
Of course, none of these teams had KERS.
This edition of the book has also taken advantage of contributions from Franco Nugnes for the engine chapter, engineer Giancarlo Bruno for suspensions and tyres. And a special thankyou goes to engineer Mauro Piccoli of Brembo for the data he provided for the brakes chapter.

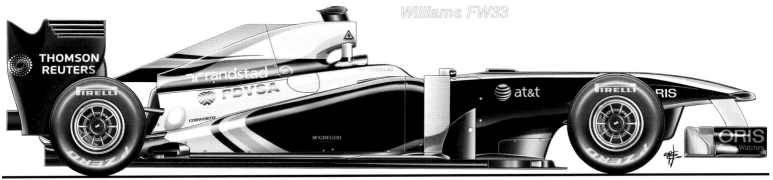

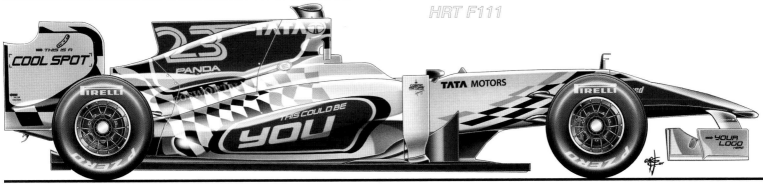

The chassis graphics have, by now, assumed a historic interest in establishing which won most in the various races. With parc fermé coming into effect between qualifying and the races in 2008 and the abolition of the spare car, there are now only the two racecars in the pits plus a completely naked spare chassis, which is kept in a case for use in extreme necessity. Remember that even if an accident happens during the first few laps of practice in the morning, the teams are not allowed to assemble the monocoque for the afternoon session, but only for the following day or race, the latter if such a thing happened on the Saturday.

## RED BULL

In 2010, Red Bull built no fewer than seven chassis, followed by Ferrari with six, Mercedes-Benz and Renault with five each and almost all the rest, surprisingly including McLaren, then Williams, Sauber, Force India, Toro Rosso and Lotus with four. In 2011, the numbers dropped to six for Red Bull – their last was never raced – and then Ferrari with five. The remainder all built four chassis each. The only exception was HRT with none, because they adapted their 2010 unit to the new regulations.

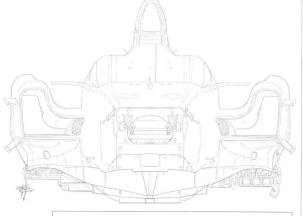

| Chassis F10 | Km completed GP |
|---|---|
| 287 | 0 |
| 288 | 8.083,4 |
| 289 | 4.187,6 |
| 290 | 9.617,9 |
| 291 | 5.950,4 |

# RED BULL • *RB7* • N° 1-2

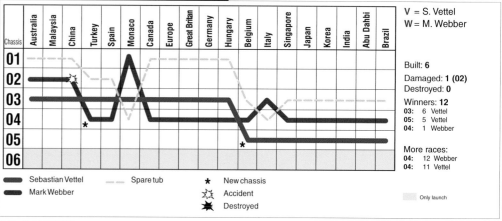

# McLAREN • *MP4-26* • N° 3-4

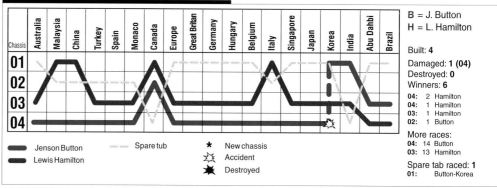

# FERRARI • *F 150 ITALIA* • N° 5-6

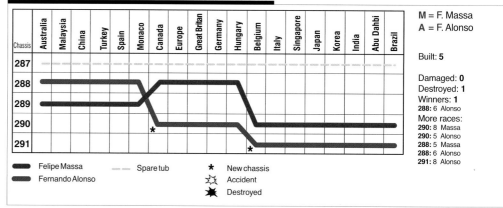

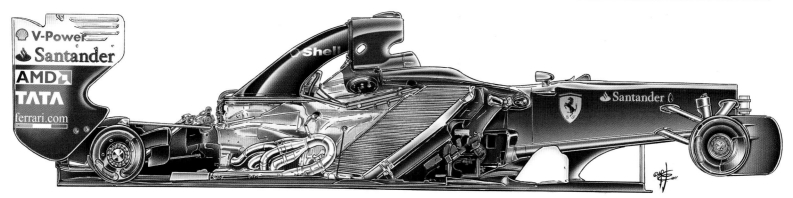

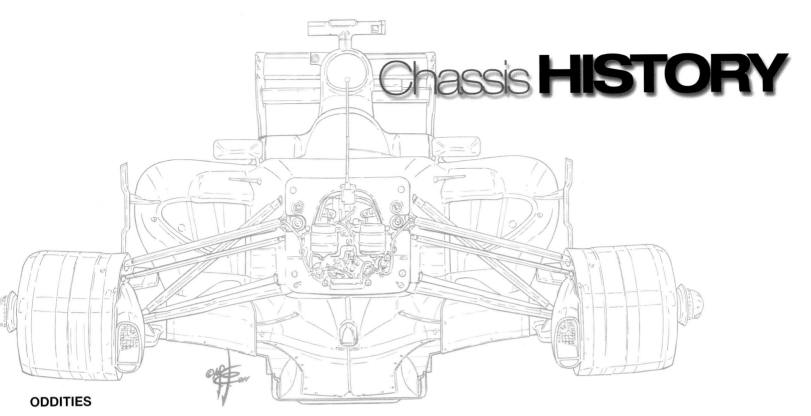

## ODDITIES

### CHASSIS DESTROYED AND INVOLVED IN ACCIDENTS

None of the top 3 teams' chassis were destroyed. Renault lost two, their 02 in a pre-championship crash test and their 03 to Petrov in Monaco; Senna's 04 was damaged in Budapest and again in a post-Abu Dahbi test. No other chassis was destroyed but there was a series of repair jobs for Sauber with two damaged by Perez – 01 in Malaysia and 03 in Monaco – and two by Kobayashi, 04 in both Canada and Singapore. Webber damaged chassis number 2 in China.
Only once did a team assemble its spare chassis for a race and that was McLaren, which replaced Button's 04 in Korea with 01 due to a problem with an engine fixing bolt.

### WINNING CHASSIS

Only three teams won at least one Grand Prix in 2011. Red Bull snapped up no fewer than 13 victories – 11 by Vettel and one by Webber – followed by McLaren with six – three for each of their drivers – and Ferrari with one win by Alonso. The award for the most successful chassis of 2011 goes, obviously, to Red Bull and its number 03 that won six GPs driven by Vettel, followed by 05 driven to five victories by the German.
Then follow three McLaren chassis: 04 took two wins, one driven by Hamilton and the other by Button, then 01 and 03 with Hamilton and 02 with Button. A single victory was achieved by Ferrari's chassis number 290 driven by Alonso and Red Bull's 04 with Webber at the wheel.

### WHEELBASES

Like the 2010 season, the longest car was the McLaren at 3,481 mm, followed in descending order by Force India (3,411 mm), a team that uses the same engine and, in particular, the same gearbox. Then come Red Bull (3,398 mm), Sauber (3,363 mm), Ferrari and Williams at 3,358, Toro Rosso (3,337 mm), Renault (3,320 mm) and Lotus (3,318 mm). The shortest of all was the Mercedes-Benz again, at just 3,208 mm as in 2010, a huge 273 mm less than the McLaren.

| | laps completed % | finishes | technical failures | accidents |
|---|---|---|---|---|
| Red Bull | 2163 (95,5%) | 36 | 1 puncture | 1 |
| Force India | 2163 (95,5%) | 34 | 2 (1)hydraulics - (1)wheel loose | 2 |
| Ferrari | 2148 (94,8%) | 34 | 2 gearbox - suspensions | 2 |
| McLaren | 2108 (93%) | 33 | 3 gearbox - wheel loose - hydraulics | 4 |
| Renault | 2025 (89,4%) | 31 | 1 exhaust | 6 |
| Sauber | 1975 (87,2%)* | 30 | 6 (3) gearbox - (1) electrics - oil leak - suspensions | 0 |
| Toro Rosso | 1957 (86,4%) | 29 | 5 (2) wheel loose - (1) engine - puncture - hydraulics | 4 |
| Williams | 1923 (84,9%) | 28 | 7 (2) gearbox - engine - (1) drive shaft - oil leak - electrics | 3 |
| Lotus | 1919 (84,7%) | 29 | 7 (2) gearbox - water leak - (1) oil leak - drive shaft - clutch | 1 |
| Mercedes | 1903 (84%) | 31 | 4 radiator - undertray - gearbox - fire in airbox | 3 |
| HRT | 1844 (81,4%) | 28 | 7 (2) alternator - (1) gearbox - electrics - rear wing - over heat - vibrations | 1 |
| Virgin | 1821 (80,4%) | 29 | 7 (2) gearbox - (1) suspension - electrics - upright - brakes - wheel loose | 2 |

*Disqualified in Australia*

The most reliable team was Red Bull, whose cars covered an incredible 95.52% of the total number of laps that comprised the 2011 world championship, with a surprising Force India boasting the same high percentage. Next came Ferrari with 94.8%, McLaren on 93%, Renault at 89.4% and Williams with 84.9%. The least reliable was HRT at 81.4%.

| | 5-6 RED BULL | 1-2 McLAREN | 7-8 FERRARI | 3-4 MERCEDES | 11-12 RENAULT |
|---|---|---|---|---|---|
| | RB7 | MP4-25 | F10 | MGP W01 | RE30 |
| **CAR** Designers | Adrian Newey<br>Rob Marshall | Jonatan Neale<br>Paddy Lowe<br>Neil Oatley | Aldo Costa*1 - Pat Fry<br>Nikolas Tombazis<br>Luca Marmorini | Ross Brawn<br>Bob Bell | James Allison |
| Race engineers | Guillaume Rocquelin (1)<br>Ciaron Pilbeam (2) | Dave Robson (3)<br>Andy Latham (4) | Andrea Stella (5)<br>Rob Smedley (6) | Jock Clear (7)<br>Mark Slade (8) | Simon Rennie (9)<br>Ayaco Komastsu (10) |
| Chief mechanic | Kenny Handkammer | Pete Vale | Francesco Ugozzoni | Mattew Deane | Gavin Hudson |
| **CHASSIS** Wheelbase | 3398 mm* | 3481 mm* | 3358 mm* | 3208 mm* | 3320 mm* |
| Front track | 1440 mm* | 1470 mm* | 1470 mm | 1470 mm | 1450 mm |
| Rear track | 1410 mm* | 1405 mm* | 1405 mm | 1405 mm | 1420 mm |
| Front suspension | 2+1 dampers<br>and torsion bars | 2+1 dampers<br>and torsion bars | 2+1 dampers<br>and torsion bars | 2+1 dampers<br>and torsion bars | 2+1 dampers<br>and torsion bars |
| Rear suspension | Pull-Rod<br>2+1 dampers<br>and torsion bars | Pull-Rod<br>2+1 dampers<br>and torsion bars | Push-Rod<br>2+1 dampers<br>and torsion bars | Pull-Rod<br>2+1 dampers<br>and torsion bars | Pull-Rod<br>2+1 dampers<br>and torsion bars |
| Dampers | Multimatic | McLaren | Sachs | Sachs | Penske |
| Brakes calipers | Brembo | Akebono | Brembo | Brembo | A+P |
| Brakes discs | Brembo | Carbon Industrie<br>Brembo | Brembo CCR<br>Carbon Industrie | Brembo | Hitco |
| Wheels | O.Z. | Enkey | BBS | BBS | AVUS |
| Radiators | Marston | Calsonic - IMI | Secan | Secan | Marston |
| Oil tank | middle position<br>inside fuel tank | middle position<br>inside fuel tank | middle position<br>inside fuel tank | middle position<br>inside fuel tank | middle position<br>inside fuel tank |
| **GEARBOX** | Longitudinal carbon | Longitudinal carbon | Longitudinal carbon | Longitudinal carbon | Longitudinal titanium |
| Gear selection | Semiautomatic<br>7 gears | Semiautomatic<br>7 gears | Semiautomatic<br>7 gears | Semiautomatic<br>7 gears | Semiautomatic<br>7 gears |
| Clutch | A+P | A+P | Sachs | Sachs | A+P |
| Pedals | 2 | 2 | 2 | 2 | 2 |
| **ENGINE** | Renault RS27-2011 | Mercedes FO108Y | Ferrari 056 | Mercedes FO108Y | Renault RS27-2011 |
| Total capacity | 2400 cmc | 2400 cmc | 2400 cmc | 2400 cmc | 2400 cmc |
| N° cylinders and V | 8 - V90 | 8 - V90 | 8 - V90 | 8 - V90 | 8 - V90 |
| Electronics | Magneti Marelli | McLaren el.sys. | Magneti Marelli | Mercedes | Magneti Marelli |
| Fuel | Elf | Mobil | Shell | Mobil | Elf |
| Oil | Elf | Mobil | Shell | Mobil | Elf |
| Dashboard | Red Bull | McLaren | Magneti Marelli | Mercedes | Renault F1 |

*1 Aldo Costa was replaced by Pat Fry after the GP of Spain    *2 Sam Michael moved to McLaren    *3 Geoff Willis moved to Mercedes-Benz

| 14-15 FORCE INDIA | 16-17 SAUBER | 18-19 TORO ROSSO | 11-12 WILLIAMS | 20-21 LOTUS | 22-23 HRT | 24-25 VIRGIN |
|---|---|---|---|---|---|---|
| WJM 03 | C29 | STR5 | FW 32 | T127 | FRT F110 | VR-01 |
| Adrew Green | James Key<br>Matt Morris | Giorgio Ascanelli<br>Ben Butler<br>Laurent Mekles | Patrick Head<br>Sam Michael*2<br>Mike Coughlan | Mike Gascoyne<br>Mark Smith | Geoff Willis*3 | John McQuilliam |
| Bradley Joyce (14)<br>G. Lambiase (15) | Marco Schüpbach (16)<br>Francesco Nenci (17) | Riccardo Adami (18)<br>Andrea Landi (19) | Tom McCullogh (11)<br>Xevi Pujolar (12) | Gianluca Pisanello (20)<br>J. P. Ramirez (21) | Angel Baena (22)<br>Richard Connel (23) | Kieron Marchant (24)<br>Lee Adams (25) |
| Andy Deeming | Urs Kuratle | Gerard Lecoq | Carl Garden | Nick Smith | Soren Morgenstern | Richard Wrenn |
| 3411 mm* | 3363 mm* | 3337 mm* | 3358 mm* | 3318 mm* | 3249 mm* | 3318 mm* |
| 1480 mm | 1460 mm | 1440 mm | 1480 mm | 1470 mm | 1425 mm | 1440 mm |
| 1410 mm | 1400 mm | 1410 mm | 1420 mm | 1405 mm | 1411 mm | 1410 mm |
| 2+1 dampers<br>and torsion bars | 2+1 dampers<br>and torsion bars | 2+1 dampers<br>and torsion bars | 2+1 dampers<br>and torsion bars | 2+1 dampers<br>and torsion bars | 2+1 dampers<br>and torsion bars | 2+1 dampers<br>and torsion bars |
| Pull-Rod<br>2+1 dampers<br>and torsion bars | Push-Rod<br>2+1 dampers<br>and torsion bars | Pull-Rod<br>2+1 dampers<br>and torsion bars | Pull-Rod<br>2+1 dampers<br>and torsion bars | Pull-Rod<br>2+1 dampers<br>and torsion bars | Push-Rod<br>2+1 dampers<br>and torsion bars | Push-Rod<br>2+1 dampers<br>and torsion bars |
| Sachs | Sachs | Koni | Williams | Sachs | Sachs | Koni |
| A+P | Brembo | Brembo | A+P | A+P | Brembo | A+P |
| Hitco - Brembo | Brembo | Brembo | Carbon Industrie | Hitco | Brembo | Hitco |
| BBS | O.Z. | O.Z. | O.Z. | BBS | O.Z. | BBS |
| Secan | Calsonic | Marston | IMI Marston | Secan | Secan | Marston |
| middle position<br>inside fuel tank | middle position<br>inside fuel tank | middle position<br>inside fuel tank | middle position<br>inside fuel tank | middle position<br>inside fuel tank | middle position<br>inside fuel tank | middle position<br>inside fuel tank |
| Longitudinal carbon | Longitudinal titanium | Longitudinal carbon | Longitudinal titanium | Xtrac longitudinal | Xtrac longitudinal | Virgin |
| Semiautomatic<br>7 gears | Semiautomatic<br>7 gears | Semiautomatic<br>7 gears | Semiautomatic<br>7 gears | Semiautomatic<br>7 gears | Semiautomatic<br>7 gears | Semiautomatic<br>7 gears |
| A+P | A+P | A+P | A+P | A+P | A+P | A+P |
| 2 | 2 | 2 | 2 | 2 | 2 | 2 |
| Mercedes FO108Y | Ferrari 056 | Ferrari 056 | Cosworth CA2011 | Renault RS27-2011 | Cosworth CA2011 | Cosworth CA2010 |
| 2400 cmc | 2400 cmc | 2400 cmc | 2400 cmc | 2400 cmc | 2400 cmc | 2400 cmc |
| 8 - V90 | 8 - V90 | 8 - V90 | 8 - V90 | 8 - V90 | 8 - V90 | 8 - V90 |
| McLaren el.sys. | Magneti Marelli | Magneti Marelli | - | - | - | - |
| Mobil | Shell | Shell | Esso | Esso | BP | BP |
| Mobil | Shell | Shell | Esso | Esso | BP | BP |
| P.I. | Magneti Marelli | Toro Rosso | Williams | Williams | Williams | Williams |

The Federation intervened heavily on the technical regulations for the 2011 season to both ban some solutions allowed the previous year, like the abolition of double diffusers and the F-Duct device, and to increase the number of overtaking manoeuvres and, therefore, the spectacle of racing. That meant they brought back KERS and introduced the adjustment of the rear flap in place of the similar device on the front wing. Result: the amount of overtaking was even considered too much during the 2011 season, but very much to the advantage of spectacle. The great unknown of Pirelli's return to F1 as exclusive tyre supplier encouraged the Federation to impose an obligatory weight distribution to avoid too much experimentation. As well as these significant new rules, many other less apparent but extremely useful new regulations came in to limit aerodynamic excess and reduce the so-called grey area in highly controversial text in which it appeared for 2010. It is easy to see them in this illustration of the 2010 car. We will limit ourselves to highlighting them in detail, using the technical rules text. In the illustrations there are examples of how much was done in 2010 to get around the spirit of the regulations in some cases.

## MINIMUM WEIGHT
The 2011 season minimum weight was increased from 620 kg to 640 kg after the return of KERS and more chassis safety measures.

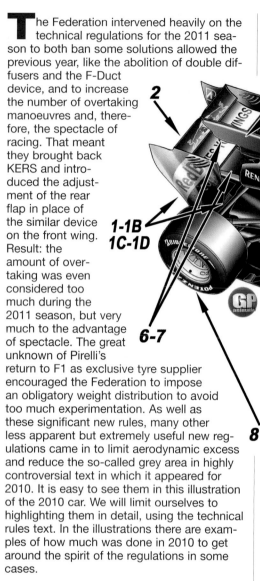

## BAN OF THE DOUBLE DIFFUSERS
### ART. 3.12.9
In the area within 450 mm from the centre line and in that delimited in a longitudinal sense between the 450 mm in front of the rear end plate of the cockpit and 350 mm behind the rear axle, every intersection of body visible from below with vertical, lateral or longitudinal planes must form a continuous line.
The only aperture permitted is that regulated by Art. 3.12.7 (the one concerning access to the starter).
The design shows well how hair-splitting was the question of the double diffusers. There just needed to be a crack of a few millimetres in the body (see the red arrow) to authorise a large dimensioned hole that fed the double diffusers, all in line with the regulation that said by observing the car from underneath one had to be able to see the sky.

### ART.3.12.10
In the area within 650 mm from the centre line and in that delimited in a longitudinal sense between the 450 mm in front of the rear end plate of the cockpit and 350 mm behind the rear axle, each intersection of the body visible from underneath with vertical, lateral or longitudinal planes must form a continuous line.

### ART. 3.12.11
The verification of this norm will be made without taking into account (Art.15.4.8) of the unsuspended mass (suspension elements).

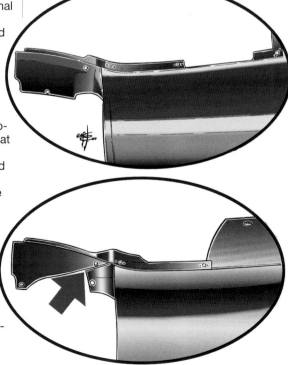

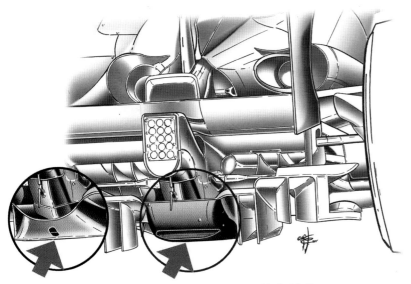

## DEFORMABLE STRUCTURE
### *ART. 15.2.4*
To avoid strange and excessive shapes of the deformable structure behind the gear-box, a maximum bulk has been imposed on the vertical of 275 mm.

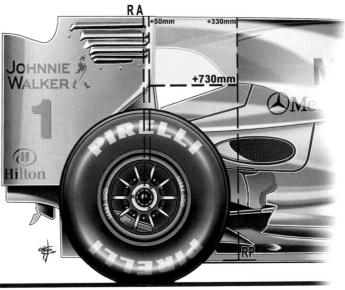

## THE STARTER HOLE REGULATED *ART. 3.12.7*
In the central channel of the diffuser there may be an aperture to access the starter motor, but that area may not exceed 3500 mm$^2$ and each point of the aperture may not be more than 100 mm from any other point of the opening.

## ADJUSTABLE REAR WING FLAP *ART. 3.18.1*
To improve overtaking, FIA introduced an adjustable rear wing flap to replace the front adjustable flap. The closed upper section closed (flap) of the rear wing may be modified in its incidence when the car is moving. The variation permits only two positions of space between the plane and flap and that is between 10 mm and 50 mm, with an ON and OFF control. The system must make the flap return to its original position in the case of an anomaly. The variation of incidence must be controlled by the driver upon authorisation of the race management (Art.3.18.2). The control may only be used when a car is at less than a second from the car that precedes it and on the authorisation of the race management. The variation of incidence is neutralised each time the driver uses the brakes.

## ELIMINATION OF THE FINS CONNECTED TO THE REAR WING
### *ART. 3.9.1*
There may be no body between the 50 mm and the 330 mm in front of the rear axle higher than 730 mm from the reference plane.

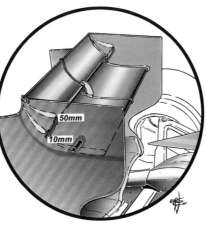

## LIMITATION OF THE REAR WING SUPPORTS
### ART. 3.10.9

The rear wing supports may have two closed symmetrical sections with a maximum of a 5000 mm² total area. The thickness of each of the two sections may not exceed 25 mm. The connection radius between these sections and the wing plane (surface defined by Art.3.10.2) may not exceed 10 mm.

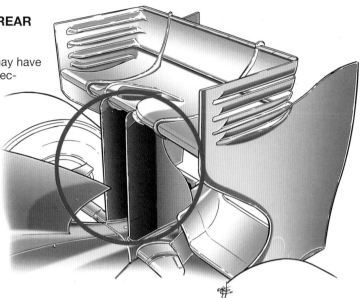

## ABOLITION OF THE REAR WING'S F-DUCT

The F-Duct system, which envisaged the possibility of stalling the rear wing flap to improve top speed, was banned given that the Federation has now brought in the incidence variation of the flap for the same purpose.

### ART. 3.10.2

The body in the area between 50 mm in front of the rear axle and situated 730 mm above the reference plane and within the 355 mm of the centre line must be located in an area which, when seen from the side, is situated between the rear axle and the 350 mm behind it.

### ART.3.18

In the lateral view, there must be no more than two sections, each completely closed. No part of either of these two in contact with the air flow may have a concave bend radius of less than 100 mm. A Gurney flap of a maximum of 20 mm may be added to the trailing edge. The higher section chord must always be less than the chord of the lower section. Instead, McLaren brought in a blower to the main plane (2) in 2009, which was in fact a double trailing edge (1) of the plain itself (illustration 6), a move copied by Williams and BMW during the same season and by Red Bull, Mercedes-Benz, Renault and Toro Rosso in 2010.

## ABOLITION OF DRIVER MANAGEMENT TYPE F-DUCT
### ART. 3.15

Apart from devices useful for the control of the car described in Art. 3.18, any movement of the driver's body that is suspected of influencing the aerodynamics of the car is prohibited: during the winter of 2010 it was suspected that some team wished to use the driver's body to interact with certain devices on the car.

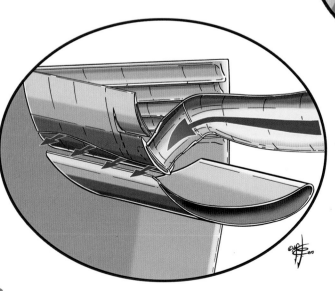

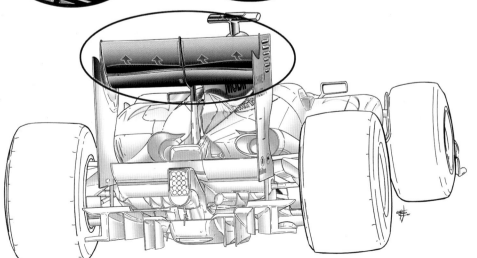

## ABOLITION OF THE LOWER BLOWN PLANE

The lower blown plane of the rear beam wing was also banned. It was used only by Williams in 2010.

### ART. 3.10.1

In the area situated beyond the 150 mm from the rear axle and between 150 mm and 730 mm in height from the reference plane, but also between 75 mm and 355 mm from the centre line, the body must fit into a limited area between 150 mm and 350 mm from the rear axle and between 300 mm and 400 mm above the reference plane. Seen from the side, the section may have a single element. The only permitted addition is that of a Gurney flap no larger than 20 mm.

**53.3/54.5 min 342kg (Q)**

**45.5/46.7 min291kg (Q)**

## MANDATORY WEIGHT DISTRIBUTION
### ART. 4.2

It was only for the 2011 season that the weight measured on the front and rear wheels was not permitted to exceed 201 kg and 342 kg respectively in qualifying (the weight measured with smooth tyres). Weight distribution must vary at between 53.3 and 54.5 at the front end and 45.5 and 46.7 at the rear.

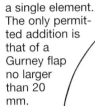

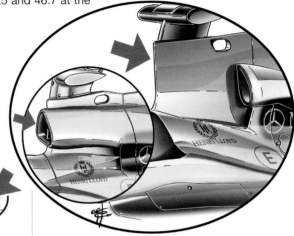

## LIMITATIONS AT THE KNIFE-EDGE ROLL BAR ART. 15.4

The roll bar for driver protection must have a minimum closed section of 10.000 mm² in its vertical projection, measured in a plane placed 50 mm above its highest point.
Its dimensions in length and width may not exceed 200 mm with a minimum thickness of 10.000 mm².
In 2011, two teams used this system: Force India and Lotus.

## NEW TEST FOR THE T-TRAY ART. 317.5

The body may have a maximum vertical flexing of 5 mm under a force of 2,000 N applied in three different points (one at the centre and two 100 mm from it). The knife edge zone under the chassis must be rigidly fixed and not contain any mechanism that permits non-linear flexing during the verification test.

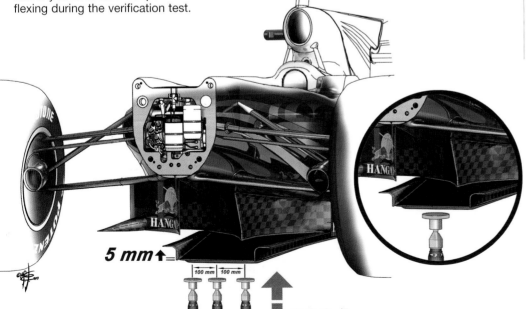

**5 mm↑**

100 mm   100 mm

**200 kg**

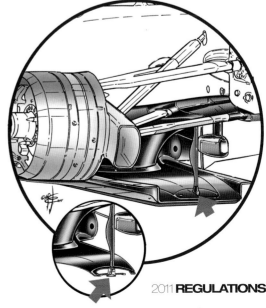

## HEIGHT OF FRONT ROLL BAR *ART. 15.2.3*

The highest point of the second safety roll bar may not exceed 670 mm above the reference plane and must pass the crash test as described in Art. 17.3

## CHASSIS HEIGHT
### *ART. 15.4.4*

The maximum height of the chassis in the points of the sections A-A and B-B may not exceed 625 mm from the reference plane.

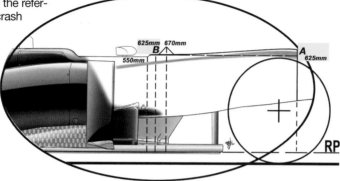

## POSITION OF THE MIRRORS
### *ART. 14.3.3*

All rear view mirror components, together with their fastening, must be contained in an area of between 250 mm and 500 mm from the waist line and 750 mm from the rear limit of the cockpit opening.

## DOUBLING OF THE WHEEL RETENTION CABLES
### *ART. 10.3.6*

To avoid the detachment of a wheel, the fastening cables must have a section greater than 110 mm$^2$. Each wheel must have two fastening cables that pass inside both suspension arms with separate mounts on both the chassis and the upright. Each cable must be longer than 450 mm and withstand a force of 70kN applied in all directions.

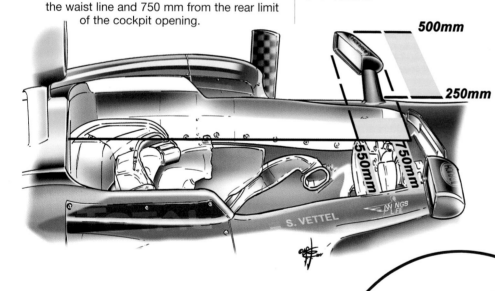

# Controversies

We chose to include this section in the new regulations chapter because there were only three solutions contested during the season even if the third, which concerned the hot blow of the engines in the deceleration phase had notable consequences and will be dealt with more specifically in the engines chapter.

## SAUBER DISQUALIFICATION

The only episode of the 2011 season that ended up in disqualification happened at the opening world championship race in Australia where the centre of attention, much to their regret, was Sauber. The cars of Perez and Kobayashi, both points scorers, were protested as it was alleged they did not respect Art. 3.10.1 and 3.10.2 that require a minim bend radius of 100 mm of the whole surface in contact with the air flow. In practice, there was only 5 mm of error in the curvature of the flap that cost the Swiss team's drivers 7th and 8th places. The defence of technical director James Key came to nothing, given the triviality of the infraction. Art. 3.10.1 requires that no part (in the area of the wing and flap) and, specifically (Art.- 3.10.2) in the two closed sections that comprise the only two planes in contact with the air flow, may have a concave radius of curvature of less than 100 mm: the exception to this restriction is the Gurney flap.

## HEIGHT OF THE REAR WING
### *ART. 3.6*

Remember that from 2009 the maximum height of the rear wing was taken from 800 mm to 950 mm in relation to the reference plane, the lowest point of the car. In practice, with the 2009 technical revolution, the rear wing was raised in line with the engine cover and the safety roll bar and nobody ever exceeded that limit.

## FERRARI BARCELONA

At the GP of Spain, Ferrari came out with a surprise – and then withdrew it – which was a rear wing that protruded 30 mm beyond the maximum permitted measurement for that component. A forcing of art. 3.10.3 in relation to the dimensions of the supports that connect the two planes that constitute the rear wing and may vary between 8 mm and 30 mm. In practice, Ferrari had applied this article's text to the letter which, in its last line, clearly states how these supports are not taken into consideration during verification and, therefore, are not affected by the dimensional limits imposed by art.3.6 concerning the height of the rear wing. Practically speaking, Ferrari had created a mono-block support that also included the transverse extension (the traditional small Gurney flap) that actually exceeds the height of the wing by 30 mm. A forcing that was first considered normal at technical verification, but which provoked a request for clarification also by the teams that "forced" the regulation in 2009 and introduced the famous holes in the diffusers.

A provocative move by Ferrari, similar to that by Mauro Forghieri in 1982 when he fielded a staggered double rear wing at Long Beach to protest against Colin Chapman's double chassis Lotus.

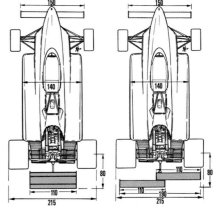

950 mm

2009

P.R.

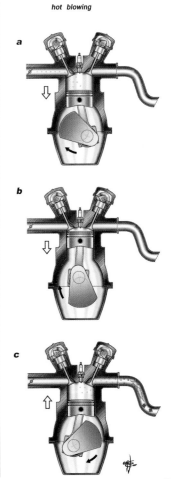

*Ferrari Long Beach '82*

## HOT BLOWING

With a view to bringing in severe restrictions of the engine blow in the diffuser channels for the 2011 season, the Federation came out with a two-phase limitation in this sector. The first took effect at Valencia with the obligation to use the same engine mapping in both qualifying and the race, seeing that some teams, especially Red Bull, had exaggerated in varying the regulation (operation envisaged by the regulation) between a single lap in practice and at race speed. The second and most anxiously awaited phase also prohibiting hot blow during the engine's deceleration to avoid the differences in downforce between power units in acceleration and not, was to have taken effect at Silverstone. Following the protests sparked off by this sudden decision, a compromise was accepted: an opening also in the deceleration phase of 20% and 10% of the throttle, depending on the revolutions. A situation that saw Ferrari able to best interpret this compromise. The illustration shows the three stages. In the first column on the left is the cycle in the acceleration phase with the throttle open. In the second is the standard deceleration phase with the throttle closed. The third and final column shows how the engine cycle was modified with hot blowing in the deceleration stage; in aspiration a component of much thinner air/petrol is sent in – (a) throttle semi-open – which is not made to explode in the combustion chamber – (b) no ignition, but subsequently is pushed into the exhaust channel where it gradually increases the temperature (c) until it catches fire, generating a flow in the extractor similar to the acceleration phase.

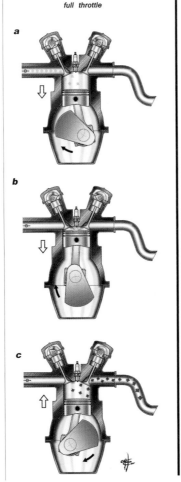

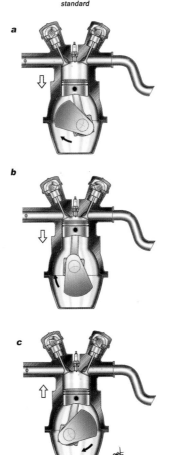

*full throttle*

*off throttle standard*

*hot blowing*

The 2011 season was one of new technical developments even if some of them were first used in the past, brought back and modernised; never before have so many reappeared again in a single season. But to tell the truth, we had a preview of this back to the old trend in 2009, when that magician Adrian Newey dusted off the pullrod rear suspension layout, which was abandoned over 20 years earlier, and turned it into the height of fashion again in 2011 with no fewer than eight of the 12 F1 teams adopting it. Newey did just that kind of thing last year by bringing back the lateral blow of the exhausts that had half-heartedly appeared on the 1985 Renault RE50. In 2011, the French constructor was again the leader in that area (as also described in the Engines chapter), followed by Red Bull, who were the first to develop exhaust blow straight into the diffusers. There were also another two new developments from the past that surfaced at the start of the season: particularly on the McLaren MP4-26 and the Toro Rosso.

The former went back to the concept of sidepods that had very high sides and were low in the centre, which was a clear reminder of the Benetton B185 and the Ferrari F310. But on the McLaren MP4-26 the concept was taken to the extreme to be able to create an

air channel towards the rear of the car and, more importantly, that worked in synergy with the lower element of the rear wing. It was a feature that brought with it a lot of complications, like the unique form of the radiators that were L-shaped, very long and narrow. Then Toro Rosso came up with a modern version of the double floor, which was first seen on Jean Claude Migeot's unfortunate Ferrari F92. The task of both projects was to improve air flow towards the rear wing zone and the diffuser. McLaren achieved its objective by drastically reducing the section in the internal area of the sidepods.

And Toro Rosso created a second air passage that energise the air flow to the rear. In fact, the sidepod part of the body was raised by the stepped bottom to create a real Venturi channel to generate downforce without negatively affecting drag to advancement. And all of it energised by a unique system of flat exhausts that blew into the lateral channel zone of the diffuser.

## NEW FEATURES

This one is not a return to the past, but it was a real surprise. It was gearbox miniaturisation by Williams with a bold project designed for aerodynamic advantages that it would have created to improve the efficiency of the rear wing group. But it was a development that was thwarted in practice due to the bulk of the Cosworth engine, which reduced those advantages.

But the biggest surprise came almost at the end of the season with the appearance of an F-Duct on the front wing of the Mercedes-Benz, which was discovered almost by chance by watching the suspicious moves of the mechanics, as described in the M-B chapter. During Friday practice for the GP of Japan, a new front wing turned up and was tested during the morning session by both drivers. Rather than a new development for the 2011 season, it was Ross Brawn's first important experiment with which to gather data for possible transfer to the 2012 car project.

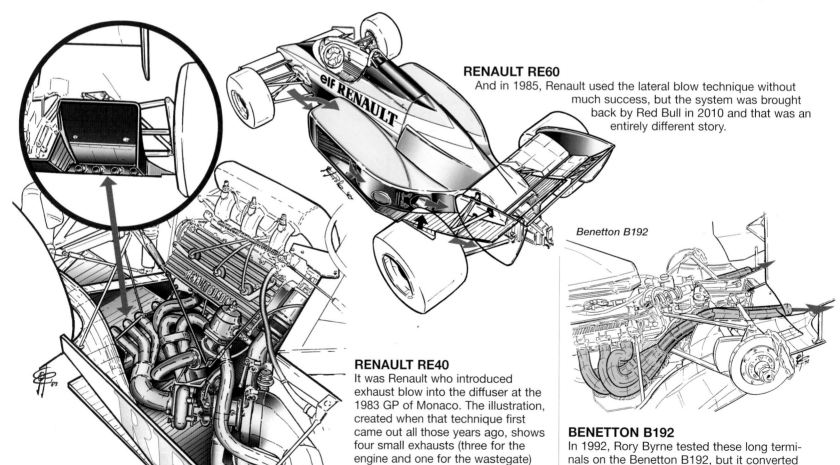

### RENAULT RE60
And in 1985, Renault used the lateral blow technique without much success, but the system was brought back by Red Bull in 2010 and that was an entirely different story.

*Benetton B192*

### RENAULT RE40
It was Renault who introduced exhaust blow into the diffuser at the 1983 GP of Monaco. The illustration, created when that technique first came out all those years ago, shows four small exhausts (three for the engine and one for the wastegate) that blew into the side channels with a sharp exit (see circle).

### BENETTON B192
In 1992, Rory Byrne tested these long terminals on the Benetton B192, but it converted no-one else and the team dropped it.

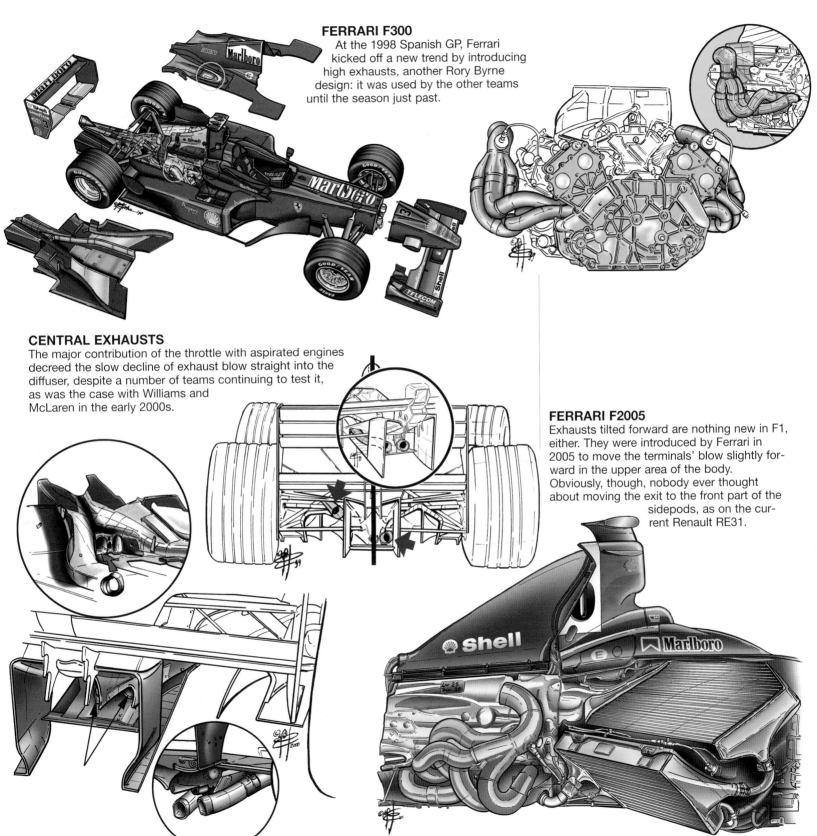

### FERRARI F300

At the 1998 Spanish GP, Ferrari kicked off a new trend by introducing high exhausts, another Rory Byrne design: it was used by the other teams until the season just past.

### CENTRAL EXHAUSTS

The major contribution of the throttle with aspirated engines decreed the slow decline of exhaust blow straight into the diffuser, despite a number of teams continuing to test it, as was the case with Williams and McLaren in the early 2000s.

### FERRARI F2005

Exhausts tilted forward are nothing new in F1, either. They were introduced by Ferrari in 2005 to move the terminals' blow slightly forward in the upper area of the body. Obviously, though, nobody ever thought about moving the exit to the front part of the sidepods, as on the current Renault RE31.

## 2011 RED BULL

Despite the severe limitations to its diffusers, blow into the lateral channels was retained, it having been introduced on the RB6 as a result of a cut in the external 5 cm of the channels conceded by the regulations.

This was most certainly one of the major contributors to Red Bull's success in 2011.

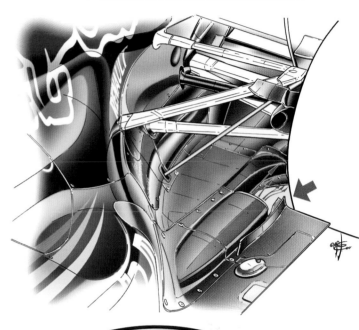

### 2010 RED BULL

Red Bull was the first to bring lateral blow back to centre stage and then, during the second half of the year, they moved on to the hot air being blown into the side channels of the diffuser. It was a technique made possible by the idea of retaining a certain blow, even when the engine was not firing so as to have no brusque load variations.

### RENAULT

Decidedly unique and extreme were the Renault RE31 exhausts, which were tilted forward and had long terminals that blew into the initial part of the car to energise air flow. It was a development that brought with it many project assembly difficulties to reduce power loss to a minimum and avoid excessive overheating in the low area of the car, which was cooled by two large ducts at the sides of the cockpit inlet.

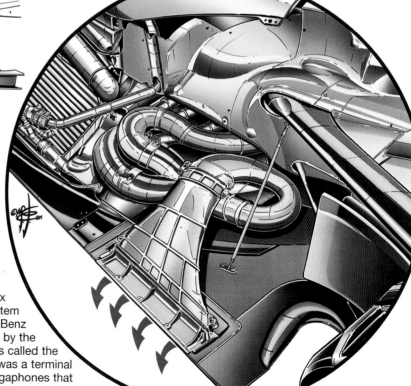

### McLAREN OCTOPUS

A new development that never made its debut in a Grand Prix was the exhaust system of the V8 Mercedes-Benz dubbed the octopus by the press, but which was called the fantail at Woking. It was a terminal with a very large megaphones that blew straight into the lower part of the bottom, in the zone in front of the rear wheels.

After many experiments at pre-championship testing, a Red Bull-type version took to the grid in Melbourne as that had immediately shown it was competitive.

## McLAREN-FERRARI F310

The double bottom was not used for the new McLaren but raised sidepods, like on the Benetton B195 and the Ferrari F310, to channel a greater amount of air towards the rear of the car. The lower area, which was less concave than on the MP4-25, boasted a Renault feature with exhausts that blew hot air into the beginning of the 'pods – as indicated by the red arrow – and was hidden by small turning vanes.

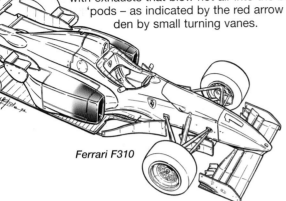

*Ferrari F310*

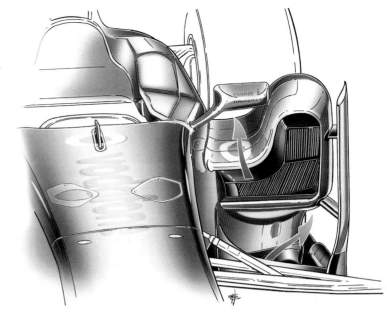

## TORO ROSSO-FERRARI F92

Toro Rosso brought back a modern version of the double bottom: the sidepods were raised and had a Venturi tube progression to create downforce while the exhausts, which were flat and long, blew into the so-called Coca-Cola zone to accelerate the air. But on Jean Claude Migeot's 1992 Ferrari, the double floor was created by a sort of second raised diffuser: that car turned out to be a disaster, not because of its unusual aerodynamics but for its chassis and suspension, which were not up to the situation.

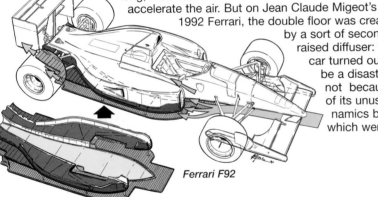

*Ferrari F92*

## WILLIAMS

The Williams was, perhaps, the most extreme example of how aerodynamics have conditioned the selection of the mechanics. Note the extreme reduction in height of the new gearbox compared to a traditional unit (shown by the dotted line), and extreme angulation of the drive shafts, which was really evident from the back view. In that way, the terminal part of the body was lower than those of all the other teams' cars: 2 cm less, for instance, than that of the RB7.

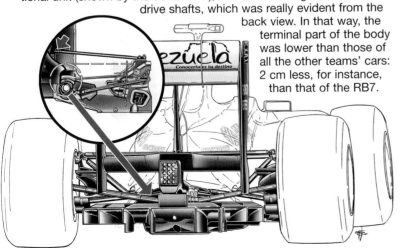

## MERCEDES-BENZ FRONT F-DUCT

The blow of the front wing with consequent 'stalling' was generated very simply. There was no need for added intakes as per the 2010 F-Duct; the system was fed through the usual aperture for cooling the cockpit. In the F-Duct version, that aperture was divided into two and was at the centre of the nose, which was split to channel the air that passes inside the support pillars through small internal channels and blow straight onto the main plane. The system was obligatorily passive, because Article 3.15 of the regulations prohibits any intervention by the driver, as took place with the 2010 F-Duct.

This was a season packed with new developments in the cockpit area, enlivened by the return of KERS and the control that operated the rear DRS flap, introduced to improve overtaking.

Steering wheels had new functions and paddles, which obliged the various teams to rationalise them and make them more ergonomic. The most significant new features came from Ferrari, which had not only slightly changed the shape of its steering wheel by making it flatter to improve habitability somewhat, but also introduced two additional rocker arms, two paddles and a further small lever to the rear of the steering wheel right from the first test. All of this, obviously, in an attempt to make the management of the various functions more immediate and intuitive for its drivers. Both Alonso and Massa preferred to operate KERS and the flap using controls moved to the back of the wheel, so that they could do so with a middle finger instead of a thumb so they did not have to break their grip of the wheel. During the season, the two Ferraristi made further changes to the wheel, with the Spaniard preferring to drop the two upper levers, partially because in the meantime the flap control was moved so that it could be operated with the left foot, but the Brazilian was given an eighth lever. Renault followed Ferrari along the road to the proliferation of levers, fitting no fewer than eight of them to the rear of their wheel from the season's first race. A left foot- operated flap control in the footrest area was installed in the Mercedes-Benz and McLaren as well as the Ferrari, which eliminated one of the six levers that first appeared in 2009, but the wheel still kept the same general. Red Bull and Toro Rosso remained true to their 'fighter plane' wheel in 2011 without the integrated display, which was positioned in the centre of the cockpit.

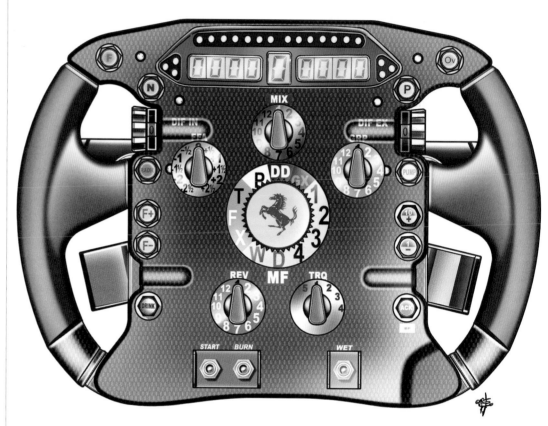

## FERRARI WHEEL

Compared to that of the F10, the F150 Italia steering wheel retained its general appearance, but it was lower and with most of the controls more concentrated in the centre to rationalise the drivers' hand movements. The most significant new feature was the rear of the wheel, as can be seen in the comparison.

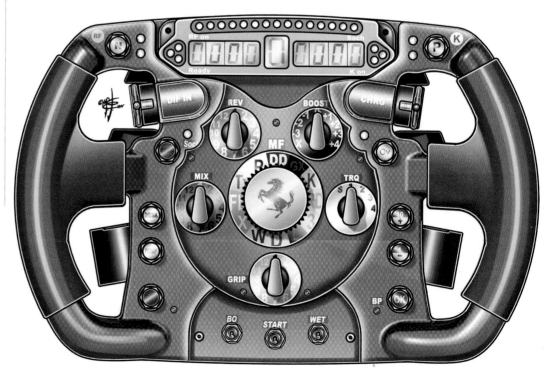

## F10-F150 ITALIA COMPARISON

The different driving positions meant a steering wheel raised in height had to be developed compared to that of the F10 (the difference in bulk is shown in yellow) to ensure more knee space as the drivers sit slightly more upright in the F150 Italia. The most notable new features were at the rear (comparison below). Below is a description of what the various controls did, but remember that they were modified in line with circuit characteristics and drivers' needs, which can differ from one another:

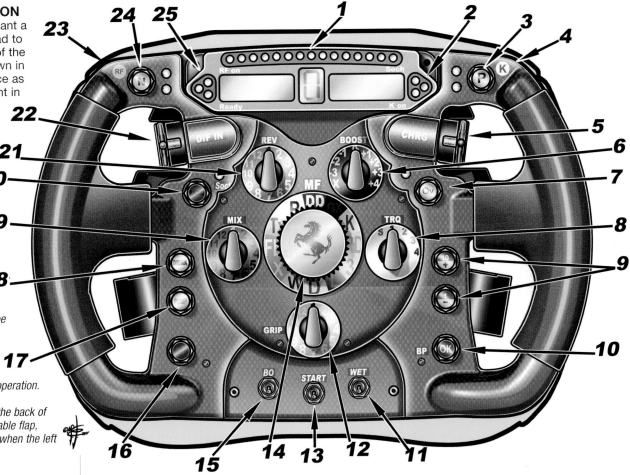

1. The display wasn't changed, given that the regulations said it should be the same on all the cars. With their sequential illumination, the LED readouts dictate the right moment to change gear.
2. Light that confirms the KERS is in operation.
3. Pit lane speed limiter.
4. Position indicator of the button on the back of the wheel that activates the adjustable flap, which stayed in that location even when the left foot control appeared.
5. KERS recharge control.
6. Regulates KERS power.
7. Ensures higher engine revolutions.
8. Adjusts engine torque.
9. Gives access to the functions to be selected on the central paddle.
10. Confirms the selection made with the paddle.
11. Inserts various wet programmes.
12. Inserts the various management programme set-ups in relation to the tyres.
13. Engages the pre-selected regulations during testing for the start.
14. Central paddle that gives access to the various management programmes.
15. Burn-out to warm up the tyres .
16. A button the purpose of which has remained a secret throughout the season.
17. Starts the oil recovery pump.
18. Gives access to the mineral salts drink.
19. Varies the air/fuel mix.
20. Radio.
21. Regulates engine revs.
22. Regulates differential management.
23. Shows the position of the flap control at the rear.
24. Inserts neutral.
25. Adjustable flap activation.

The most significant new features on the Ferrari wheel were hidden behind it, where there were seven levers compared to the four of the F10. There were also new paddles to activate KERS (1) and the adjustable flap (2), even if this was operated by a control on the footrest to the left of the pedals. Levers 3 and 4 were also new and regulated the differential. The gear levers (5) were back to being split instead of the F10's single rocker arm, permitting the management of the gears by using even one hand; now, changing up through the gears was on the right and changing down on the left. 6) Double clutch paddles, which were unchanged. The driver could manage the start in two distinct phases; one with lever to move the car, the other to manage the traction with its modulator. 7) Introduced during the last pre-season test session at Barcelona, there was also a lever behind the wheel the purpose of which remained secret.

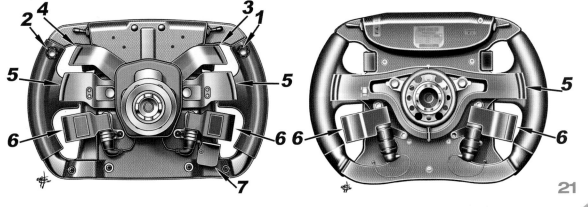

## ALONSO-MASSA COMPARISON

As with the 2010 season, the Ferrari drivers were in a different driving position, especially concerning the steering wheel and its distance from the chest. Fernando Alonso preferred to have his wheel closer and drove with his arms more bent, while Felipe Massa kept his arms slightly less so. That is why the connection spacers at the steering column were notably long and fairly different between the two drivers, having been more or less the same in 2010.

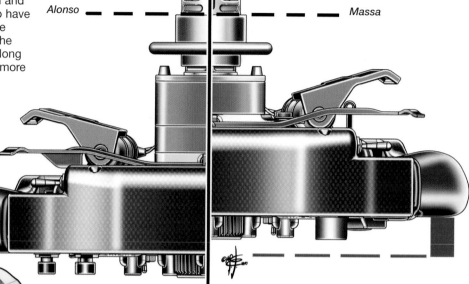

Alonso         Massa

## FERRARI

Not satisfied with having seven levers at the rear, mid-season Massa used a steering wheel with an eighth lever (see red arrow), while Alonso often used a wheel without the two new levers at the top .

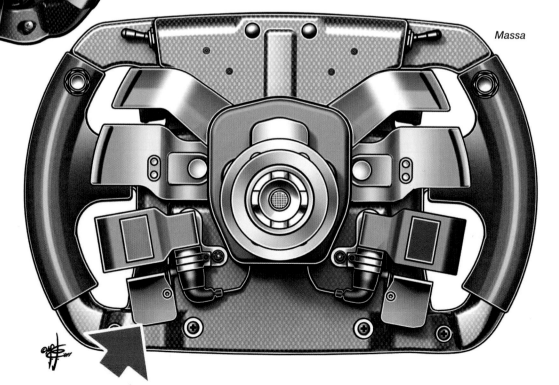

Massa

## RENAULT

To the seven levers at the rear of the Ferrari steering wheel computer, Renault responded from the first race of the season with eight. And in this case it was Vitaly Petrov and Nick Heidfeld who suggested the idea to their technicians. The two small paddles down low, almost hidden by the others, were both used to operate the rear wing flap and ensure easy control with one of the two hands, depending on the wheel's position at the time. Of course, the two central levers were for the gearbox, the lower one for the clutch and the two uppers for the differential as on the 2010 Renault, because the team was the first to follow McLaren and introduce six levers at the 2009 GP of France.

*2009*

## McLAREN

Having brought in the new six lever feature to the rear of their steering wheel (right) in 2009, McLaren eliminated one of them for 2011 and moved the flap control to the base of the footrest, to be operated on the straight by the driver's left foot; this was also to better synchronise the move under braking when the adjustable flap must return to the 'load' position to avoid blocking the rear wheels. Note the different shape of the gear levers (see circle) required by Jenson Button.

## McLAREN

The shape of the McLaren's steering wheel was unchanged: it had been open in the lower area since the 2010 season to make as much room as possible for the drivers' legs.
Note how McLaren uses fewer paddles than the Ferrari, but also the extreme neatness of the MP4-26 inside, with the brake division controls on the left.

## FERRARI

Ferrari split the DRS insertion control: as well as the button behind the steering wheel operated with the left index finger, a new one operated by the left foot was added.
It was more functional, made for improved synchronisation of the moment in which the flap has to return to the "load" position, because that moment was determined obligatorily by the foot shifting over to the brake pedal.

## RED BULL

A photograph taken during Webber's Monza accident revealed that the Red Bull did not have the flap that could be operated with the left foot and that the RB7's pedals were completely conventional. Note how the pedals take the shape of the driver's feet on all the other cars, complete with anatomic stoppage for the heels.

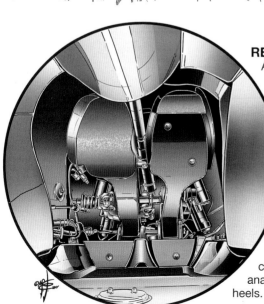

# RED BULL

The Red Bull steering wheels were practically unchanged in relation to those of 2010, despite the introduction of KERS and rear wing flap management.

Among other things, Red Bull was the only team – together with their 'cousin' Toro Rosso – to have no display incorporated into the shape of the 'wheel, which continued to be the horizontal X.

There was only a slight difference in the shape of the gear lever (above) between the cars of Sebastian Vettel and Mark Webber. The decision to 'dirty' the adjustable flap lever with red paint on the German's car to avoid mistakes seemed strange.

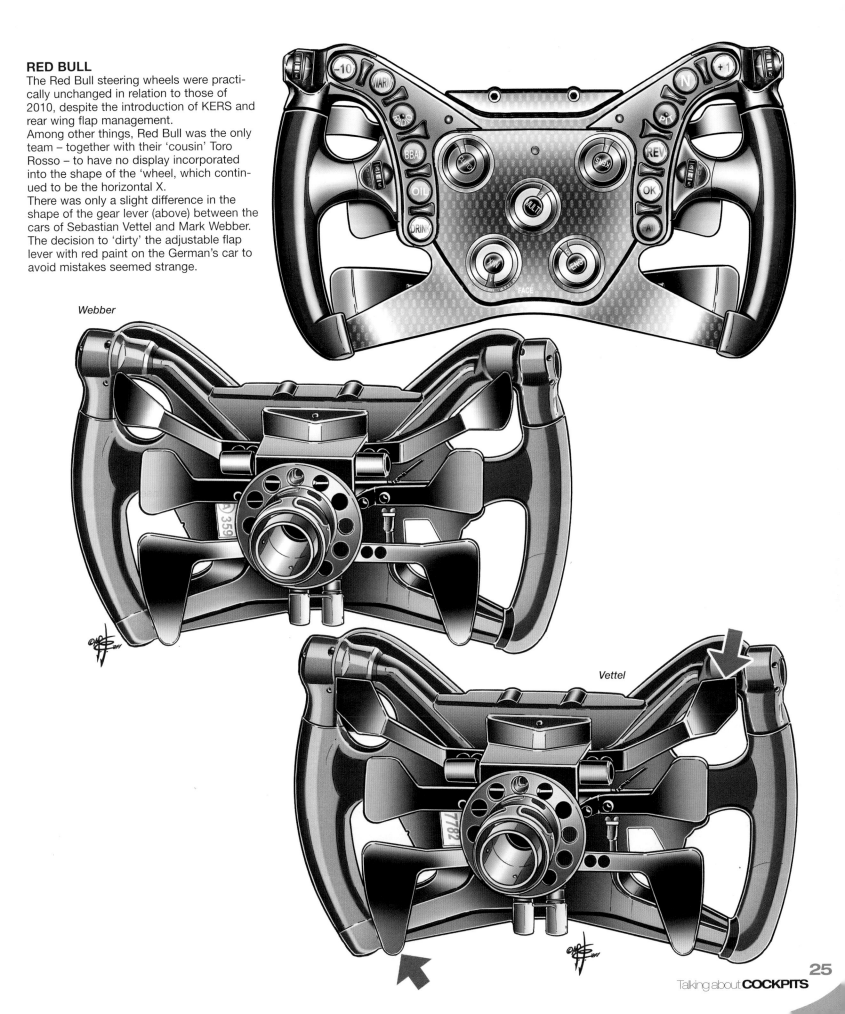

*Webber*

*Vettel*

# Brakes

The development of braking systems for 2011 had to take four main factors of change into account compared to the previous season: the switch in tyre supplier from Bridgestone to Pirelli, the return of the KERS energy recovery system, the introduction of the adjustable rear wing with the consequent ban of the F-Duct and the prohibition of the double diffuser. All of those elements had their effect on the car's variation of grip and speed, as well as a direct involvement on the rear braking couple in the case of KERS, making a considerable impact on the performance demanded of the braking system. Right from testing in Abu Dhabi at the end of 2010, the move to new tyres made the different behaviour of the car evident under braking. If the Bridgestones guaranteed an extremely high lateral grip, allowing the driver to carry cornering speed and manage the braking in the entry phase, the Pirellis turned out to be more exploitable in a longitudinal

direction, favouring straight wheel braking to maximise deceleration. This, together with a lower speed through the corners, translated into a greater cornering force to the front wheels and a consequent movement of the braking balance.

That behaviour was further emphasised, even if to a slightly lower degree, by the reintroduction of KERS, which subtracts from the braking couple of the rear axle during its battery recharging stage, from the abolition of the double diffuser that drastically reduced aerodynamic force at the rear and the introduction of the mobile wing, which had its

impact on top speed and, consequently, the braking power demanded by the car. Anticipating the change in performance caused by those elements, Brembo directed its development towards the increased performance of the front braking system and lightening that of the rear, with the objective of optimising and harmonising the system's behaviour to the new distribution characteristics of division. For that purpose, the company carried out determined simulations on the handling of the car, which allowed it to define a clear target at which to aim its development work.

## RED BULL

This was the only team, together with its Toro Rosso cousin, to retain the prone position of the brake calipers at the front, despite the experiment carried out at the GP of Japan with them fitted in the vertical overhang position. It was a technique that enabled them to lower the suspension's centre of gravity and did not cause the reliability problems of the 2010 season. Of the small teams, the same solution was used by Lotus.

## 4 PISTONS

From the GP of Spain, Toro Rosso had adopted four piston calipers for the rear, which had been used by Red Bull in 2009 before they decided to return to the normal six piston set-up of the subsequent two seasons.

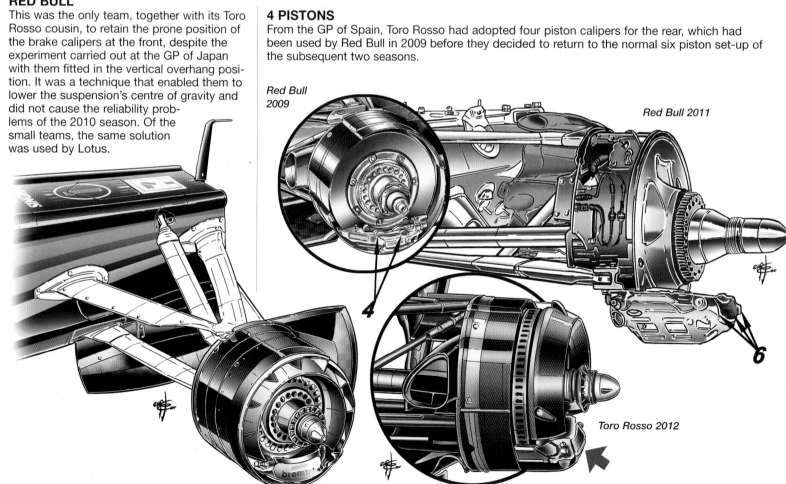

*Red Bull 2009*

*Red Bull 2011*

*Toro Rosso 2012*

# BRAKES, TYRES and ENGINES

The most obvious example of that imposition was the choice of Toro Rosso, which opted for a four piston caliper at the rear that was introduced at the GP of Barcelona on Jaime Algersuari's car and at Monte Carlo on both, replacing the common six piston system that was used previously. Similar technology had already been used by Red Bull in 2009. KERS and the mobile wing also pressed for a really versatile braking system to ensure better management in all conditions. Those two elements represented a usage variable on the track – for example, the mobile wing could be used at all points of the circuit in qualifying, but only on the main straight during the race

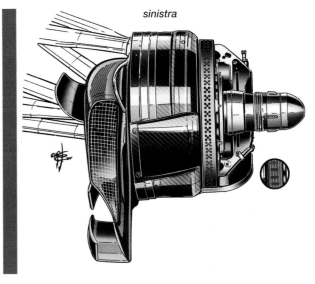

*destra*

*sinistra*

### BREMBO DISCS

Brembo supplied customised brake calipers to Ferrari, Red Bull, Mercedes-Benz, Sauber, Toro Rosso and HRT. It also provided its discs to Jenson Button (McLaren) his team mate Lewis Hamilton – but only for Hungary and Belgium – and Heidfeld (Renault).
For the other races, McLaren used the French company C.I.'s discs, fitted exclusively on the Williams and Lotus, while Renault and Virgin chose the American HITCO's products.
A great deal of work was carried out on disc ventilation.

### McLAREN

McLaren conducted a strange experiment to improve tyre temperatures, especially those at the front. We even saw asymmetric brake ducts at the front from the GP of Germany to verify the interaction between the heat of the discs, tyre behaviour and their possible degradation. Similar experiments were also carried out by Force India.

### FORCE INDIA

Force India kept its odd position of its brake calipers, which are usually vertical but above the front axle but positioned between their axes. Not an optimum technique for cooling them.

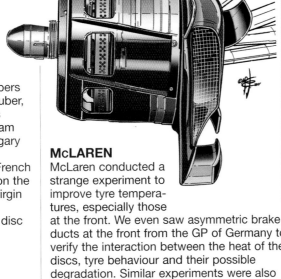

*Montreal*

*Monaco*

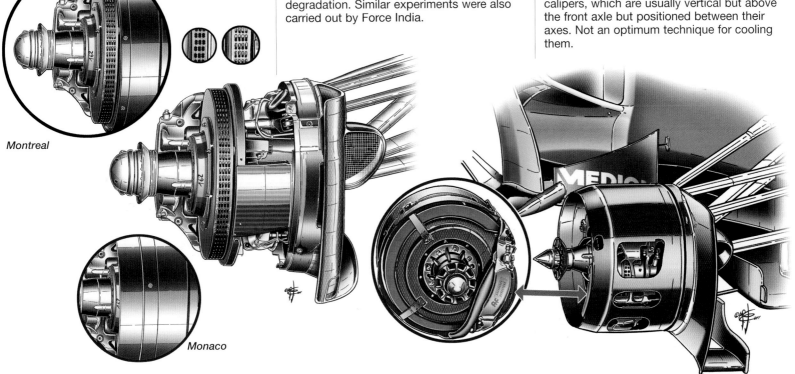

– and pursued the maximisation of consistency and repeatability of the system in the various conditions of couple and temperature. For that reason, one of the major development areas in 2011 was continuous research into the improvement of disc ventilation, leading to the appearance of new designs for the units' holes.

The Italian company works with its clients by offering consultancy on the CFD and personalising disc design in line with a car's specific characteristics and its air intakes. It also takes into account the increasing importance of air flow dynamics inside the rim to better manage the aerodynamic load and tyre temperature.

A fundamental contribution to ventilation is guaranteed by the fixing system developed by Brembo in recent years for its carbon fibre discs. Known as spline fixing, the technique has the bell and brake disc directly connected and 'engaged' through a toothed profile, contrary to the traditional system of using titanium pins to unite the two elements.

With this new technique, the air entry point becomes completely free in its internal diameter, so it is no longer interrupted by fixings, substantially increasing the values of capacity and, therefore cooling, bringing with it temperature improvements of over 100°C; and it also had a more robust feed under torque.

So it can easily be understood how the management of the performance variations of the car under braking, further aggravated by the

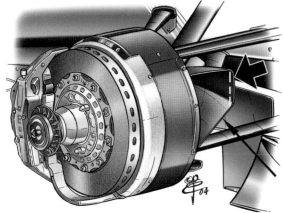

*Toyota 2004*

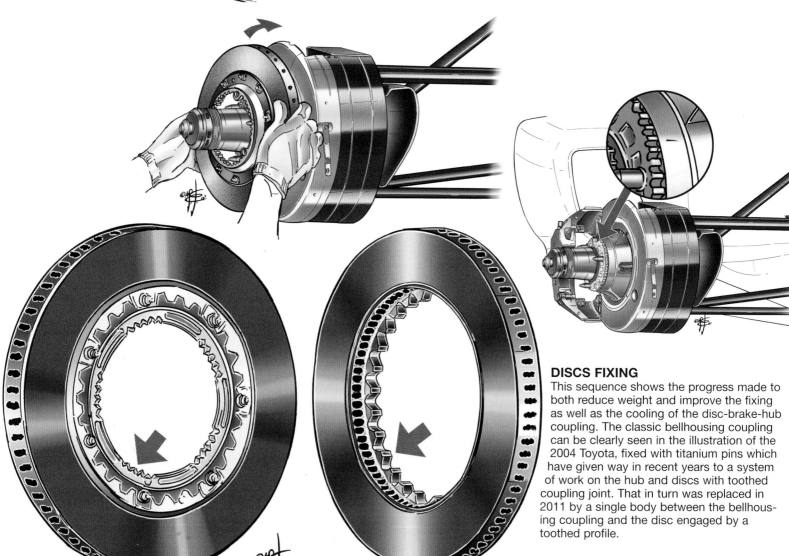

## DISCS FIXING

This sequence shows the progress made to both reduce weight and improve the fixing as well as the cooling of the disc-brake-hub coupling. The classic bellhousing coupling can be clearly seen in the illustration of the 2004 Toyota, fixed with titanium pins which have given way in recent years to a system of work on the hub and discs with toothed coupling joint. That in turn was replaced in 2011 by a single body between the bellhousing coupling and the disc engaged by a toothed profile.

greater degradation of the new Pirelli tyres compared to the Bridgestones, have provided a fundamental aspect in the development of the braking system. The opportunity of offering an increasingly refined adjustment of the braking balance and easy intervention by the driver, who uses these devices many times even during a single lap, has led the teams to work on the controls that operate the distribution of hydraulic pressure between the two systems. In some cases, a control paddle has been added to the traditional means of adjustment using a small lever, which enables the driver to work faster on brake balance.

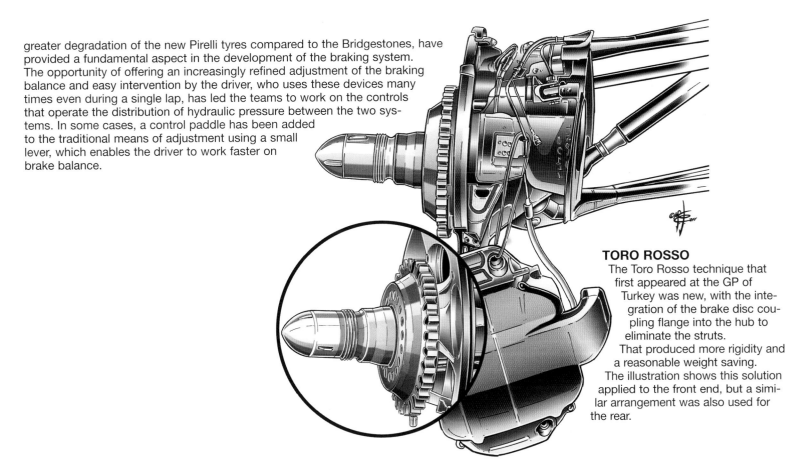

**TORO ROSSO**
The Toro Rosso technique that first appeared at the GP of Turkey was new, with the integration of the brake disc coupling flange into the hub to eliminate the struts.
That produced more rigidity and a reasonable weight saving.
The illustration shows this solution applied to the front end, but a similar arrangement was also used for the rear.

# Tyres

The mission assigned to Pirelli on its return to Formula 1 after success in world championship rallying and GT racing was the somewhat difficult one of enlivening the maximum formula's races and making them more exciting.

That task, which had never ever been given to any other tyre maker, was to design and construct covers that guaranteed more overtaking, more pit stops and different race strategies.

Compared to the Bridgestones, the dimensions of the Pirelli fronts stayed the same at 245/660x13", but the rears became slightly narrower at 325/660x13" keeping the rolling radius the same. Naturally, the shape of the section of the tyre changed, being creature of a different tyre manufacturer's philosophy. Pirelli's first objective was to ensure top level

safety, followed by high speed performance; those two characteristics had to combine with a well-defined degradation of performance that could add another parameter to the race strategies of the various teams, but also more uncertainty.

One of the technical difficulties was to identify which should be the various components of the tyres and in what quantity, to avoid their wear rate taking too long, but also to ensure that it was not too short.

From the design point of view special attention was paid to the shoulders, which were developed using new technology to ensure they could withstand the new slip angle, and the design of the carcass in composite material, able to increase the overall structural rigidity.

On that score, it should be remembered that

the wide use of blown exhausts, with boiling hot air directed to the inner sidewall of the tyre, caused tyre problems in some circumstances; this induced the technicians to set a maximum limit of about 130°C on the temperature of the shoulders with a view to avoiding damage or failure.

The production process can be summarised in three segments – the 'Formula', Compounding and Vulcanising – each one of which has behind it extensive studies, computer simulations with mathematical models,

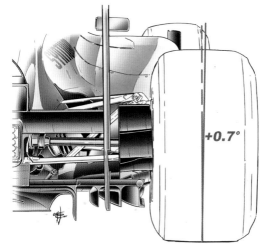

**MERCEDES-BENZ**
In Brazil, the last Grand Prix of the season, Mercedes-Benz and Red Bull tested< with positive static camber angles of about 0.7°, while the other teams kept a negative camber, but one that was very low in this case, too. The reason was in seeking to preserve the rear tyres even more, increasing the footprint on the ground. On the mixed sections of the track, where there is comparatively little lateral stress with the addition of a greater tendency to oversteer, it was particularly the rear right tyre that came under stress. The result was that its behaviour was improved, even if there was a slight degradation on the external area of the tyre where there is generally greater wear in the inner zone.

prototypes, indoor testing and, finally, testing on the track.

With regard to the 'Formula', for every four dry compounds envisaged for the season – Super Soft, Soft, Medium and Hard – the number of components expected to be used between natural and synthetic was 18 to 20, with some common with more compound.

During the Compounding stage, the various components are brought together to respond to specific needs of the mix and, lastly, after having been through other production phases, the tyre is placed in the vulcaniser at a suitable pressure and temperature.

These constructional stages take place in two plants, the prototypes in Milan and the tyres destined for testing and the Grands Prix in Izmit, Turkey, all called Pirelli P Zero Formula 1.

At Izmit, there are rigorous quality controls that prevent tyres with a weight difference of more than 100 grams over the established values – from a minimum of 8.35 kg per front slick to a maximum of 12.35 kg for a rear rain – from being delivered.

For immediate compound recognition, the tyres' sidewalls are painted with strips of different colours: Red for Super Soft, Yellow for Soft, White for Medium and Grey for Hard.

Of the rain tyres, the Intermediates are Blue painted and the rains Orange.

Right from the first race of 2011, teams and drivers have had to devise new tyre range management procedures covering pressures when cold, the temperature of the heaters, the length of time they stay on, warm-up on the track to achieve the required grip in the predicted times through to the driving style to obtain the expected performance and wear rate.

The tyres' warm-up phase has appeared rather critical, as confirmed indirectly by the spins of the various drivers after leaving their pit garages, a clear sign of the need to play into the covers gradually to achieve the start of optimum grip .

To help meet the need for complete exploitation of the tyres, at every GP Pirelli supplied a document with tyre management 'prescription', as well as the suggested pressures for when the tyres were cold and hot, optimum temperatures and functional maxims, camber values with a view to ensuring safety, but also to safeguard the tyres' performance.

The teams and drivers most receptive to these indications were able to achieve the best performance, especially in the race; so we saw Grands Prix of reasonably stable performance with a certain compound for a certain number of laps, which varied from track to track.

After that phase, we usually saw an increase in times that would not change for the next six to eight laps, followed by a clear fall-off in performance that could hardly be envisaged and was not progressive, with an increase in lap times of even two to three seconds.

It was this last phase that seemed less predictable and, therefore, less manageable by the drivers, who lost numerous positions in some cases for having delayed a tyre change, even by a single lap.

On the other hand, changing tyres earlier sometimes led to a driver to clawing back lost positions – like Nico Rosberg in the Grand Prix of China – and finish high up the results table.

As requested by the teams, on some tracks where the tyres came under extremely high stress, the number of pit stops was high – as many as four in the GP of Turkey.

Another characteristic of the Pirellis was the creation of so-called chips or marbles, which were pieces of rubber that came off the tyres when in use.

They filled the track outside the line of trajectory during a race; it was calculated that something like 10,200 kg of rubber was deposited on the tracks of the world in this way during the season.

After the first few races, the technicians identified the different behaviour of the various compounds and modified a number of them. The difference between one compound and another was, on average, around 1.0-1.2 seconds and this rather made certain strategic race decision obligatory.

In some cases, they were associated with the particular adaptation of a driver and the limited aggressiveness of the car on the tyres selected, requiring one pit stop less during the race to enable a team to achieve more significant places in the final results.

As early as the Grand Prix of Spain, a new hard compound was adopted that gave more performance at wear rate parity, to reduce the gap between it and the medium mix.

Usually, an extra set of new compound tyres was supplied to each team for testing during Friday practice, as well as the 11 sets dictated by the regulations. This to enable the squads to compare the new compound with a reference mix, as happened in Canada, where the new Medium was tested and compared for the first time and then made its debut in Valencia.

And it was in Canada that the full wet tyres were used for the first time in a race that saw the safety car take to the track no fewer than six times and the Grand Prix suspended; it was eventually won by Jenson Button on the last lap after four hours.

The intermediates made their debut at Silverstone, but they were only used until the 12th or 13th lap and were then replaced by Softs after track conditions had improved. The same went for the Hungaroring, where the intermediates gave way to the Supersofts between the 10th and 13th lap.

In development terms, new Soft compounds were tested at both the Nürburgring, and then at the end of the season, at Abu Dhabi. They were developed for a minimum difference in performance, but gave an increased mileage return. The Soft mix tried at Bahrain made its first Grand Prix appearance in Brazil, where a new Hard was also used in 2012 pre-configuration. The compound, on two sets of tyres supplied on the Friday morning, was slightly harder than the Medium, therefore coming closer to the operating fields of the four mixes.

At the end of the season, the statistics confirmed that the initial objective was amply met: there were almost 1,100 pit stops that peaked at 88 in Hungary with a minimum of 35 at Monza.

The same goes for overtaking manoeuvres, at more than 1,100 during the season with an incredible 126 and 125 during the Grands Prix of Turkey and Canada respectively.

The new tyres forced the teams' engineers, aided by the 'instructions' supplied by Pirelli's technicians, to also explore new camber angles that adapted better to the cars' characteristics, but which produced also improved performance and reduced wear.

On average, the maximum values recommended were about -4.0° for the front, which was sometimes exceeded by some teams, and -2.5° for the rear.

With regard to the rear, on average the teams adopted values close to -1.0°, with some exceptions, due to the need to increase the tyres' footprint on the ground.

In Brazil, Mercedes-Benz and Red Bull even tested positive static camber angles, above +0.5°.

Considering the recovery of camber in the compression of the wheel, this value was dynamically reduced to close on 0°.

That permitted a maximum footprint and, therefore, improved traction on exiting slow corners without having to use excessively loaded aerodynamic configurations and, therefore, penalising the car on the straights.

*Giancarlo Bruno*

## RED BULL

Adrian Newey devised the stratagem of taking hot gasses to the diffuser, over-lengthening the exhaust terminals almost like those of the Renault, even though they introduced the opposing concept. They were no longer of round but rectangular section, so that they could be immersed in the carbon fibre of the car. That is how the blowing effect created a kind of thermal mini-skirt, which enabled him to create much more sophisticated aerodynamics.

# Engines

To Enzo Ferrari, a Formula 1 car had to have the best engine to be able to win. Power was the maximum expression of competitiveness, but in 2008 FIA froze V8 power unit development to significantly reduce the cost of a season, avoiding the aberrations of qualifying engines that could only be used during such sessions. So engines have increasingly become an 'accessory' to the F1 car, while previously they were its heart and often even the soul of it.

Those restrictions imposed the creation of engines that were really similar, but not the same: it is true that the technicians have no chance of intervening on the internal components of the power units, but they do have the freedom to adapt the 2400 cc V8 to the car's layout. The monocoque mounts, oil pump and many other organs are moved year by year in line with the needs of the chassis men and aerodynamicists. So the fusion of the crankcase can be redesigned before each season. To have a more tapered rear end, in 2011 the Ferrari technicians worked on the

056 placing the service pumps in a new position, but the great revolution that conditioned the season was introduced by Red Bull Racing, taking the concept of the exhaust blow even when the engine is in release, to the utmost degree.

The ingenious Adrian Newey transformed a defect of the Renault engine into an aerodynamic advantage: Red Bull Racing's technical director decided to subjugate the French 8-cylinder to specific aerodynamic needs with the convinced complicity of the Frenchmen. The RS031 V8 was already forced to consume more fuel than necessary, because a part of the petrol was used to cool the head and avoid reliability problems.

The British genius considered that was a waste of energy, which could be used for better performance. How? By manipulating the exhaust gasses so that they blew into the rear diffuser to generate increased vertical load. The idea was not completely new, given that it had already been

developed by Jean Claude Migeot for a Renault in the early Eighties, as can be seen in the New Developments chapter.

But the English technician had solved the problem of the loss of downforce in the release stage by 'dedicating' one of the five mappings of the MES electronic management system to operate so that the exhaust gasses could blow hot air into the diffuser, when the engine was in release or the driver took his foot off the accelerator.

Even if the pedal remained untouched, the butterflies of the V8 stayed 80% open, making petrol and air flow in the combustion chamber. To ensure there was no combustion, an electronic programme was developed that cut the electricity transmitted to the spark plugs and retarded the advance to the maximum. The cut-off meant between four and six cylinders were

## LOTUS RENAULT

Without doubt, credit must go to Lotus-Renault for having adopted the most unconventional feature of the season. It inverted the route of the exhausts, making them run forward to beneath the radiator mouths, where they were curved outwards so that hot air fed the acceleration of air that was directed towards the diffuser by the turning vanes, mounted on the outside of the sidepods. In theory, it should have created a more constant downforce, but in effect it created serious reliability problems. Note that at the ends the long exhaust terminals of the two opposing developments are similar, if not identical.

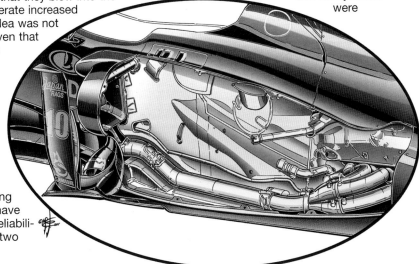

switched off: the mixture was subjected to the pre-ignition of one cylinder per bank before ending up in the exhausts, where the temperature can exceed 800°C. It is here with auto-combustion that the ignition took place and the F1 exhausts transformed that into a kind of post-burner, which emitted a scorching energy that had to be carried effectively to the rear diffuser.

Newey was the first to realise it is possible to generate a Venturi action useful in augmenting aerodynamic load. To obtain the sucking effect at the rear end, it is not enough to blow the hot gases into the diffuser. Working in the wind tunnel, the Briton found it was possible to create a sort of 'thermal mini-skirt' that curbed the general turbulence generated by the rear wheels in movement, directing the exhaust gasses to the bottom of the rear tyre. The 'thermal mini-skirt', which is non-existent when verified with the engine switched off, enabled the Red Bull Racing designer to elaborate the strange set-up of the RB7, which was useful in augmenting the amount

of air that passed under the rear diffuser. But this technique, which is difficult to set up, did not only create advantages: the blown gasses increase the Renault engine's fuel consumption from 5% up to 10%, while both Ferrari and Mercedes-Benz never reached such value limits. So Newey accepted that he should start with a heavier car – in F1, 10 kg more costs an average of 0.3 seconds a lap – knowing that he would have greater benefits from the aerodynamic efficiency of the RB7. There have never been exact estimates, but the word is an advantage of up to one second a lap.

If Red Bull Racing decided to direct the hot gasses to the diffuser by disproportionately lengthening the exhaust terminals, which were no longer round but of rectangular section to be 'drowned' in the depths of the car's carbon fibre, Lotus-Renault tried to develop an alternative idea. The Enstone team had its exhausts run forward to just below the radiator mouths, where they were curved outwards to feed the flow of hot gasses to the acceler-

ation of air that was directed towards the extractor by turning vanes mounted in the outer area of the sidepods.

The idea produced good results in the early races, but it created major reliability problems because all the parts in carbon fibre closest to the exhaust blow broke and became a danger. No other team followed Lotus-Renault's example, but almost all of them tried their own interpretation of the Red Bull Racing concept. McLaren achieved good results with the Mercedes-Benz engine, but we cannot say the same of Ferrari.

Maranello was never able to find that second that distanced them from the RB7 – especially in qualifying – and they had to be happy with an improvement of half that due to the objective difficulty of making the wind tunnel and track data work.

Newey did not stop, but always forged ahead further developing the concept, differentiating the way the exhausts work at blowing in the engine release phase (braking), but also during initial acceleration on exiting a corner or

## HOT BLOW

### OPEN ACCELERATOR CYCLE

The first column shows the cycle during the acceleration phase (a = butterfly open) in which the entire quantity of the air/petrol mixture is compressed in the cylinder and the spark plug (b) makes it explode; at that point, the gasses generate the energy needed to push the piston downwards while in the subsequent (c) stage; when they are still very hot they are pushed into the exhausts making them scorchingly so; at the end of the cycle, the gasses channelled into the diffuser increase the negative lift effect.

### RELEASE CYCLE

The second column represents the standard release stage, where (a = butterfly closed) air is still aspirated due to the drive shaft/piston rotation effect, but being without the petrol component, despite the ignition of the spark plug (b), it produces no energy of any kind; at this point, the air is made to flow in the exhausts but without the 'blow' effect (c) into the diffuser.

### HOT BLOWING

In the third and last column, we see how the engine cycle is modified with hot blowing in the release phase; in aspiration, there is a much thinner air/petrol component (a = butterfly part-open at about 80%) and it is not made to explode in the combustion chamber (b – no ignition) but is subsequently pushed into the exhaust pipe where it gradually increases in temperature to about 800°C until it ignites, generating a flow into the diffuser similar to that of the acceleration phase (c).

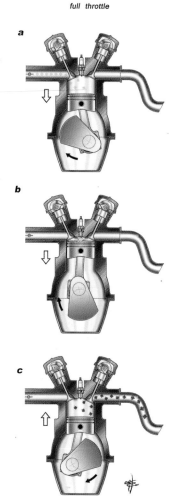

full throttle

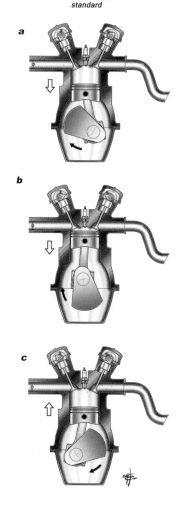

off throttle
standard

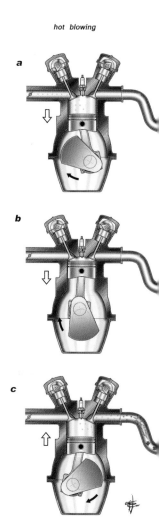

hot blowing

curve. Due to the cut-off, he was able to reduce engine torque that would have made the rear wheels spin due to excessive power: he dispersed the surplus energy into the exhausts, so increasing the aerodynamic load at the rear end and ensuring greater torque, therefore more traction, without having to use wings with incidences that were too loaded. Many recognised the deep sound of the Renault V8 in the chicanes due to the ignition cut-off in the cylinders: even if indirectly, the French were able to recreate a sort of traction control, which is banned by FIA.

When it realised it was being made a laughing stock, the Federation tried to intervene by maintaining that engines were not allowed to influence aerodynamic behaviour.

Charlie Whiting, the organisation's technical delegate, also held that it was not permitted to change the mapping of the electronic management system between qualifying and the race, given that it was only in testing that they used the anticipation values that would have created reliability problems.

There was some tough in-fighting on this one and it led to the prohibition of exhausts blow for the Grand Prix of Great Britain – the Silverstone race was subjected to three regulation changes in a single weekend – and it was not by chance that the Ferrari 150 Italia scored its only success of the season in that GP, driven by Fernando Alonso.

But the attempt to ban exhaust blow came to nothing, because Renault's specialists and then those of Mercedes-Benz were able to demonstrate to FIA – even producing 2009 telemetric graphs – that certain anticipated values were indispensible in guaranteeing the tightness of the engines, given that the open butterflies have always been used to cool the valves.

At every GP we saw very different and ever more refined exhaust solutions. Knowing that the evolution of hot blowing could cost about 30 hp – the terminals were too long and not of the most efficient shape – the engine specialists tried to recoup at least part of the amount of power dispersed in favour of aerodynamics. For example, Ferrari experimented with a sort of closed chimney below the four terminals per cylinder bank, which was useful in compensating for the energy load created by the post combustion effect.

The paradox was that F1 regulations allow the use of eight engines per driver per season. So the saving that was made was wasted in 2011 with continuous bench testing to work out the new exhaust configurations.

It is said that Mercedes-Benz used benches with two work cycles per day, while Ferrari decided on a weekly long run.

And when they say long run they do not limit themselves to the duration of a GP, but a complete vital cycle of an engine. So we are talking about a distance of over two-and-a-half GPs.

Every new exhaust design required bench test work and resolution with the develop-

## FERRARI

Starting from the Grand Prix of Belgium, Ferrari experimented with a kind of closed chimney below the four terminals per cylinder bank, which was useful in compensating for the charges of energy that it created due to the effect of post-combustion.
It is a feature that was transferred to the 2012 car project, for which season hot blowing was prohibited by the Federation.

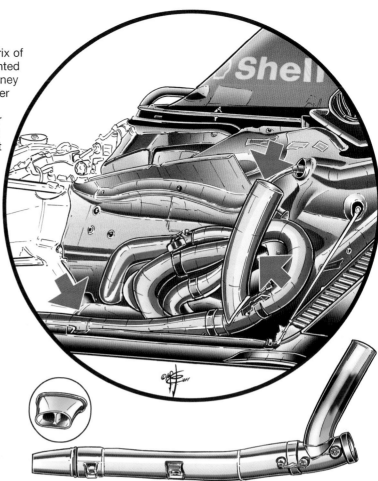

ment of at least a long run. To all of this was added the need to develop electronic solutions in line with the modifications carried out on the terminals, creating ad hoc mapping every time.

So it is clear that the investment to support the development of kinds of performance like exhaust blow was considerable.

During the experiments, valves or pistons sometimes gave way, further increasing the work cycle. But the engine specialists did not so much go looking for performance as the ability to tolerate the kind of 'torture' necessary to take post combustion to the extreme. Basically, Formula 1 wants more ecological engines but tolerated the use of a much polluting V8 – substances not correctly burnt in the combustion chamber release others into the atmosphere that damage health – thanks to KERS. Although limited by the regulations, the engine men also tried to improve performance by concentrating on the reduction of the friction coefficient in the moving parts. Mercedes-Benz, for example, used silver alloy for clamping the connecting rods, while Ferrari worked with the same material in the seal between the crankcase and the head. Substantial attention was also paid to lubricating oil, the viscosity of which was much reduced, as was the quantity necessary for the correct working of the power unit.

With the reduction of friction, power was slightly increased: the Mercedes-Benz V8 was credited with 760 hp at 18,000 rpm and Ferrari's 056 was not far off that, even if the Maranello unit was designed with an 11:1 compression ratio against 13,0:1 of other F1 motors.

We should, of course, remember that the Formula 1 World Championship was won by Renault with Red Bull Racing and has about 10 hp less than other top line teams.

We are talking about maximum power, while the French technicians are committed to finding the best fulfilment at medium revs, the ones most frequently used on modern circuits.

The use of KERS also changed after it returned from a year's absence: it is no longer used at maximum power as in its debut year of 2009 with its kinetic energy recovery, but at average speed to enable the cars to reach their top performance quicker.

On the question of reliability, it should be remembered that the current V8s limited their power loss from one GP to another: it was once the case that an engine competing in its third race could lose 30 hp, but now the fall-off is down to 1% or just 7 hp.

A value a driver is unlikely to notice, but which could be significant in a race.

*Franco Nugnes*

# KERS

KERS is short for the Kinetic Energy Recovery System, which recuperates kinetic energy during braking when the driver exerts a pressure of 2 bar on the pedal and the throttle is not in use. It is transformed into electric energy for use as an overboost of power. KERS reappeared in Formula 1 in 2011 after an initial debut in 2009.
The exorbitant cost of its development pushed the smaller teams into taking a tough stance, which led FIA to suspend the use of KERS in 2010. But in reality, the system was never cancelled from the technical regulations and, as required by FIA president Jean Todt, it went back into action in 2011 even if as an option.

Nine teams out of 12 adopted KERS for 2011, the odd ones out being Lotus Racing, Virgin and HRT. Ferrari and Renault, two of the four manufacturers, made themselves available to supply the whole system at a political price of 1 million euro per season.

So the Federation fixed expenditure rules: five million euros for research plus one million for each team to be supplied. Ferrari had set a budget of eight million, Mercedes-Benz had interpreted the norm differently and budgeted an investment of 18 million – six million for each of the teams it supports, Mercedes itself, McLaren and Force India.
In the end, agreement was reached on 12 million euros per producer.

Ferrari provided KERS for its client teams Sauber and Toro Rosso and Renault supported Red Bull Racing as well as the Enstone team; Williams came up with its own system, combined with the Cosworth engine.

The 2009 KERS technical norm was unchanged: it was possible to use energy of 400 Kj per lap, with a maximum power of 60 Kw or about 80 hp. But the year when it was not used enabled the technicians to develop lighter systems. The first year, a complete KERS system – motor-generator, batteries, cables and electronic management system –

weighed about 30-35 kg, but in 2011 that had been pared down by 30% as it did not exceed 20 kg.

The major improvement in quality, which saved a lot of money, was in the length of time the components lasted. In 2009, the KERS system was practically replaced after every Grand Prix, but in 2011 the teams used the same kit for five or even six races.

The exploitation strategy had changed in the search for maximum performance: the use of the system was adjusted in relation to the characteristics of the various tracks.
The philosophy on the basis of which the extra boost was used changed: it did not just produce a continuous charge of 60 Kw on a straight when the V8 is delivering maximum power, it also parcelled up the energy in packets to use on the exit from corners in the acceleration phase. In 2009, the teams sought maximum speed with which to overtake, but then they realised it was better to make top speed as fast as possible.
This is a factor that made Sebastian Vettel's Red Bull RB7 such a winner: Adrian Newey had solved the KERS reliability problems that had dogged the Milton Keynes cars' performance at the start of the season, especially on Mark Webber's car.

## 2009 FERRARI KERS

Ferrari set the trend over the installation of KERS and its accessories. In fact, in 2009 the F60 had a battery pack housed in a singular element positioned inside its fuel tank, meanwhile Mercedes-Benz, McLaren and BMW had separate elements in their sidepods. A decision that ensured safety and a good concentration of the mass near the centre of gravity, which continued on the F150 Italia with a lighter, smaller 'case'.

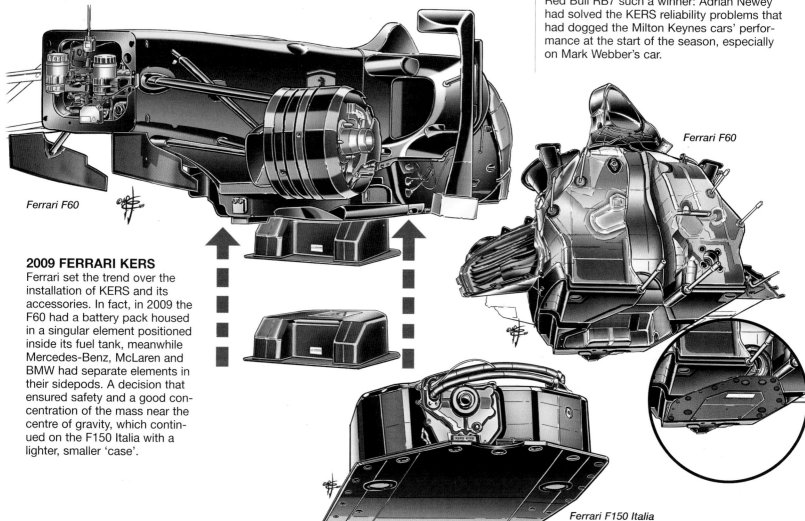

*Ferrari F60*

*Ferrari F60*

*Ferrari F150 Italia*

## 2009 McLAREN KERS

In 2009, Mercedes-Benz and BMW had divided batteries in the sidepods, but for 2011 they opted for the Ferrari system with a single battery pack inside the fuel tank.

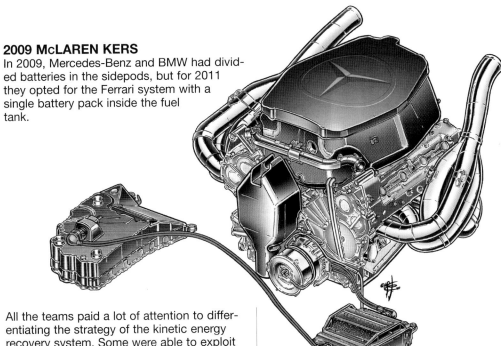

All the teams paid a lot of attention to differentiating the strategy of the kinetic energy recovery system. Some were able to exploit 800 Kj in a lap; it was possible to discharge 400 Kj before the finish line and the same again immediately afterwards, which was ideal on circuits with really long straights, where it was possible to try to overtake.

So KERS became a useful instrument in optimising performance. For example, its use is not advisable when exiting a corner if the car has traction problems – the advantage would disappear with a loss of grip or wheelspin – but it can be useful in 'filling in' torque holes that some engines can have at certain rpms, for those which are their fluid mechanics characteristics.

As can be seen, KERS became an element that also interacted directly, even with the layout of the car. All those that use it install the system in the most protected area of the car: Ferrari indicated the right direction when it

housed the entire system inside a small 'case' below the fuel tank between the driver and the engine, the safest place if hit from behind.

On the other hand, Red Bull Racing went for a more creative solution in that it decided to distribute the batteries in various areas of the rear end: on the left side of the Renault engine and inside the carbon fibre gearbox, near the clutch bellhousing. It seems right that it is easier to accommodate many small boxes rather than a single case, without affecting the capacity of the fuel tank.

If the KERS contribution could be pegged at about three tenths of a second the first year, its value grew in performance stability: the

efficiency of the system would have reached 90% - a thermal motor gets up to 35% at the most - an indication that the batteries had a much greater autonomy than in the system's debut year.

That result was possible by refrigerating the system: the accumulator, which is the most critical component, was stabilised at a temperature of 60°-70°, while the motor-generator could peak at 250° as it turned at double the revolutions of the V8: 36,000 against 18,000 of the thermal engine.

Another aspect that the technicians spent time on was recharging: we said that KERS stores energy under braking.
So to all effects and purposes, the system is an added depository that contributes to slowing the car. So it was not easy to 'tune' the detachment of the driver with the system, because in 2009 many of them complained about the discontinuity of braking, perhaps because the system became detached during the manoeuvre.

With its sophisticated software, the KERS electronic management system, manages complex strategies designed by specialist engineers that interface in real time with the designers of the car. The tendency is to charge energy with every release so as not to create any 'surprises' for the driver, but the charge surplus can be dissipated in heat.

The recovery of energy is a fascinating aspect, because it is one that is hidden within the car.

## RED BULL

Just for a change Adrian Newey, who rejected KERS for the 2009 car, went against the trend! The RB7's batteries were divided, miniaturised and placed in a useful area to both weight distribution and the car's aerodynamics – but logistical trouble maker.
He positioned the two packs in one of the hottest points of the car, behind the exhausts.
To improve cooling, there was a complicated system of internal channelling within the chassis and the engine cover. Result: as well as having more complex recharging, Red Bull's KERS was the RB7's only Achilles heel on more than one occasion.

The return of Pirelli tyres to Formula 1 after a 19-year absence forced the technicians to take a different approach to suspension design but, during the season, also to a form of car set-up management that could better adapt itself to the characteristics of the new covers.

The technical regulations had been somewhat modified, increasing the car's minimum weight with the driver to 640 kg, reducing the inclination of the diffuser – which in turn diminished aerodynamic downforce – and set the weight distribution so that the front axle did not weigh less than 291 kg and the rear no less than 342 kg.

These limits, which were the equivalent to a static division of 45.5% at the front but could reach a maximum of 46.6%, reduced the possibility of working on the car's set-up by switching ballast around.

From the suspension lay-out point of view, the pushrod system was adopted universally at the front once again; pull rod was used for the rear, as it was considered more suitable to have a means of moving the mass downwards and optimise the aerodynamics.

This layout was selected by seven teams, although Ferrari, Sauber, Virgin and HRT continued to use pushrod.

Our analysis begins with the front suspension. It is interesting to note how, at layout parity, there were different interpretations and distribution of the suspension elements by the various designers. That went especially for the position of the steering box and relative steering arms, to the location of the pushrod on the hub and to the anti-dive angles.

But these different layouts are 'children' of choice that can optimise aerodynamic efficiency and do not derive from any particular need of kinematic mechanisms of the suspension.

In some cases, like those of Lotus Renault and McLaren, the drive box was moved to the lower area of the chassis to keep down the weight of the suspended mass.

The steering arms on the Lotus ran parallel with the front lever of the lower wishbone and were fixed at a height just below the centre wheel line on the hub side. In the top view it is clear how the mounts on the side of the chassis were almost aligned and formed a symmetrical V in relation to the front wheel axle with the pushrod oriented towards the front part of the car. The side view shows the choice of inclination angles, which are higher for the lower wishbone than the upper to increase the anti-dive effect.

On the other hand, in McLaren's case the mount of the front lever of the lower wishbone on the chassis was further down in respect of the steering arm; again the top view shows how the V of the wishbones is extremely narrow, with the front arms almost parallel with the front wheel axis.

## WEIGHT DISTRIBUTION

With the arrival of Pirelli tyres, the Federation imposed fixed weight distribution parameters, shown in the illustration: on the front axle no less than 291 kg were to be calculated and on the rear at least 342 kg. Those limits, which are the equivalent to a static distribution of 45.5% at the front but that may reach a maximum of 46.6%, reduced the possibility of intervening on the car's set-up and working on the movement of ballast.

## FERRARI

While still with the same suspension layout, there was a different interpretation and distribution of its elements by the various designers, with particular reference to the drive box position and relative steering arms. Ferrari abandoned the position of the arms at the same height as the upper wishbone to move on to one with the steering arm fixed to the hub that was higher than the wheel centre.

**53.3/54.5**
**min 342kg (Q)**

**45.5/46.6**
**min291kg (Q)**

Consequently, the pushrod is oriented towards the back of the car.

In this case, the side view shows how the inclination of the upper wishbone is greater than that of the lower unit.

To be highlighted the position of the steering box outside the chassis, with the steering arm mount on the hub lower than the wheel's centre line, and that of the inerter, of generous dimensions.

On the Ferrari, the steering box was also installed high up and inside the chassis, with the steering arm fixed to the hub higher than the wheel's centre line. Its wishbones were of a fairly symmetrical V shape in respect of the axle; the pushrod was slightly angled towards the rear and its mount on the wheel hub ended up in a lower position to the rim's centre line and very close to the lower wishbone.

In the side view, the Ferrari's suspension wishbones show the greater inclination of the upper units in relation to the lowers in search of higher anti-dive angles.

On the Force India, which had similar geometry to that of the Ferrari, there was an asymmetric V of the wishbones, as visible in the top view. The front arms were almost parallel with the wheel axis and pushrod oriented towards the car's nose. In this case, the drive box was on the outside of the chassis and, therefore, easily accessible.

Red Bull's layout was also similar to Ferrari's, the difference being that the steering box was almost at mid-height between the suspension's wishbones. The side view shows a greater inclination of the upper wishbone compared to the lower unit.

The position of the steering box on the Sauber was at the same height as the upper lever. The top view shows the symmetrical lay out of the suspension wishbones with a fairly narrow V and the pushrod slightly oriented

*McLaren*

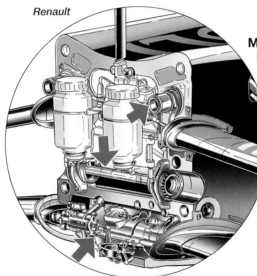
*Renault*

### McLAREN AND LOTUS RENAULT
Both McLaren and Renault moved the steering arms into the lower zone of the monocoque to keep down the weight of the suspension mass. On the MP4-26 the lower wishbone was once more set lower. On the Lotus Renault, the steering arms ran parallel with the front lever of the suspension's lower wishbone and were fixed at a height just below the wheel centre line on the hub. Note the anti-roll bar outside the monocoque.

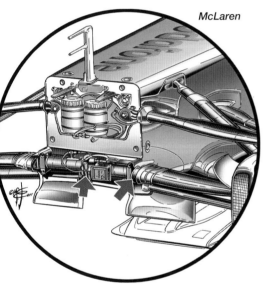

### McLAREN INERTER
During front suspension assembly operations it was possible to see the generous dimensions of the inerter or inertial damper of the McLaren. The position of the steering box is worth pointing out: it was outside the monocoque with the steering arm mount on the hub, lower than the rim centre line.

### McLAREN AND RED BULL
From this top view, it is clear how the mounts on the monocoque's side were almost aligned and formed a symmetrical V in relation to the front wheel axis, with the pushrod oriented towards the car's rear.

towards the car's rear end.

And on the Air Asia, at layout parity, the wishbones had high angles of inclination when seen from the side; the steering arm hub mount was extremely high, those of the pushrod and the peak of the lower wishbone well below the wheel centre line.

The Williams layout was unusual, with the steering box moved to the inside of the chassis mid-way between the chassis' wishbone mounts; the torsion bars as in 2010, have one end slotted into the rocker arm and the other connected through a metal element to the other bar. When movement is purely bump, rotating in discordant directions, the two bars stressed the traction bar and, therefore, bent in function of their rigidity, permitting the suspension's compressing movement.

With roll motion, one of the suspension compresses and the other extends; not being linked to the chassis, the bars rotate in the same direction, causing a horizontal movement of the small connecting bar; so the roll stiffness is controlled by the anti-roll bars linked to the rocker and a third damper.

Now we'll move on to analysing the rear suspension, discussing first those with pushrods. In this case, too, the layouts were fairly similar, with an upper wishbone that had a rear arm practically parallel with the axis of the wheel and the front connected to the gearbox in a reasonably advanced position, very close to the connection between the engine and the gearbox.

The small anti-steering arm, usually attached to the carbon fibre configuration of the rear

deformable structure, was in a set back position towards the lower wing plane and aligned in height with the wheel's centre line, The pushrod was really long and inclined forwards; its fixing on the rocker, especially the Ferrari's, was very close to the front mount of the upper wishbone.

The lower wishbone had very high mounts on the gearbox and, in the top view, they made up the geometry of the upper wishbone, but with a reduced V-shaped opening.

By the GP of Canada Ferrari started to test with a modified the geometry having worked on the rear top arm, which was shorter, fixed at a higher point than the hub and closer to the longitudinal axis of the car. This modified a number of parameters

## FORCE INDIA
The steering arms of the Force India were in a very similar position to those of the Ferrari, but the drive box was external to the monocoque and, therefore, more easily accessible.

## FERRARI: TOP VIEW
The wishbones on the Ferrari were V-shaped and reasonably symmetrical in relation to the wheel axis; the pushrod was only just oriented towards the rear and its mount on the hub ended in a lower position than the wheel centre line, very close to the lower wishbone mount.

## RED BULL
The Red Bull had a suspension that was very similar to that of the 2010 car. Compared to Ferrari, the steering box was almost at mid-height between the wishbones. In the side view, the upper wishbone's inclination was greater than that of the lower unit.

characteristic of the suspension, especially the camber change, increased the scrub of the wheel during compression, work carried out to generate more lateral force and, therefore, greater temperature and grip.

The geometry with pull rod proved to be more effective, enabling the heavier elements of the suspension to be kept in a low position and freeing the area of the flat bottom, where space had been made for the exhausts that exploited the blown effect .

The best interpreter of this technique was, of course, Red Bull, which adopted and

developed it over a number of years.

The layout had an upper wishbone with a rear arm parallel to the axis of the wheel and connected with that of the other side on the gearbox's carbon fibre structure; but the front arm outstretched in a decisive manner towards the gearbox by a fixing located in proximity with that which connects engine and gearbox.

The lower wishbone mounts on the gearbox were notably high, with both the arms fixed to the gearbox in a higher position than the drive shafts and with a V-angle in the top view that was much narrower in relation to the upper wishbone. On the hub side, the fixing point was in a position under the wheel centre line, but still fairly high up to permit the location of the caliper in a horizontal position, all to the advantage of cleanliness of the area where the cold aerody-

namic air stream flows, as well as hot flow generated by the exhausts.

Note the much advanced position of the pull rod in metal, outside the lower wishbone, equipped with a regulator with shims to vary the height from the ground. That controls the rocker placed in a very low position on the gearbox, with an extremely long lever arm to activate the damper and permit a non-excessive speed of the stem.

In a more advanced position and higher than the front mount of the lower wishbone was the anti-roll bar housing, controlled by opportune internal leverage on the gearbox.

A solution very similar to that of Red Bull is present on the Air Asia; all the other cars with same lay out had the pull rod inside the upper wishbone.

Williams deserves a special mention as they designed and produced a gearbox with a very low positioned differential. That brought with it an evident lowering of the rear end below the engine cover and a suspension design in line with this new geometry.

The drive shafts were much inclined downwards in relation to the wheel centre line and they were oriented slightly towards the back; the rear mounts of the upper wishbone and the anti-steering arm were no longer connected to the gearbox, but to the central pillar that supported the rear wing.

Given the ban on adjusting the suspension, Mercedes-Benz created a passive hydraulic interconnection able to react to loads exerted on them; the hydraulic unit, composed of a tank and a group of valves, was connected to elements that presumably perform like dampers, ensuring the fluid did not move from one of the damper's upper chambers to the other, but through tubing as far as the valve block. Depending on how the upper and lower compartments on the left side were connected to the corresponding chambers on the right side, the system reacted differently to the impulses that came from the suspension, so opposing resistance to the roll motion or vertical bump and rebound.

In terms of height from the ground, it should be said that the tendency – initially explored by Red Bull and then adopted by the other teams – was to use a particularly unusual set-up with the extremity of the diffuser at a height of around 240 mm from the ground. This set-up was developed to be able to best use the exhaust blow; working in the diffuser zone, the hot gases favoured the extraction of air to create increased aerodynamic load.

*Giancarlo Bruno*

2010

## WILLIAMS

Williams kept more or less the same position for its steering arms in relation to the suspension's wishbones; only the steering box was moved inside the monocoque. The metal connection between the mounts of the torsion bars was also retained.

2011

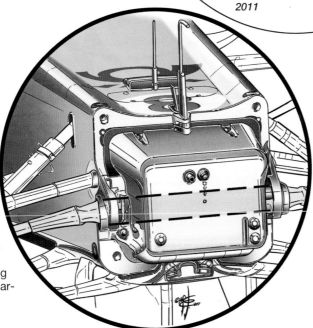

## MERCEDES-BENZ

The steering links were also separate from the suspension's wishbone fairing on the Mercedes-Benz and the steering box was external, covered by carbon fibre fairing.

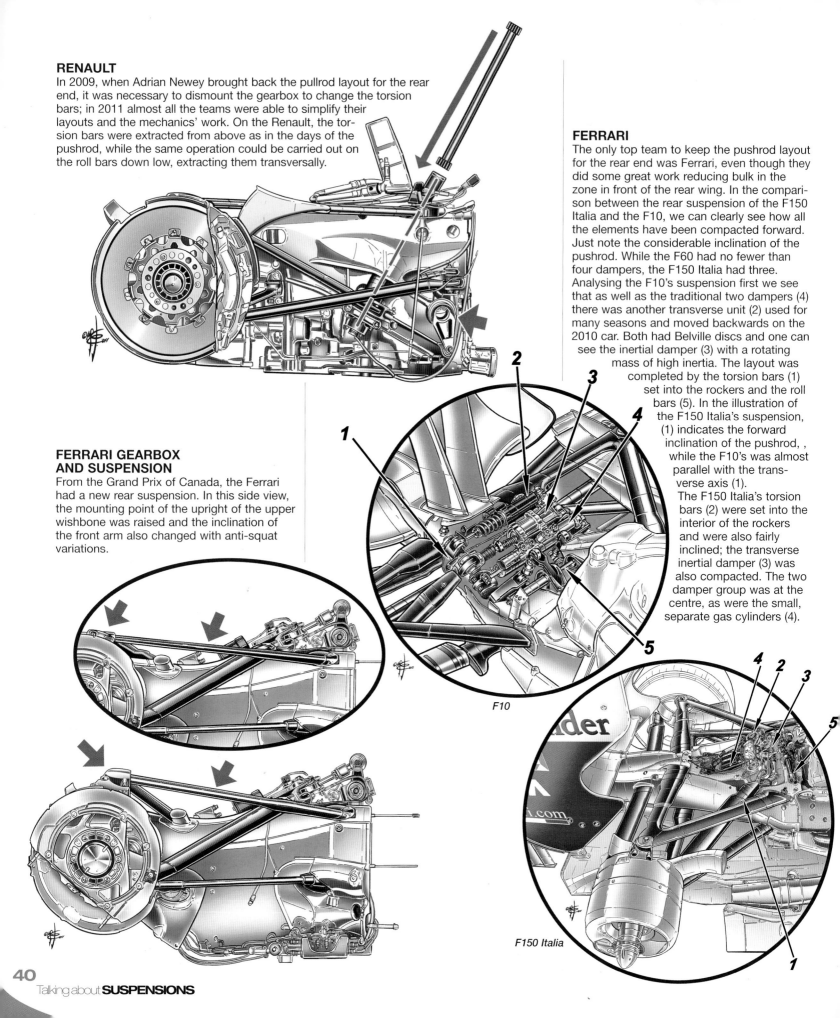

## RENAULT

In 2009, when Adrian Newey brought back the pullrod layout for the rear end, it was necessary to dismount the gearbox to change the torsion bars; in 2011 almost all the teams were able to simplify their layouts and the mechanics' work. On the Renault, the torsion bars were extracted from above as in the days of the pushrod, while the same operation could be carried out on the roll bars down low, extracting them transversally.

## FERRARI GEARBOX AND SUSPENSION

From the Grand Prix of Canada, the Ferrari had a new rear suspension. In this side view, the mounting point of the upright of the upper wishbone was raised and the inclination of the front arm also changed with anti-squat variations.

## FERRARI

The only top team to keep the pushrod layout for the rear end was Ferrari, even though they did some great work reducing bulk in the zone in front of the rear wing. In the comparison between the rear suspension of the F150 Italia and the F10, we can clearly see how all the elements have been compacted forward. Just note the considerable inclination of the pushrod. While the F60 had no fewer than four dampers, the F150 Italia had three. Analysing the F10's suspension first we see that as well as the traditional two dampers (4) there was another transverse unit (2) used for many seasons and moved backwards on the 2010 car. Both had Belville discs and one can see the inertial damper (3) with a rotating mass of high inertia. The layout was completed by the torsion bars (1) set into the rockers and the roll bars (5). In the illustration of the F150 Italia's suspension, (1) indicates the forward inclination of the pushrod, , while the F10's was almost parallel with the transverse axis (1).

The F150 Italia's torsion bars (2) were set into the interior of the rockers and were also fairly inclined; the transverse inertial damper (3) was also compacted. The two damper group was at the centre, as were the small, separate gas cylinders (4).

F10

F150 Italia

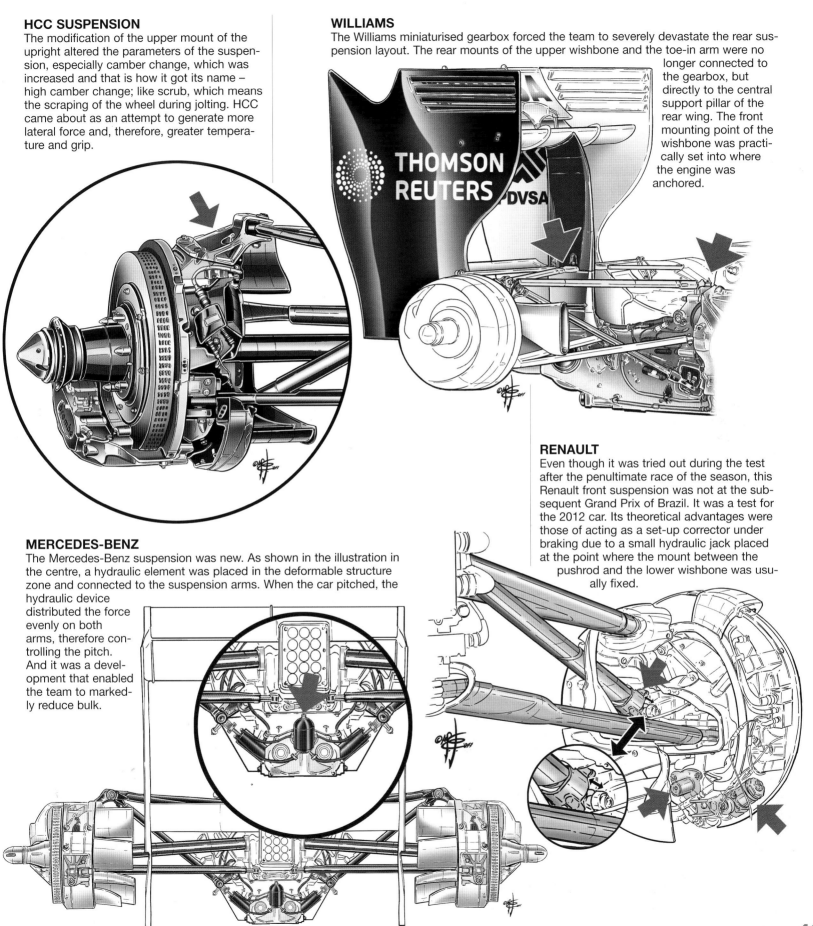

## HCC SUSPENSION

The modification of the upper mount of the upright altered the parameters of the suspension, especially camber change, which was increased and that is how it got its name – high camber change; like scrub, which means the scraping of the wheel during jolting. HCC came about as an attempt to generate more lateral force and, therefore, greater temperature and grip.

## WILLIAMS

The Williams miniaturised gearbox forced the team to severely devastate the rear suspension layout. The rear mounts of the upper wishbone and the toe-in arm were no longer connected to the gearbox, but directly to the central support pillar of the rear wing. The front mounting point of the wishbone was practically set into where the engine was anchored.

## MERCEDES-BENZ

The Mercedes-Benz suspension was new. As shown in the illustration in the centre, a hydraulic element was placed in the deformable structure zone and connected to the suspension arms. When the car pitched, the hydraulic device distributed the force evenly on both arms, therefore controlling the pitch. And it was a development that enabled the team to markedly reduce bulk.

## RENAULT

Even though it was tried out during the test after the penultimate race of the season, this Renault front suspension was not at the subsequent Grand Prix of Brazil. It was a test for the 2012 car. Its theoretical advantages were those of acting as a set-up corrector under braking due to a small hydraulic jack placed at the point where the mount between the pushrod and the lower wishbone was usually fixed.

Once again Red Bull achieved both its goals by winning the drivers' and constructors' F1 world championships with the perfect RB7. Their collection of victories and pole positions was extensive in any man's language and is featured in the introduction to this book. What interests us more than anything else from the technical point of view is that, as well as being the most competitive car of all, the RB7 also turned out to be the most reliable. Just one retirement during the whole season for Sebastian Vettel and that was due to a rear tyre, perhaps connected with exhaust blow. Rather than an evolution of the previous season's car, the RB7 seemed to be a direct descendent of the 2009 RB5, the one designed for the single diffuser and which, without Ross Brawn's discovery, would have dominated that season. The gearbox went back to being slightly wider but it was lower, all to the advantage of the miniaturised rear end that married better with its blown exhausts. That was the technical feature on which Adrian Newey concentrated his entire design from August 2010 onwards. To give maximum privilege to the car's aerodynamics, he avoided installing the KERS components inside the fuel tank so as to have neither negative consequences as far as wheelbase dimensions were concerned nor variations in the height of the tank and, therefore, the centre of gravity. The installation of KERS was a laboured affair and was the only weak point of this perfect car. So as not to alter the shape if his project, Newey miniaturised the various KERS components and positioned two mini-batteries at the sides of the gearbox, which was unfortunately a hot area near the exhausts, obviously cooled by suitable channelling, although that created some inconve-

nience, especially in the first part of the season.
To sort out the problem, Newey introduced channelling that took air from two small windows low down on the chassis in a sort of stepped area formed between the nose and the chassis mount, which ran along almost the whole car to cool the electronic management system and the batteries. In part, it was reminiscent of

the 2010 F-Duct layout, with channelling that ran along the whole chassis to ensure blow into the rear wing's flap.
The other RB7 project starting point was its swooping set-up, which had already been introduced in 2010 and became one of the strong points of the new car.
A swooping set-up and blown exhausts formed a perfect sym-

biosis, given that the exhaust blow into the diffuser's side channels worked like a thermal mini-skirt that sealed the greater space between the diffuser's end plates and the ground, compensating for the excessive height from the ground determined by that particular set-up.
A camouflaged version of the Red Bull was unveiled at the official lunch of the car in Valencia; it

*Red Bull RB6*

*Red Bull RB7*

*Red Bull RB7*
*Melbourne*

*Red Bull RB7*
*Barcelona*

| CONSTRUCTORS' CLASSIFICATION | | | |
|---|---|---|---|
| | 2010 | 2011 | |
| Position | 1° | 1° | = |
| Points | 498 | 650 | +152 ▲ |

had a small fin on the engine cover and almost traditional exhausts, but a few days later a new cover arrived plus exhausts that blew into the lateral channels in which the last five centimetres were cut to privilege the blow. And immediately after that, along came a new diffuser with a mini-flap in the trailing edge that Newey simply copied from the Toro Rosso. The ingenious designer has never hidden the fact that he is the usual attentive observer of all the cars to winkle out features that could improve his projects' designs. That was the case with the fringes under the rear wings, which had been reintroduced from the start of the season by Sauber, taken up by McLaren and fitted to the RB7 from the Spanish GP.

Returning to the links with the 2009 RB5, the suspension layout and position of the brake calipers were unchanged, with the fronts laid flat despite the experiment with vertical calipers at Suzuka. Development during the season was maniacal, with the appearance of new features at just about every race.

The GP of Spain was the stage on which the first important element came out, with a new engine cover and hot air outlets, a unique diffuser that was tested by Vettel, new rear wing end plates with McLaren-style fringes and, surprisingly, front rims with rings of the Ferrari school.

And on more than one occasion, the Red Bull drivers had three or four versions of the front wing available to them that were different in both the shape of the central pillars, the planes and the end plates, as was the position of the TV camera.

The same went for the rear wing and diffuser, with at least two variants taken to every GP. And in Belgium there was a semi-revolution that passed by almost unobserved.

The initial part of the sidepods was drastically modified, not so much in shape as the section of the brake in the lower area, which was notably increased to guarantee a better air flow towards the rear; a change that required the repositioning of all the internal elements of the sidepods.

The modification of the diffuser at Monza was significant, with the addition of a mini-flap in the end plate area. This guaranteed more load and the use of a wing with a reduced chord, compared to the one at Spa, without losing downforce. So the Red Bulls built up their advantage in sections two and three of Monza, permitting them the luxury of operating with Vettel's car a seventh shorter, which produced 'just' 327.7 kph against the more than 342 kph of the Ferraris.

In some cases like Japan, they even used materials in extremis, sending them by scheduled flights and then by helicopter from the airport to the track.

Red Bull RB7
Valencia

Red Bull RB7
Spa-Francorchamps

Red Bull RB7
Monza

Red Bull RB7
Suzuka

## RED BULL RB7

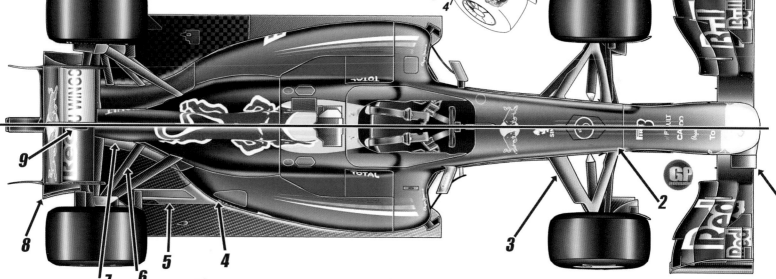

Rather than having been derived from the car that won the 2010 world championships, the RB7, the best F1 car of recent years, was a direct descendent of the RB5, which astonished observers with its innovative features even if it did have to give way to the Brawn GP and its double diffuser. The 2011 Red Bull took all the basic principles of the RB5 to become a clear evolution of that earlier car in every detail. Despite the introduction of KERS, its wheelbase was practically the same, as was the disposition of the prone brake calipers at the front end (1) and the similar general outline from both the aerodynamics and installation of the various components points of view. For example, the radiators (2); the same goes for the exhausts (3), but only at the Valencia presentation and for the very low line of the whole rear end (4) due to a gearbox that went back to being wider but much lower (5) while on the RB6 it was narrower and higher to work better with the double diffusers then banned for 2011.

## TOP VIEW

The principal differences can be seen from the top view. (1) The nose is slightly wider and flatter and has the cameras mounted on its sides, while on the RB6 they were moved to the inside of the wing support pillars (2). As the regulations required, the chassis was of a different shape and no longer had protrusions at the sides. (3) The suspension was of different geometry. (4) The whole of the rear end was completely revised with a more accentuated tapering, to the point at which it obliged the use of heat protection panels, the bodywork being in contact with the exhausts. (5) After the 'camouflaging' at the launch, right from the first tests Red Bull introduced brand new, very long exhaust terminals that blew into the sides of the diffuser's side channels. (6) The rear suspension was also new, with a thinner basic lower wishbone. (7) There were enormous lateral channels at the sides of the gearbox to improve air flow towards the end of the car. (8) The new diffuser was limited in height throughout its width. (9) Adjustable flap.

## REAR VIEW

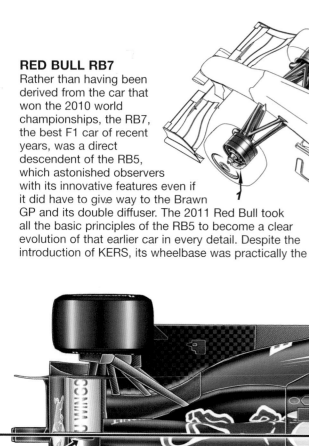

The regulation limit (1) imposed by the Federation for 2011 is shown in yellow. In the new diffusers, the central channel (2) is at the same height, where last year there was the central double diffuser (3), blown by a hole in the lower area. (4) The progression of the zone inside the wheel was also very different and allowed the passage of hot air from the exhausts. (5) The brake ducts were also new, with the inner part of the rim more faired. (6) The hot air vent was also different; in Malaysia, the bigger horizontal oval section aperture was used.
(7) The rear wing flap had less chord and could be adjusted by the driver to help him overtake.

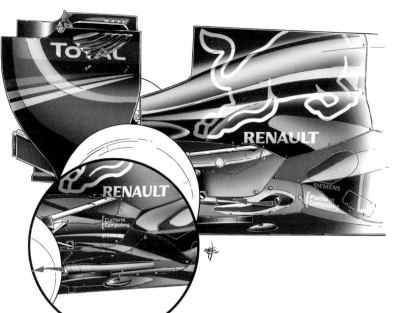

## EXHAUSTS

At the Valencia launch, the Red Bull RB7 seemed to be a simple evolution of the 2010 car with fairly traditional exhausts, but in the days that followed it brandished – even if briefly – a new exhaust system that was retained for the first race of the season. Adrian Newey was able to repeat the phenomenon of the exhaust blow into the inside of the diffuser by simply cutting a small portion of the bottom in the area near the wheel so that the long, flat exhausts blew not just towards the lateral channels of the diffusers, but also in their lower area. However, that was not enough: along came a new engine cover that was very different in its terminal area compared to the one at Valencia. In place of the small vertical fin there was a cover that was further lowered and terminated with a large oval hole from which the side-pods' hot air exited.

## BLOWING EXHAUSTS

This was Red Bull's devastating weapon, which was developed during the winter and immediately applied to the RB7. To be able to blow both above and below the side channels of the diffuser, from Barcelona the initial part of its lateral channels was cut (5 cm as permitted by the regulations). The brake ducts were new, with end plates that shielded the interior of the wheels from the heat incorporated a kind of flap in the upper area. The cutaway reveals the great deal of work carried out not only by Red Bull but also Renault in support of Newey's design. The exhausts have been turned round to then return towards the rear and blow through long, straight terminals in the area in front of the diffuser's side channels.

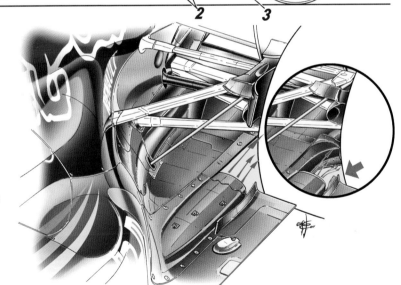

## SUSPENSION-GEARBOX

These two illustrations confirm just how much maniacal research was carried out by Newey in his attempt to reduce to a minimum the amount of bulk in relation to the car's aerodynamics. The KERS batteries were split and one was placed on the exterior of the gearbox and the other inside the spacer between the engine and gearbox. It was a difficult position to cool and subject to major stress, which created quite a number of problems in the early races. With no more double diffusers there was a need to compact all the mechanics, many suspension elements of the RB7 were external like, for example, the rockers (1), the pair of dampers (2) and the roll bar (4). In the quest to reduce weight and bulk, the adjustment of the height of the car from the ground was made on the Friday with a special tie rod that was then replaced on the Saturday by a lighter, simpler one. In the 2010 car's gearbox all the suspension elements were hidden inside the 'box, which was narrower but higher.

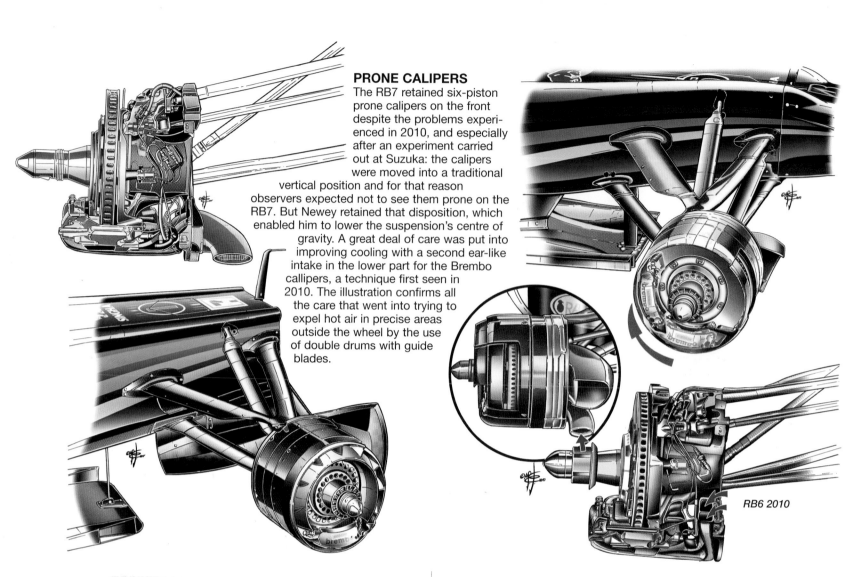

## PRONE CALIPERS

The RB7 retained six-piston prone calipers on the front despite the problems experienced in 2010, and especially after an experiment carried out at Suzuka: the calipers were moved into a traditional vertical position and for that reason observers expected not to see them prone on the RB7. But Newey retained that disposition, which enabled him to lower the suspension's centre of gravity. A great deal of care was put into improving cooling with a second ear-like intake in the lower part for the Brembo callipers, a technique first seen in 2010. The illustration confirms all the care that went into trying to expel hot air in precise areas outside the wheel by the use of double drums with guide blades.

*RB6 2010*

## SEPANG

At the early race weekends, Red Bull often tested two different front wings, as was the case at Sepang where each driver had two wings available to him. The one selected for the race had end plates (see oval) with a single external window.

## DIFFUSER

And at Sepang we also saw a new diffuser with a rounded link between the horizontal and side vertical parts. The RB7 did not fully exploit the chance of descending with its lateral walls to the plane of the stepped bottom, right in the area where, among other things, the exhaust blow was directed. That would have made the car less sensitive to pitch, especially in relation to the particular rake set-up of the RB7 on the track. Also note the blow (in yellow) of the small flap applied to the upper part of the diffuser.

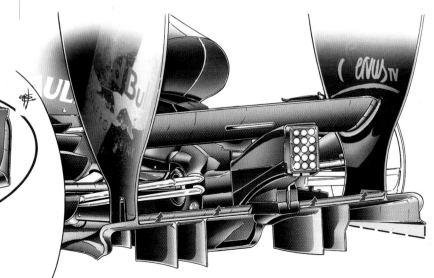

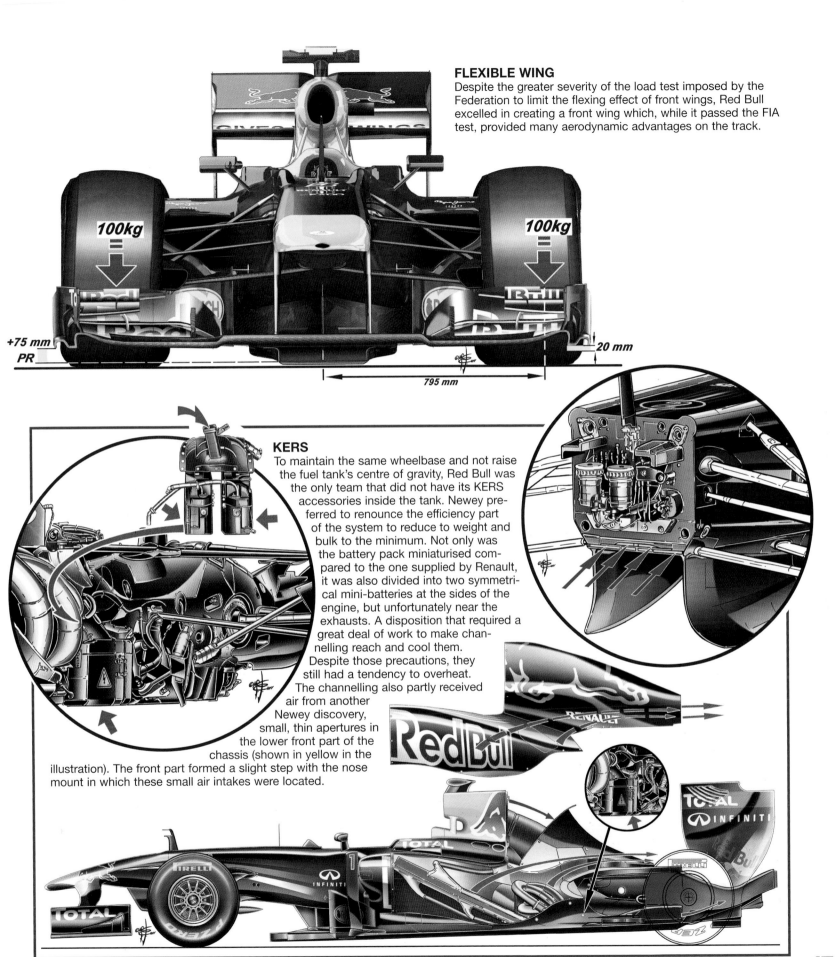

## FLEXIBLE WING

Despite the greater severity of the load test imposed by the Federation to limit the flexing effect of front wings, Red Bull excelled in creating a front wing which, while it passed the FIA test, provided many aerodynamic advantages on the track.

**100kg** **100kg**

+75 mm
PR

20 mm

795 mm

## KERS

To maintain the same wheelbase and not raise the fuel tank's centre of gravity, Red Bull was the only team that did not have its KERS accessories inside the tank. Newey preferred to renounce the efficiency part of the system to reduce to weight and bulk to the minimum. Not only was the battery pack miniaturised compared to the one supplied by Renault, it was also divided into two symmetrical mini-batteries at the sides of the engine, but unfortunately near the exhausts. A disposition that required a great deal of work to make channelling reach and cool them. Despite those precautions, they still had a tendency to overheat. The channelling also partly received air from another Newey discovery, small, thin apertures in the lower front part of the chassis (shown in yellow in the illustration). The front part formed a slight step with the nose mount in which these small air intakes were located.

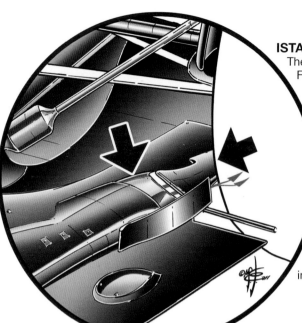

## ISTANBUL

The new exhaust system fitted to Vettel's car on the Friday morning in Turkey ended up in bits after Vettel's car flew off the track and was destroyed. Its brief lifespan brought a more detailed observation to an end. It had longer terminals which, in practice, almost sealed with an extension of a brake air intake wing. All of this to better direct exhaust blow into the lower area of the extractor planes; the 'traditional' version that was used in qualifying had a blow that brushed the upper part of the side channels. There was a long sensor with which to monitor the tyre temperature during Vettel's experiment.

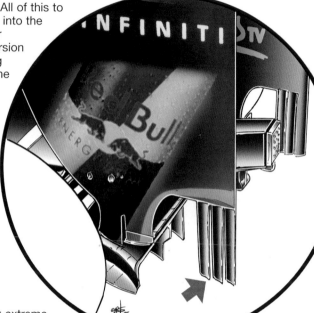

## BARCELLONA

At the GP of Spain, the most extreme exhaust blow was used again after Vettel destroyed it during Friday morning practice in Turkey. What seemed like a simple rod was a fin integrated into the brake duct that separated the flow in this zone, with the exhaust terminal lengthened and gently touching it. But it was an experiment that was not taken any further.

## REAR WING

For Barcelona, Red Bull and Ferrari both adopted the McLaren-Sauber-type fringes in the lower part of their end plates which, in the RB7's case, were square shaped.

## MONTREAL

At Montreal Red Bull brought back new, wide supports of the Ferrari school, but only for the Saturday morning.
They had been tested briefly at Monaco and were combined with a new front wing for the Canadian track. Both drivers qualified and raced with that configuration.

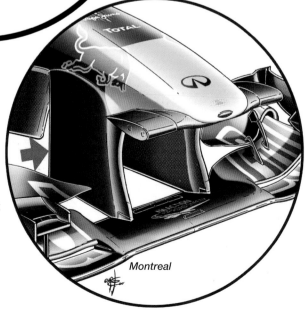

*Montreal*

*Monaco*

## FRONT WINGS

Vettel destroyed his new front wing (above) during Friday morning practice in Montreal, while Webber tested another completely different one. They varied in this way: (1) the main plane was different and in the new version had a sort of step in its central zone that was less curved towards the lower area of the car. (2) The blow between the main plane and the first flap (see the version below) was different. (3) Both the flaps were of new conception, with Webber's more differentiated compared to the previous version. (4) These small raised flaps were only on the destroyed wing, with the section near the mini-lateral screen curved and its vertical support inclined. (5) The plane in the zone close to the end plates was different and had no mini-fin (6), which was present on the version below. (7) The blow of the second flap was more extensive and twisted.

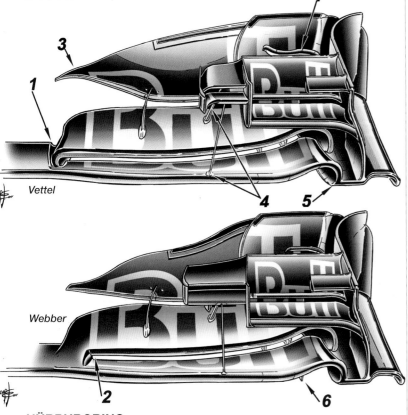

Vettel

Webber

## NÜRBURGRING

In Germany, Red Bull had two new front wings with wide vertical pillars. The difference between the two was the twisted small end plate (see circle) inside the raised flaps. This was the version used for both qualifying and the race.

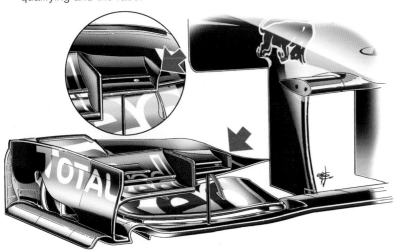

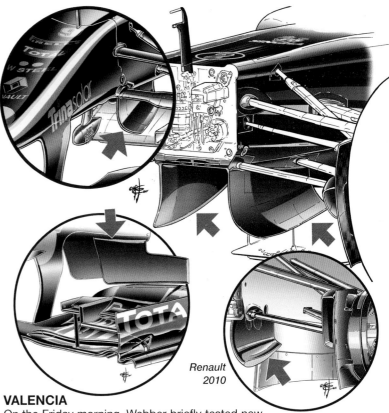

Renault 2010

## VALENCIA

On the Friday morning, Webber briefly tested new front aerodynamics with the turning vanes under the central part of the nose taken off and replaced by two elements and applied to the lower part of the chassis. It was a feature first used by Renault (below) the previous year and also retained for 2011's RE31. Surprisingly, this solution was refitted for qualifying and the race. The illustration below right shows Renault's 2010 technique and above is the 2011, while below left are the old turning vanes under the nose, fitted to the RB7.

## BUDAPEST

Many experiments were carried out on the Red Bull's front wing in Hungary, some of them seen previously. On the Friday, the team tested the Nürburgring unit, with its large support pillars (1), turning vanes under the chassis introduced at Valencia and the new plane that made its debut in Germany as well as new, twisted internal end plates (3). In the afternoon, Vettel tested a much curled flap with a long Gurney flap, but that was dropped. Then on the Saturday there was a real revolution, a mixture of old and new developments: they went back to the old pre-Valencia nose with its narrow pillars and the turning vanes underneath (2) even if the new planes still remained.

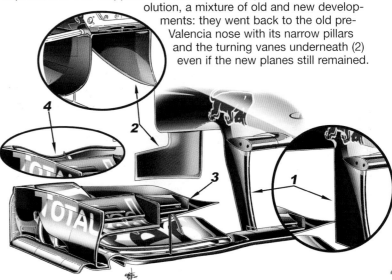

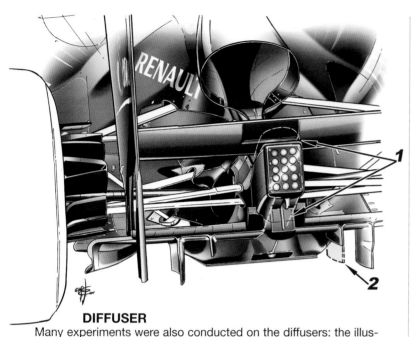

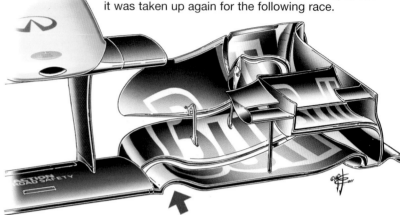

## FRONT WING
On the Friday, Vettel tested this wing at Spa. It had a prominent rounded 'step' in the portion that linked with the neutral central zone like that of the Williams and, partially, the McLaren. It was an experiment that only lasted a few laps, but it was taken up again for the following race.

## DIFFUSER
Many experiments were also conducted on the diffusers: the illustration shows the Nürburgring one used by Vettel on the Friday, plus the old deformable structure. In the afternoon the new one was fitted and then taken off to be replaced by the Valencia unit. Webber retained both the new deformable structure (1), suspension and diffuser (2), indicated by the dotted line.

## SPA-FRANCORCHAMPS
Following in McLaren footsteps in the sophistication of its drum brake air intakes, Red Bull turned up in Belgium with two versions at the rear end and a more complex one (see illustration) for Vettel. The latter had a rather prominent box (arrow) in the central zone (before the disc) and special stepping to direct air flow to a specific point on the wheel, recreating the wheel cover effect that was banned the previous season.

## MONZA
A new diffuser was taken to Monza by Red Bull to compensate for the reduction of rear end downforce due to the new back wing, which was less loaded than the one at Spa. A small flap was also added (indicated by the arrow) in the external zone linking with the lateral seal to guarantee more downforce.

## SPA-FRANCORCHAMPS
A new development that was not noticed was the reconstruction of the sidepods' front, which was much more tapered in the lower area and that also involved rebuilding all of the interior.

## FRONT WING

A new front wing brought back a feature first seen on the McLaren at the 2010 GP of Singapore: it was this additional plane (1) to better manage the air flow in the area.

Note the diminished amount of main flap chord (3), especially in the central zone.

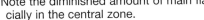

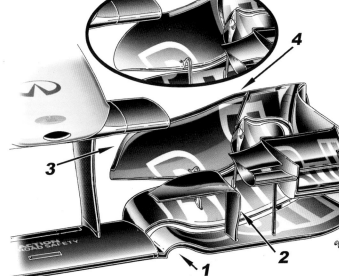

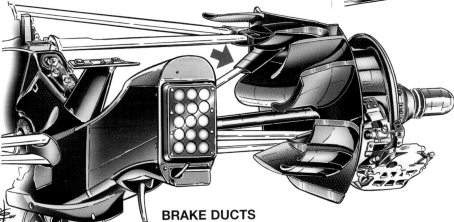

## BRAKE DUCTS

It is no secret that brake ducts increasingly became aerodynamic devices. Inside the Red Bull's rear duct there were no fewer than eight small downforce planes with negative lift to create more vertical load. Also note the small faired section of the suspension tie rod, which was limited by the regulations.

## SINGAPORE

Red Bull began the weekend with no fewer than three front wings, one like that used in Hungary and two brand new ones. The latter were both derived from the stepped plane of the McLaren school (1), which were used briefly by Vettel at Spa. The one used by Webber on the Friday had an extension inside the raised flaps – similar to the one seen on the Toro Rosso at Monza – while Vettel had a McLaren-type L-shaped flap (2) fitted to his wing at Monza. There was more chord on the main flap (3) of both versions and they had long Gurney flaps located differently in relation to the rest. (4). That was the solution adopted by both cars for the race.

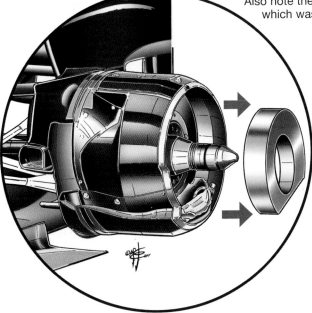

## PRE HEATED DRUMS

At the season's finale, Red Bull began to pre-heat the central part of the suspension-brake group to bring the bell coupling up to temperature even when the car was standing still. It was a method used mainly in qualifying and was a kind of return to the concept of heating the inside of the rim introduced by Sauber in 2006 and then prohibited by the regulations, except that in this case the heat support was directed to the wheel, hub and disc assembly.

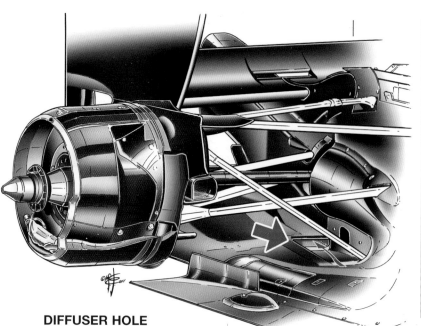

## SUZUKA

Red Bull took two examples of a new front wing to Japan, but Vettel destroyed one of them during Friday morning practice and that forced the team to continue testing with both cars fitted with the same kind of unit as in Singapore so as not to show favouritism. Twenty minutes before Saturday testing new replacement components arrived from Britain, so the team was able to assemble the two new wings. The end plates were different, in particular, with a straighter progression in a vertical sense and with a smaller blow in the rear. The oval below shows the old method used until Singapore.

## DIFFUSER HOLE

Controversy was sparked off by the dimensions of the hole in the central zone of the diffuser, where the regulations permit a well limited aperture to give access to the starter; but there was no actual official protest over the matter.

## REAR WING

This is the version of the high load rear wing with a much curved main plane and a flap that had more chord.

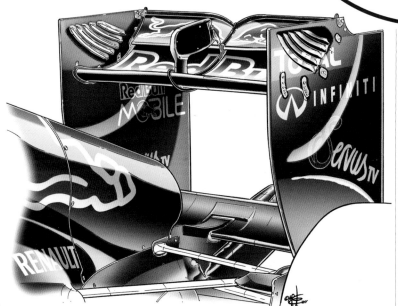

## DRUM DUCTS

In the second part of the season, Red Bull took on a feature brought in by McLaren and used two semi-drums and left the discs uncovered. It was an approach that made the front tyres reach operating temperature more quickly. A comparison of the closed solution with the directional blade between the two drums, partly open towards the exterior.

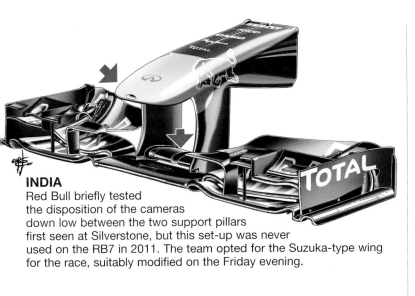

## INDIA
Red Bull briefly tested the disposition of the cameras down low between the two support pillars first seen at Silverstone, but this set-up was never used on the RB7 in 2011. The team opted for the Suzuka-type wing for the race, suitably modified on the Friday evening.

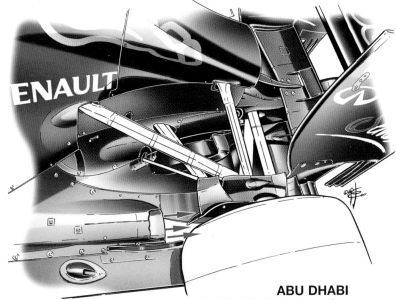

## ABU DHABI
The Abu Dhabi race was the penultimate for exhausts blowing straight into the side channels of the diffusers, a technique that was banned for 2012.
That development created a sort of thermal mini-skirt that sealed the lower aerodynamics to the ground, even with the raked set-up first adopted by Red Bull. The small inlet that blew into the central part of the diffuser that caused some controversy at Monza was of diminished dimensions.

## DIFFUSER FROM BELOW
In this view from below, we can clearly see the different materials used for the bottom in the zone near the wheels (5 cm) partially cut to permit hot blown air to pass above and below the lateral channels. The flat zone that delimits the channels was accentuated and had three small vertical curved fins.

## RAKE SET-UP
One of Red Bull's winning developments was its much raked set-up, with the rear end a good deal higher from the ground than the front in order to recreate a sort of long Venturi tube. Among other things, the RB7 did not fully exploit the possibility of its lateral walls descending as far as the stepped bottom in the zone where the exhaust blow was directed and acted as a thermal mini-skirt. The rake set-up and blown exhausts were, therefore, in perfect harmony with each other. Without the thermal mini-skirt effect created by the exhausts, the one with negative lift would have been too sensitive to pitch. And this set-up made the diffuser's angle of inclination and the incidence of the wings more accentuated. It is for the latter that the Red Bull cars were never the fastest on the straight. Also note the blow (in yellow in the circle) of the flap applied to the upper part of the diffuser.

125

**c** = 240 mm   **b** =120mm   +50 mm   **a** = 40mm

McLaren's was a stirring season, one packed with excitement that characterised the various stages of the world championship before it became clear that the Woking constructor was the only serious rival of the stratospheric Red Bull. After the clamour of the MP4-26's 'shock' launch, in particular due to its unusual L-shaped sidepods, observers soon became disappointed during initial track testing before euphoria broke out all over again as a result of a real technical revolution that erupted in extremis with the first race of the season just around the corner, when the car suddenly became miraculously competitive. The new project was built around the concept of maximum exploitation of the exhaust blow effect, had a decidedly long wheelbase – the longest of all the season's cars – and an exhaust system unofficially called the octopus, although its factory designation was the MK1.

It had a kind of megaphone terminal that blew air downwards in a long window to the area at the floor, in front of the rear wheels. This project, the reproduction of which it is possible to show thanks to a contribution from the team's technical director Paddy Lowe, never worked but what was even worse, not even the basic layout of the exhaust system was reliable.

In pre-championship testing, McLaren was never able to do its simulations to cover a whole race distance. "It was the worst winter of my career for many reasons; similar to the one we went through at Williams in 1988, when we were dealing with the first active suspension and the Judd engine", Lowe admitted after Jenson Button's win for the team in Canada. Then came the drastic decision to set this ambitious project to one side and go hell for leather for the design of exhausts similar to those of Red Bull.

So a real miracle happened in the Melbourne pit garage, not only due to the final result of work carried out, but especially because that work demanded the complete assembly of the entire rear end. Burning the midnight oil at Woking, the diffuser and the whole exhaust system were re-designed to result in a sort of Red Bull copy.

McLaren MP4-25

McLaren MP4-26

McLaren MP4-26
Test

McLaren MP4-26
Melbourne

The new parts were even assembled for the very first time in the Melbourne pits without being able to do a single test lap, yet everything worked as it should except that which had been labelled as a wrong project. Among other things, it was precisely the need to make components quickly that meant they had to drop the use of Pyrossic, the expensive material supplied by a French company to all the teams, because there was not enough time to produce it.

So McLaren opted for titanium which, with its clear colour, made the shape of the MP4-26's lower aerodynamics highly visible. So exhaust blow became a McLaren ace in the hole, to the point that at Silverstone, when the regulations were changed leading to the drastic limitation of blow, the MP4-26 suffered the most. Another McLaren strong point was its KERS, which had been the best of all of them in 2009. For 2011, its overall weight was reduced by about 10%, but better still its installation had been improved with a single element inside a specific area in the fuel tank and no longer with separate elements placed in the sidepods.

| CONSTRUCTORS' CLASSIFICATION | | | |
|---|---|---|---|
| | 2010 | 2011 | |
| Position | 2° | 2° | = |
| Points | 454 | 497 | +43 ▲ |

McLaren MP4-26
Barcelona

McLaren MP4-26
Valencia

McLaren MP4-26
Nürburgring

McLaren MP4-26
Monza

An indispensible modification, given the unusual shape of the 'pods that required a different radiator installation, which were oblique, also L-shaped and certainly longer than those of the MP4-25.

Development continued with the non-stop refinement of the front wing area and the DRS, an unusual system introduced during practice at Silverstone and then not used in racing until Spa. A B version of the MP4-26 made its first appearance in Spain with completely re-designed aerodynamics for all components, starting with the central area of the nose, its lower zone modified to integrate with two mini-appendages applied to the lower chassis. The position of the main plane was also new in relation to the nose, a choice that forced the team to incline the support pillars forward; equally new were the end plates that also had new parameters in both their components and the flaps – those that were raised and the others on the main plane, in which the position of the fin had been modified, hiding the adjustment of the third plane. The sidepods were profoundly modified, with the end part re-designed to accommodate the different progression of the exhausts. The whole rear end was tapered partly due to the smaller dimensions of the new gearbox, which was fully crash tested as required by FIA.

That allowed the introduction of new rear suspension and a modified diffuser. After going for the Red Bull exhaust blow, another programme also kept Paddy Lowe's staff busy: it was research into the rake set-up of the rival RB7, which did not produce brilliant results at the start of the season. Working jointly on the front wing, it had a brusque upswing that heightened the brake air intakes, not only to improve the aerodynamics but also to better exploit the tyres. Open drums were increasingly seen at the front, half open, even asymmetric, developing that which had only been a 2009 experiment to bring the tyres up to the correct operating temperatures at cold circuits.

At the Nürburgring in particular, Hamilton tested drums with asymmetric holes and brake discs more or less visible, to direct hot air towards the interior of the rims and, therefore, influence the operating temperature of the tyres. The development continued until almost the season's last race with the debut of ad hoc refinements for the front wing, engine cover, exhausts and diffuser at every race.

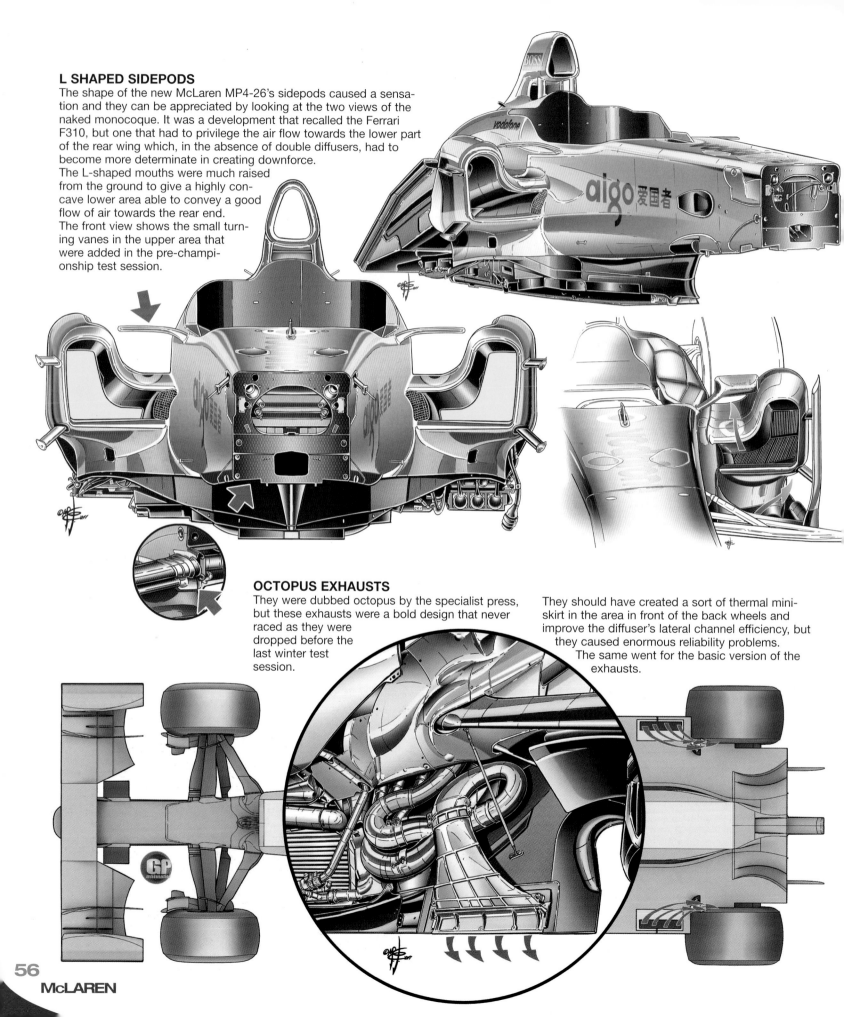

## L SHAPED SIDEPODS

The shape of the new McLaren MP4-26's sidepods caused a sensation and they can be appreciated by looking at the two views of the naked monocoque. It was a development that recalled the Ferrari F310, but one that had to privilege the air flow towards the lower part of the rear wing which, in the absence of double diffusers, had to become more determinate in creating downforce.

The L-shaped mouths were much raised from the ground to give a highly concave lower area able to convey a good flow of air towards the rear end.

The front view shows the small turning vanes in the upper area that were added in the pre-championship test session.

## OCTOPUS EXHAUSTS

They were dubbed octopus by the specialist press, but these exhausts were a bold design that never raced as they were dropped before the last winter test session.

They should have created a sort of thermal mini-skirt in the area in front of the back wheels and improve the diffuser's lateral channel efficiency, but they caused enormous reliability problems. The same went for the basic version of the exhausts.

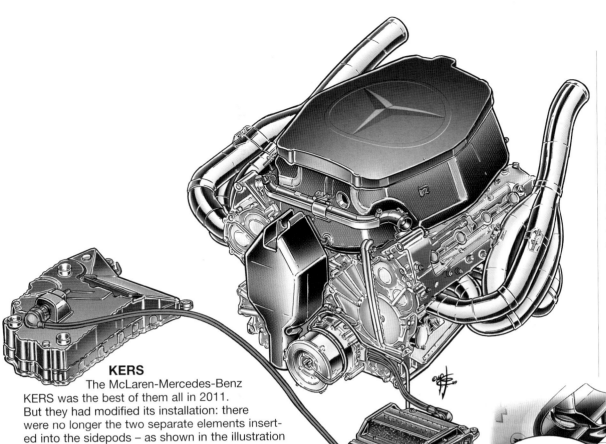

## MELBOURNE

McLaren did an incredible amount of work to recover competitiveness and return to an efficient exhaust system for the MP4-26. They opted for a Red Bull-type version, with the reconstruction of the whole rear section. The mechanics assembled this version of the car for the first time in the Melbourne pits and pulled off a real technical miracle. Given the impossibility of having a timely supply of Pyrossic – the special insulating material used in such cases – the team opted for a diffuser in titanium of a rapid prototype variety, which enabled observers to understand its real shape.

## KERS

The McLaren-Mercedes-Benz KERS was the best of them all in 2011. But they had modified its installation: there were no longer the two separate elements inserted into the sidepods – as shown in the illustration of the 2009 layout – but a single small battery package in the fuel tank, which was slightly lengthened. For that reason, the McLaren maintained the generous dimensions of the previous MP4-25's wheelbase.

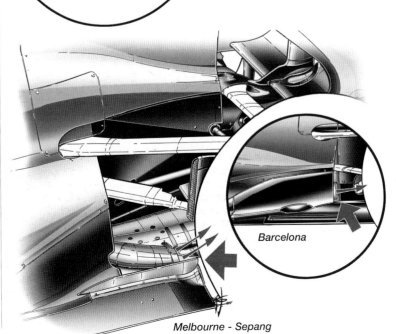

*Barcelona*

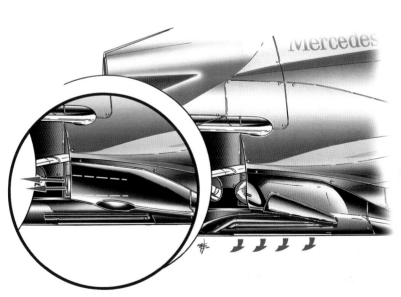

## EXHAUST TEST

This illustration shows the two versions of the exhausts tried out during winter testing, but they failed so badly that they were not even used for a distance trial. Both versions, the traditional straight units in the circle and the one called the octopus, broke repeatedly. It was a real nightmare for Paddy Lowe and his colleagues.

*Melbourne - Sepang*

## SIDEPODS

These horizontal finlets arrived during the last pre-season tests to straighten the air flow in this zone and convey it towards the rear end.

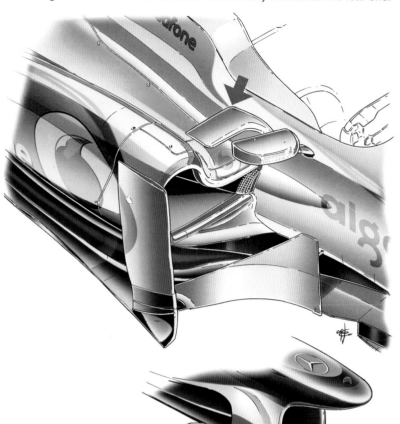

## BARCELONA

The car taken to Barcelona was almost a B version of the original. It had a new nose, sidepods, gearbox, suspension and diffuser.
The sidepods were different, both for the fact that they hosted various exhaust manifolds and because they were even more tapered due to the new, narrower gearbox. The suspension mounts to the deformable structure and the differential box were changed; that is why it was necessary to conduct another rear crash test.

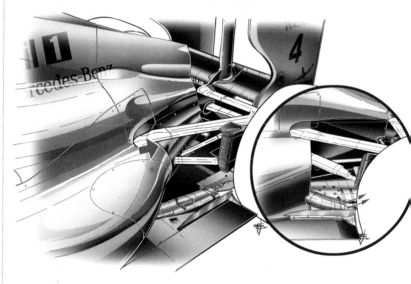

## FRONT WING

McLaren kept the 2010 unit (see circle) with a kind of deflector in the lower part of the nose; but the nose's shape and dimensions were profoundly modified for the Spanish GP. The front wing taken to Barcelona was different in all its components, starting with the shorter external part of the end plates (1), which made the internal one (2) protrude more in the trailing edge. (3) Both the traditional raised flaps (4) and the more twisted ones were also new and the curvature increased. Also new was the position of the adjustment (5) of the third element, which also acted as a small turning vane in that area. The position of the main plane was different and that forced a forward inclination (6) of the central pillars.

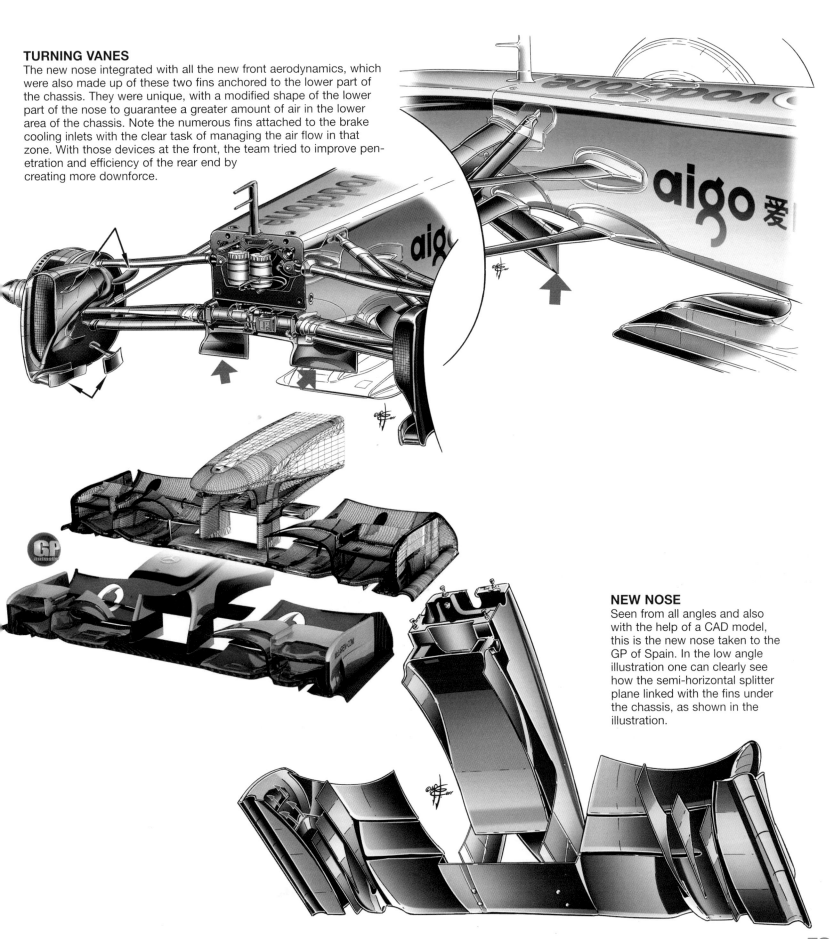

## TURNING VANES

The new nose integrated with all the new front aerodynamics, which were also made up of these two fins anchored to the lower part of the chassis. They were unique, with a modified shape of the lower part of the nose to guarantee a greater amount of air in the lower area of the chassis. Note the numerous fins attached to the brake cooling inlets with the clear task of managing the air flow in that zone. With those devices at the front, the team tried to improve penetration and efficiency of the rear end by creating more downforce.

## NEW NOSE

Seen from all angles and also with the help of a CAD model, this is the new nose taken to the GP of Spain. In the low angle illustration one can clearly see how the semi-horizontal splitter plane linked with the fins under the chassis, as shown in the illustration.

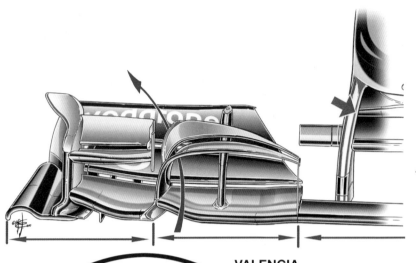

## VALENCIA

McLaren maintained the arched shape and divisions in two sections of the width of the main plane, first seen in Singapore in 2010.

A new front wing (above) made its debut in Valencia, based on the main plane of the previous unit of which the end plates and raised flaps were modified. In the detail, the external end plate (1) had two vertical windows instead of one and it was shorter so that a third (2) window appeared, applied to the internal end plate. The position and width of the raised flaps were different, as shown (3) by a link point with the more internal main plane.

The front view (see circle) shows the different position of the internal raised flaps, which are more detached compared to the external ones, as revealed by the small step at the linkage point with the main plain. The outline of the second flap is also different and does not have its predecessor's Gurney flap.

The different position of those flaps compared to the principal plane and external elements is shown in yellow.

## BUDDH INTERNATIONAL

There was a real revolution in India concerning the front wing which, until that moment, had been subjected to normal adaptations to comply with the different tracks. In the main plane of the McLaren front wing the step (1), which was introduced at Silverstone in 2010 and kept on all subsequent versions, had disappeared (1). The two drivers made different choices: Lewis Hamilton used the new wing, which obviously also had the support pillars (2) of the raised flaps, longer and straighter, while Jenson Button kept the Suzuka unit.

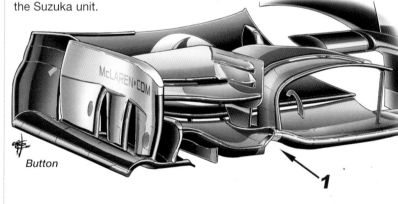

*Button*

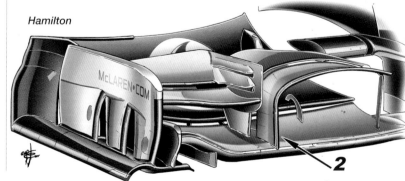

*Hamilton*

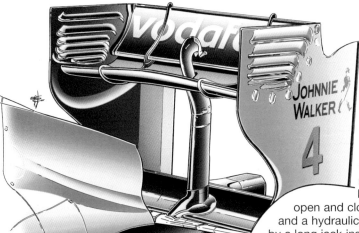

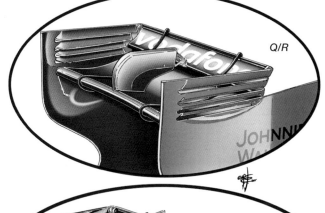

### REAR WING

During the first part of the season, McLaren used a rear wing with a greater chord on the adjustable flap compared to all other cars; this to have a major difference between the open and closed positions and a hydraulic control operated by a long jack inside the central pillar.

Q/R

Silverstone

### SILVERSTONE

At Silverstone, McLaren moved on to use a different control for the flap and a smaller chord but the new rear wing, inspired by that of Mercedes-Benz, did not work. The illustration clearly shows how the chord of the principal plane was bigger and so the flap was smaller and had an electro-hydraulic control without a central pillar. After the umpteenth comparison made on the Saturday morning with Hamilton, who used it, and Button, who preferred the old unit, the team decided not to fit it for qualifying or the race.

### SPA-FRANCORCHAMPS

The new rear wing at Silverstone that McLaren did not use in the UK finally made its debut at Spa. There were two versions: one with more neutral planes and end plates identical to those at Silverstone with five lateral gills, and one with even less loaded planes (above) and new end plates, with only four gills of different design. For qualifying and the race the second alternative was selected.

### SUZUKA

A brief parade of a new generation of rear wings introduced at Silverstone ended for McLaren with the one used at Suzuka. It had a flap with its chord reduced to increase top speed the moment it was opened. The end plates were completely new and were joined with the part connected to the main plane and the cut in the area regarding the flap.

Race

### SINGAPORE

Here, McLaren tested two rear wings. On the Friday, Hamilton had these small planes –15 mm wide, in line with regulations – fitted at the height of the lower plane of the wing that was first seen at Silverstone and then Spa, while Button had the Budapest rear wing. The team opted for the Hamilton wing for the race, but without those added small planes.

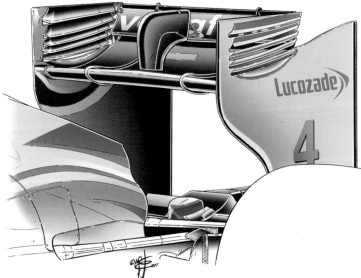

**McLAREN**

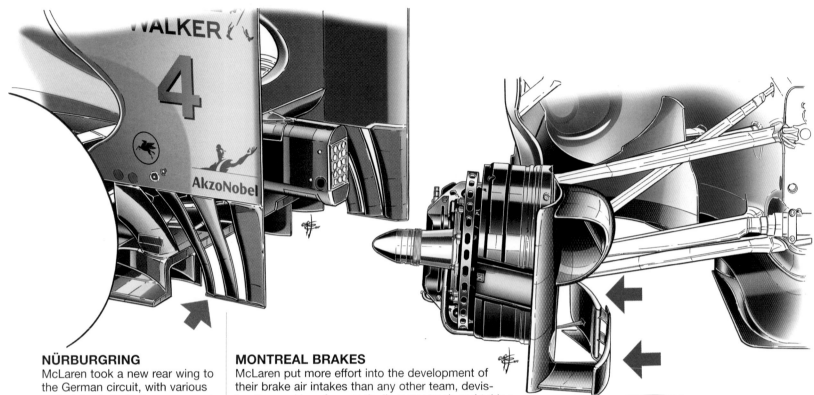

## NÜRBURGRING

McLaren took a new rear wing to the German circuit, with various end plates in both the upper part (see side view) of introduction and the lower area, where the fringes inserted from the first Grand Prix of the season were subjected to notable evolution: they became wider and had an arched progression.

## MONTREAL BRAKES

McLaren put more effort into the development of their brake air intakes than any other team, devising them ad hoc for practically every track and taking up once more the work begun two years earlier.
In the circle is the one used in the 2010 season, which even then had discs in view that were then adopted for all tracks which are hard on the brakes or that had low ambient temperatures. The discs can be easily compared, given that Hamilton and Button often used different material (see the Brakes chapter). Among other things, the absence of the drum ring permitted an increase in the tyre temperature with the hot air from the radial apertures, which they shot to the inside of the rims and, therefore, the tyres.

*right*

*left*

## NÜRBURGRING

At the German circuit, McLaren even tried asymmetric cooling on Hamilton's car, combined with brake discs by Carbon Industrie. The purpose was to improve the operating temperature of the less stressed front wheels with greater heat support from the more uncovered discs. The solution on the left was selected for the Saturday, so with drums that stop before the disc, which had been used in the past, but combined with Brembo discs (see small circle) that were normally used by Button.

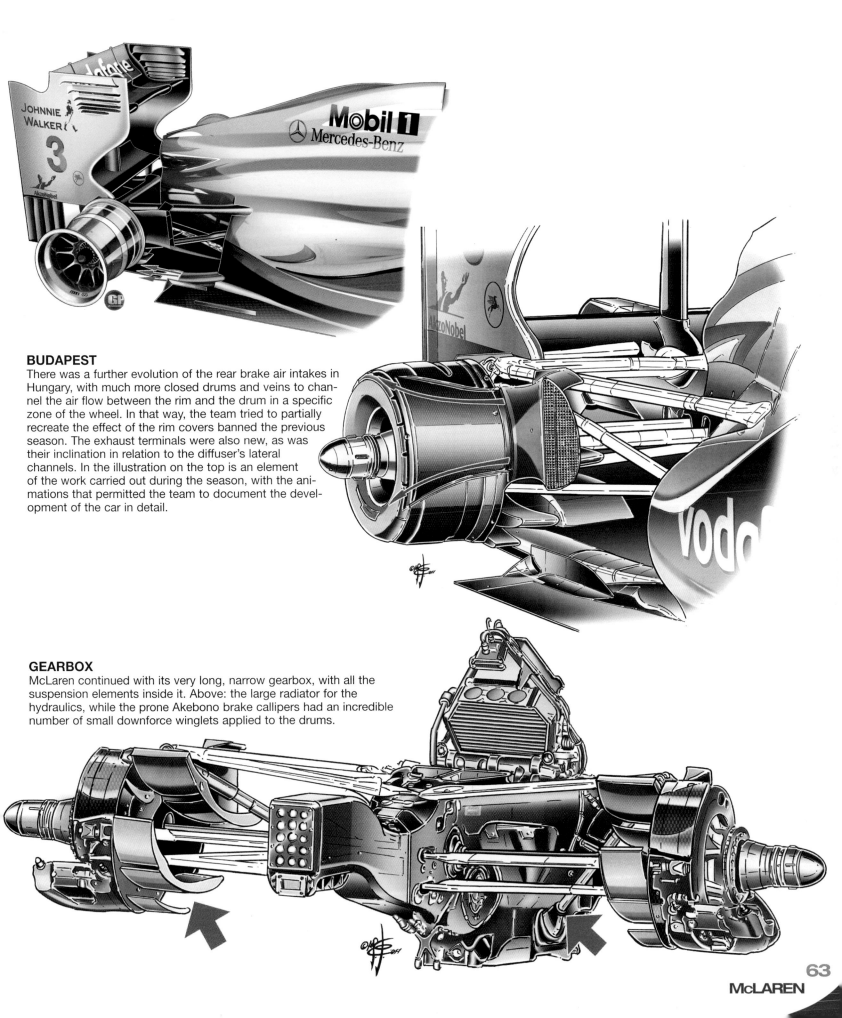

## BUDAPEST

There was a further evolution of the rear brake air intakes in Hungary, with much more closed drums and veins to channel the air flow between the rim and the drum in a specific zone of the wheel. In that way, the team tried to partially recreate the effect of the rim covers banned the previous season. The exhaust terminals were also new, as was their inclination in relation to the diffuser's lateral channels. In the illustration on the top is an element of the work carried out during the season, with the animations that permitted the team to document the development of the car in detail.

## GEARBOX

McLaren continued with its very long, narrow gearbox, with all the suspension elements inside it. Above: the large radiator for the hydraulics, while the prone Akebono brake callipers had an incredible number of small downforce winglets applied to the drums.

The 2011 was the worst season in Ferrari's recent history. Despite having maintained the same position in the constructors' championship, the F150 Italia was unable to make the technical recovery the team had achieved the previous year with the F10. Both cars appeared to be clearly inferior to the Red Bulls, but the technical run-up by the men from Maranello in 2010 was such that it enabled Fernando Alonso to fight with Sebastian Vettel for the world title at the last race of the season with the complicity of mistakes made by the Red Bull men during the year.

There were two fundamental stages in the recovery of the F10: one was at the GP of Valencia with the introduction of low exhaust blow and the other at the Belgian GP with the arrival of the new gearbox and diffuser. Unfortunately, all the work carried out on the F150 Italia to make it competitive had no positive effect; they were even late with the basic project compared to the best teams, Red Bull and McLaren. While the F10 had some new features despite everything, like the angled engine that meant greater exploitation of space for the double diffusers, the F150 Italia was just a logical evolution of that previous project. On the eve of the presentation, observers expected to see a radically new car with a pullrod rear suspension layout and avant garde exhaust developments. Instead, it soon became clear that the 'camouflaged' version at the presentation was really not so different from the car that began the 2011 season.

The decision to retain the pushrod layout at the rear end also conditioned the Sauber which, using both the Ferrari engine and gearbox, was forced to adopt the same system. It is a fact that Ferrari and Sauber were the only teams – with the exception of the minors Virgin and HRT – to retain the pushrod system. The delay in the arrival of Red Bull-type exhausts was surprising, because in 2010 the move to that technology was determinate for the recovery of Ferrari, more so than the adoption of the F-Duct. With the ban of double diffusers, the support exhaust blow was underestimated to the point that research in that area only started in December, while Red Bull had already launched into theirs in August 2010.

And there was another difficulty, which was admitted by Pat Fry: it was the lack of a perfect correlation between data gathered in the wind tunnel and verification on the track, which often led to the dismissal of new developments tried in the tunnel as early as Friday practice.

This was a problem associated with the move from 50% scale models to those of 60%, which obliged Ferrari to also use the Toyota wind tunnel as well as forcing it into doing an incredible

Ferrari F10

Ferrari F150 Italia

Ferrari F150 Italia
Melbourne

Ferrari F150 Italia
Barcelona

| CONSTRUCTORS' CLASSIFICATION | | | |
|---|---|---|---|
| | 2010 | 2011 | |
| Position | 3° | 3° | = |
| Points | 375 | 396 | -21 ▼ |

amount of work to calibrate data once more.

Another major problem was the inability of the car to exploit its hard tyres. The crucial moment in the season on that score was at the GP of Spain where, as a result of an exceptional start by Alonso the F150 Italia took the lead and kept it in the two first stints of the race on soft tyres, but came fifth and was even

lapped with hards.

That cost chief technician Aldo Costa and aerodynamics boss Mario De Luca their jobs. From that GP onwards, Pat Fry became the team's technical director and simulations expert Neil Martin, who had been at McLaren with Fry, arrived from Red Bull to reinforce that Maranello sector.

It is worth remembering that

Ferrari was certainly more seriously affected than any other team by the abolition of tests that enabled them to verify new developments on the Fiorano and Mugello circuits while their opposition had to carry out the same work with CFD simulations, and it is from here that the formulation of simulation programmes came long before Maranello was able to achieve

them. One of the positive technical turnarounds came at the GP of Canada with the introduction of a project that was started in Aldo Costa's day, the new rear suspension that brought a greater recovery of camber. Tested on the Friday morning at Valencia, this suspension was part of the package that brought Maranello its only victory of the season in the subsequent British GP. And that was a win partially favoured by the reduction of hot blow imposed by the Federation for that one race, giving Ferrari an advantage over its opposition. A lot of work was also carried out in two other sectors: front wings and exhaust blow, leading to testing a bold solution with double blow both onto and under the diffuser's lateral channels during practice in Belgium.

It was a technique that was also tried unsuccessfully by Red Bull. Used in the Spa race, it was not brought out again until practice for the GP of Japan, but it did not race. The last stage in the development of the F150 Italia in Korea – or perhaps it would be more correct to call it the first experiment for 2012 – was the introduction of a Red Bull-type 'flexible' wing, which revealed a few problems of excessive flexing, especially on Massa's car. But it was a clean break from the past, with some developments inspired by other cars and some brought in the week before by Red Bull. A starting point for the 2012 car.

Ferrari F150 Italia
Monaco

Ferrari F150 Italia
Silverstone

Ferrari F150 Italia
Monza

Ferrari F150 Italia
Yeongam

## FERRARI F150 ITALIA: TOP VIEW COMPARISON

The F150 Italia immediately looked like a simple, even logical development of the 2010 car. But from the top view, differences from the old F10 soon made themselves known despite the car still appearing 'camouflaged' at its presentation and first track test. The higher nose was combined with the old wing planes that first appeared at Silverstone. (1) The new developments began with the front suspension, in particular the steering arms which, for the first time, were not set into the upper wishbone's fairing. (2) The driver sat slightly further forward and that was certainly the case with the hoop that forms part of the seat back and determines the higher position of the chest to ensure good visibility. That, among other things, allowed the team to make a little more space for the fuel tank without increasing wheelbase dimensions. (3) The front of the sidepods was different, with much raised air intakes and a rectangular horizontal shape, the side safety structures were also increased. (4) The narrowing achieved in the zone in front of the wheels compared to the F10 was notable, with exhausts that blew low (the illustration shows those used for the first track tests). (5) The whole damper-torsion bar group was advanced and miniaturised to make an especially reduced dimension rear area, as revealed by the substantial inclination of the pushrod links; that enabled Maranello to obtain some of the advantages of the pullrod system used by Red Bull. (6) In practice, the rear ended in an extremely tight V ensuring greater air flow efficiency to the wing and the diffusers. (7) The rear wing, shown at the car's launch and envisaged for testing at Valencia, was just a first experiment leading to a development designed for the start of the season.

F150 Italia

F10

## REAR SUSPENSION

Ferrari was the only top team to also keep a pushrod layout at the rear end – apart from Sauber, obviously, as they use the same gearbox. But despite that, the cleanliness of the entire upper area of the gearbox was considerable. The forward inclination of the pushrod shown in yellow enabled the team to compact all the suspension elements in the zone behind the engine, as can be seen in the detailed illustration of the rear suspension.

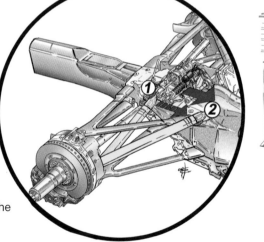

## FRONT SUSPENSION

Raising the chassis and, consequently, the anchorage of the suspension's wishbones forced the team to position the steering arms slightly lower in relation to the upper unit to guarantee greater suspension efficiency.
Note that the retention cables were doubled, as required by the regulations.

## EXHAUST TEST

Before the season began, Ferrari tested various exhaust systems: the first had oval section terminals exiting low down on the sidepods that were suitably lengthened. Note the cut at the bottom (1) of the starter opening area with insulation material (2) at the sides of the gearbox.

## MELBOURNE

In spite of the promise kept to field a very different car at the first race compared to the one at the presentation and the first three pre-season test sessions, the F150 Italia was late compared to the cars of other top teams. In the side view comparison (above is the GP of Australia version) one immediately notes the many differences.

(1) The most striking new developments were these two large fins connected to a front wing all of the components of which were new, including the end plates (2). The initial parts of the sidepods were much more concave (3) with a doubling of the small vertical fins (4) in the lower area. Seen from the side, the narrowing of the body was given away by the more extended surface (5) of the insulation material. The body (6) was slightly longer and from here the long exhaust terminals exit (7) in place of the short ones of the basic version (below). The diffuser (8) was, of course, also new and integrated between the body and the rear wing support pillars.

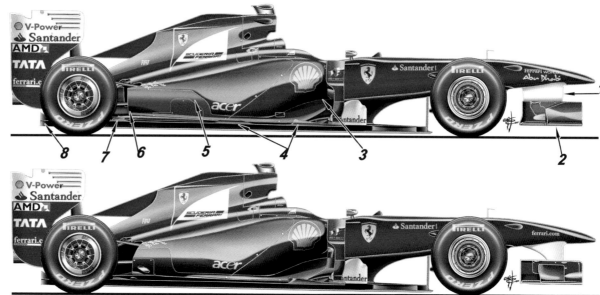

## MELBOURNE EXHAUSTS

In the last pre-championship test at Barcelona, Red Bull-type exhausts were used the fairing of which was integrated into the distribution of the new body.
In the circle, there is a comparison with the original version, which was retained for the first three winter test sessions.

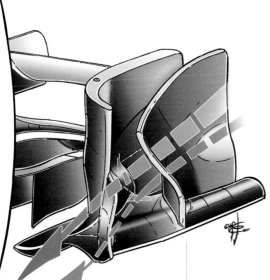

## FRONT WING

The front wing was also new, with two different end plates to better manage the air flow in that delicate area. The dotted yellow lines show the section of the apertures that convey air both under and to the sides of the front wheels.
The difference between the two planes was, however, verifiable in its lower part.

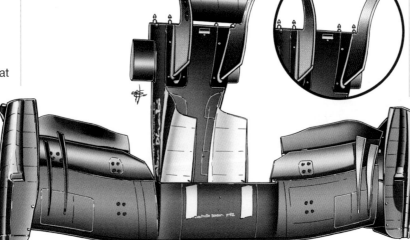

## SEPANG

Ferrari had already added this small flap to the inside lower part of the two turning vanes in Australia, as shown in the view from below. Only two small modifications were made in the end plate area for Malaysia, as well as a different second flap tested briefly by Fernando Alonso on the Friday.

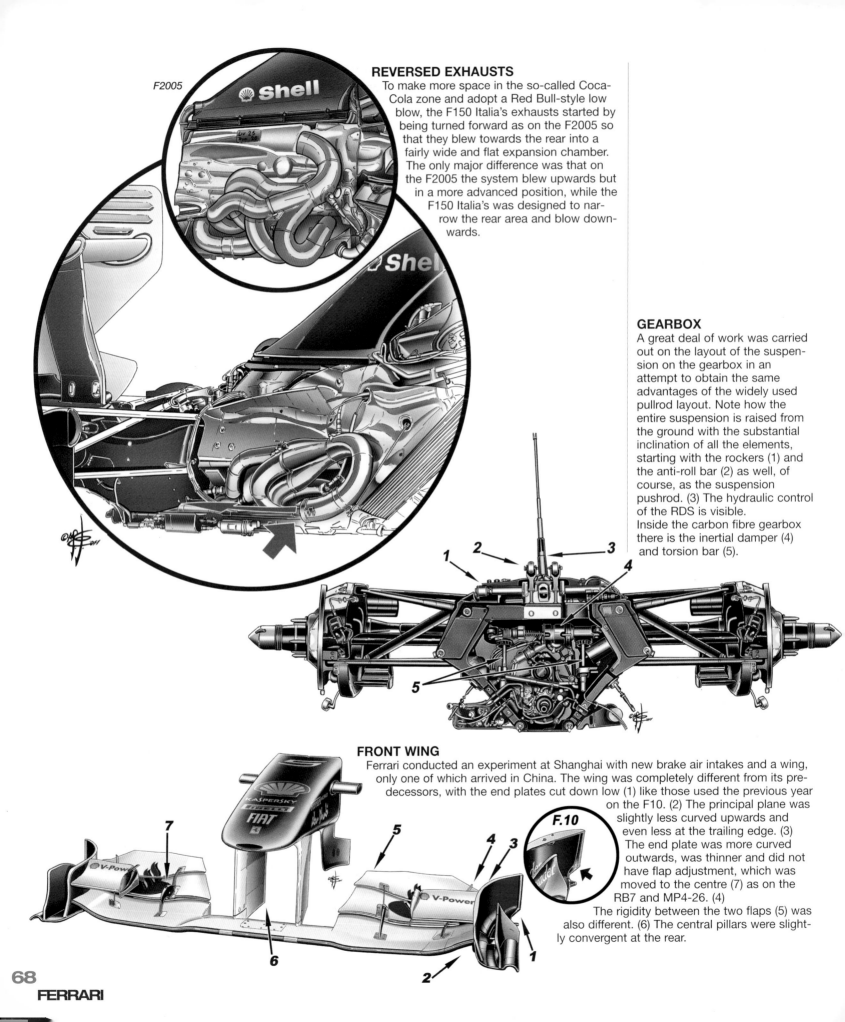

*F2005*

## REVERSED EXHAUSTS

To make more space in the so-called Coca-Cola zone and adopt a Red Bull-style low blow, the F150 Italia's exhausts started by being turned forward as on the F2005 so that they blew towards the rear into a fairly wide and flat expansion chamber. The only major difference was that on the F2005 the system blew upwards but in a more advanced position, while the F150 Italia's was designed to narrow the rear area and blow downwards.

## GEARBOX

A great deal of work was carried out on the layout of the suspension on the gearbox in an attempt to obtain the same advantages of the widely used pullrod layout. Note how the entire suspension is raised from the ground with the substantial inclination of all the elements, starting with the rockers (1) and the anti-roll bar (2) as well, of course, as the suspension pushrod. (3) The hydraulic control of the RDS is visible.
Inside the carbon fibre gearbox there is the inertial damper (4) and torsion bar (5).

## FRONT WING

Ferrari conducted an experiment at Shanghai with new brake air intakes and a wing, only one of which arrived in China. The wing was completely different from its predecessors, with the end plates cut down low (1) like those used the previous year on the F10. (2) The principal plane was slightly less curved upwards and even less at the trailing edge. (3) The end plate was more curved outwards, was thinner and did not have flap adjustment, which was moved to the centre (7) as on the RB7 and MP4-26. (4) The rigidity between the two flaps (5) was also different. (6) The central pillars were slightly convergent at the rear.

*F.10*

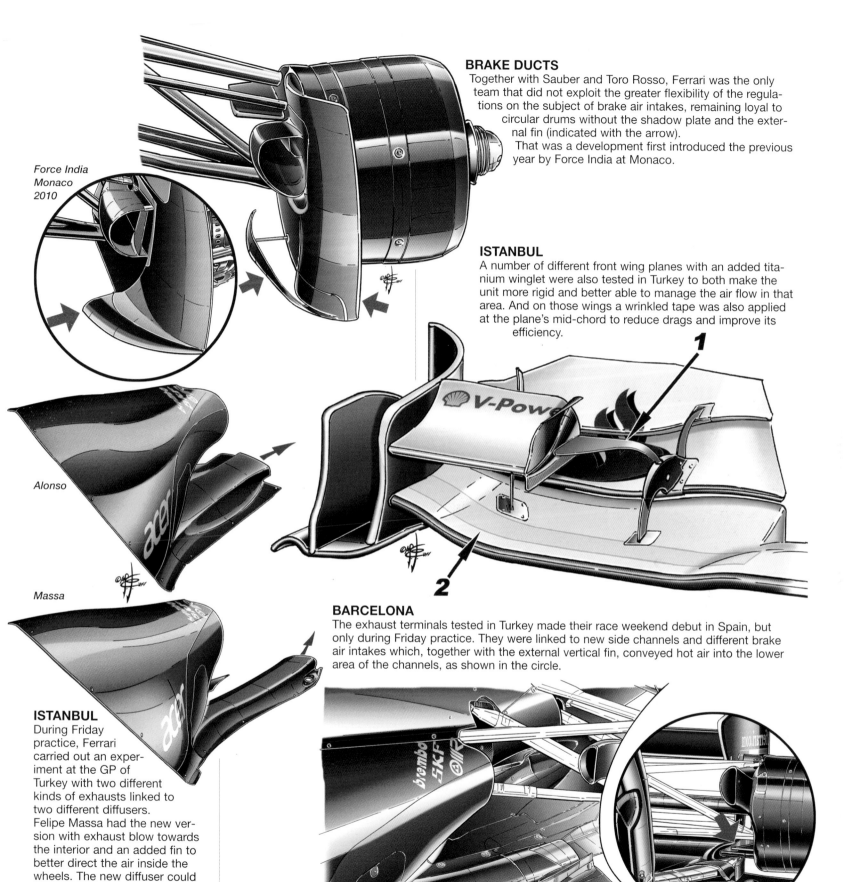

## BRAKE DUCTS

Together with Sauber and Toro Rosso, Ferrari was the only team that did not exploit the greater flexibility of the regulations on the subject of brake air intakes, remaining loyal to circular drums without the shadow plate and the external fin (indicated with the arrow).

That was a development first introduced the previous year by Force India at Monaco.

*Force India Monaco 2010*

## ISTANBUL

A number of different front wing planes with an added titanium winglet were also tested in Turkey to both make the unit more rigid and better able to manage the air flow in that area. And on those wings a wrinkled tape was also applied at the plane's mid-chord to reduce drags and improve its efficiency.

*Alonso*

*Massa*

## ISTANBUL

During Friday practice, Ferrari carried out an experiment at the GP of Turkey with two different kinds of exhausts linked to two different diffusers.
Felipe Massa had the new version with exhaust blow towards the interior and an added fin to better direct the air inside the wheels. The new diffuser could be recognised by its mini-flap at the trailing edge, as on the Toro Rosso and Red Bull.

## BARCELONA

The exhaust terminals tested in Turkey made their race weekend debut in Spain, but only during Friday practice. They were linked to new side channels and different brake air intakes which, together with the external vertical fin, conveyed hot air into the lower area of the channels, as shown in the circle.

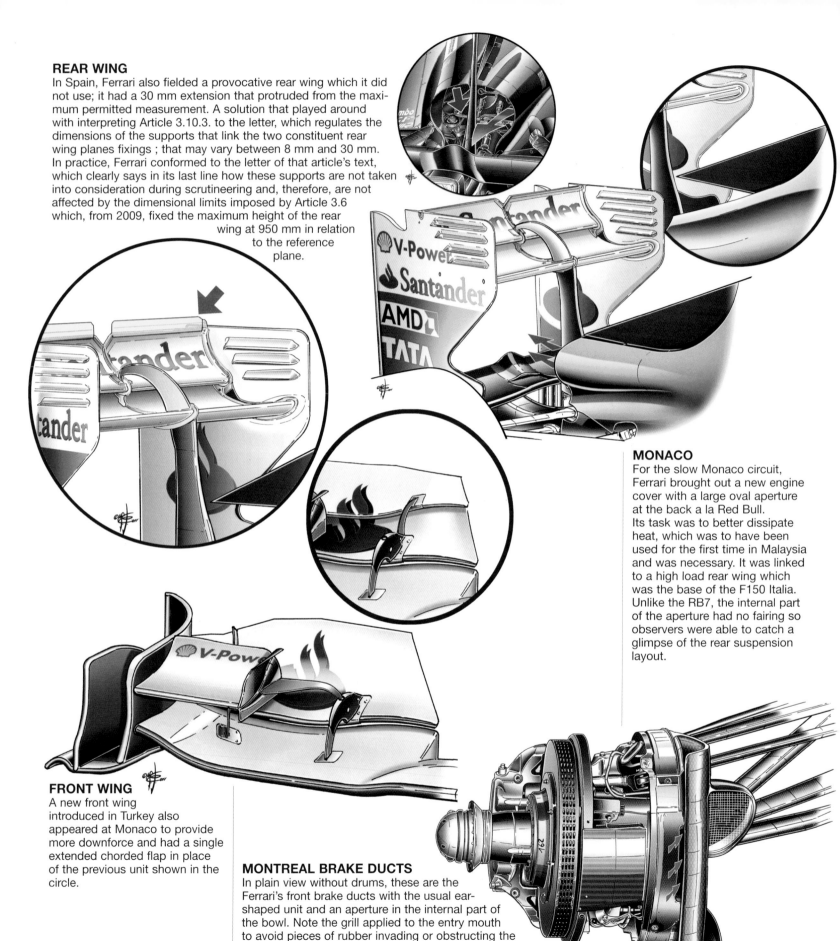

## REAR WING

In Spain, Ferrari also fielded a provocative rear wing which it did not use; it had a 30 mm extension that protruded from the maximum permitted measurement. A solution that played around with interpreting Article 3.10.3. to the letter, which regulates the dimensions of the supports that link the two constituent rear wing planes fixings ; that may vary between 8 mm and 30 mm. In practice, Ferrari conformed to the letter of that article's text, which clearly says in its last line how these supports are not taken into consideration during scrutineering and, therefore, are not affected by the dimensional limits imposed by Article 3.6 which, from 2009, fixed the maximum height of the rear wing at 950 mm in relation to the reference plane.

## MONACO

For the slow Monaco circuit, Ferrari brought out a new engine cover with a large oval aperture at the back a la Red Bull.
Its task was to better dissipate heat, which was to have been used for the first time in Malaysia and was necessary. It was linked to a high load rear wing which was the base of the F150 Italia. Unlike the RB7, the internal part of the aperture had no fairing so observers were able to catch a glimpse of the rear suspension layout.

## FRONT WING

A new front wing introduced in Turkey also appeared at Monaco to provide more downforce and had a single extended chorded flap in place of the previous unit shown in the circle.

## MONTREAL BRAKE DUCTS

In plain view without drums, these are the Ferrari's front brake ducts with the usual ear-shaped unit and an aperture in the internal part of the bowl. Note the grill applied to the entry mouth to avoid pieces of rubber invading or obstructing the effectiveness of the system.

## MONTREAL

Ferrari further cut the F150 Italia's brake drums, which had already been drastically reduced at Monaco: before that, they were almost completely closed in the external area. They were very similar to those that McLaren had used on all tracks that were severe on the brakes or in low ambient temperatures. Both teams kept the discs tested at Monaco, with their new apertures. The absence of the drum ring enabled the team to increase tyre temperatures with the hot air from the radial apertures that shot towards the interior of the rims and, therefore, the tyres.

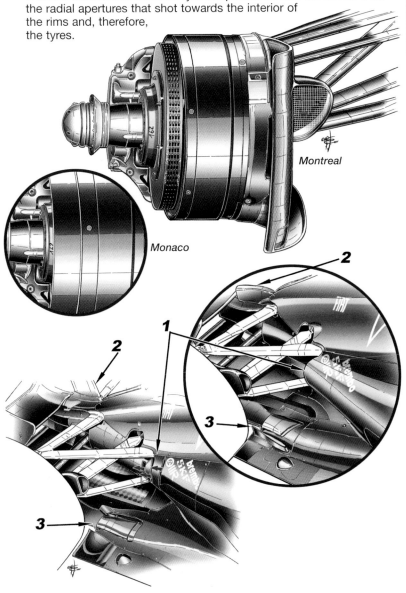

Montreal

Monaco

**2**

**2**

**1**

**3**

**3**

## SILVERSTONE

Ferrari brought an important package of modifications to the GP of Great Britain. This illustration shows the new developments in the terminal areas of the sidepods (1); they were lengthened to improve air flow quality in that area, which was also given three gills from which to dissipate more heat; the new rear wing eliminated the vertical support (2), which was replaced by a box of the electro-hydraulic system for flap control. Two different exhaust positions were tested, after which the one in the large illustration (3) was adopted, with its different progression of the terminal area of the manifold that no longer had the small lateral shielding fin.

## REAR SUSPENSION

And in Canada, Ferrari introduced a new rear suspension, which was tested by Alonso on the Friday and recalled that of Mercedes-Benz. To have a different camber change and a lower roll centre, it was moved higher and inside the connection of the upper wishbone mount, which then became shorter and more inclined. The gearbox mounts were unchanged, so the anti-squat characteristics were the same. But on the Saturday, the team went back to the original solution, shown in the illustration by the dotted lines.

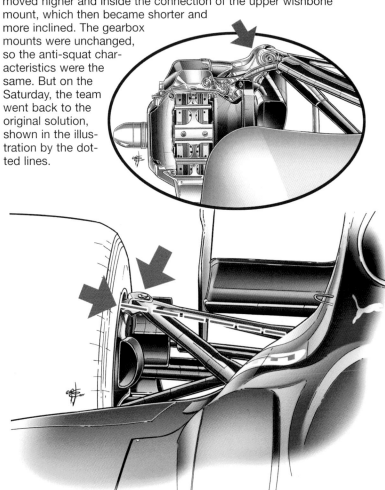

## REAR WING

At Silverstone, Ferrari also debuted a new control system for the rear wing flap, which ensured greater precision and speed of movement. So there was no longer a hydraulic jack inside the central pillar – which was eliminated – but an electro-hydraulic control worked by a box, as on the Red Bull, Renault and Force India.

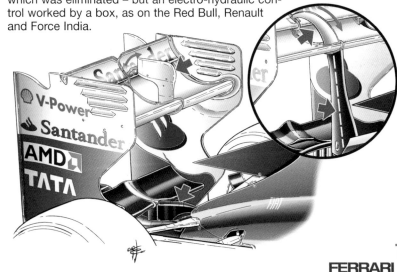

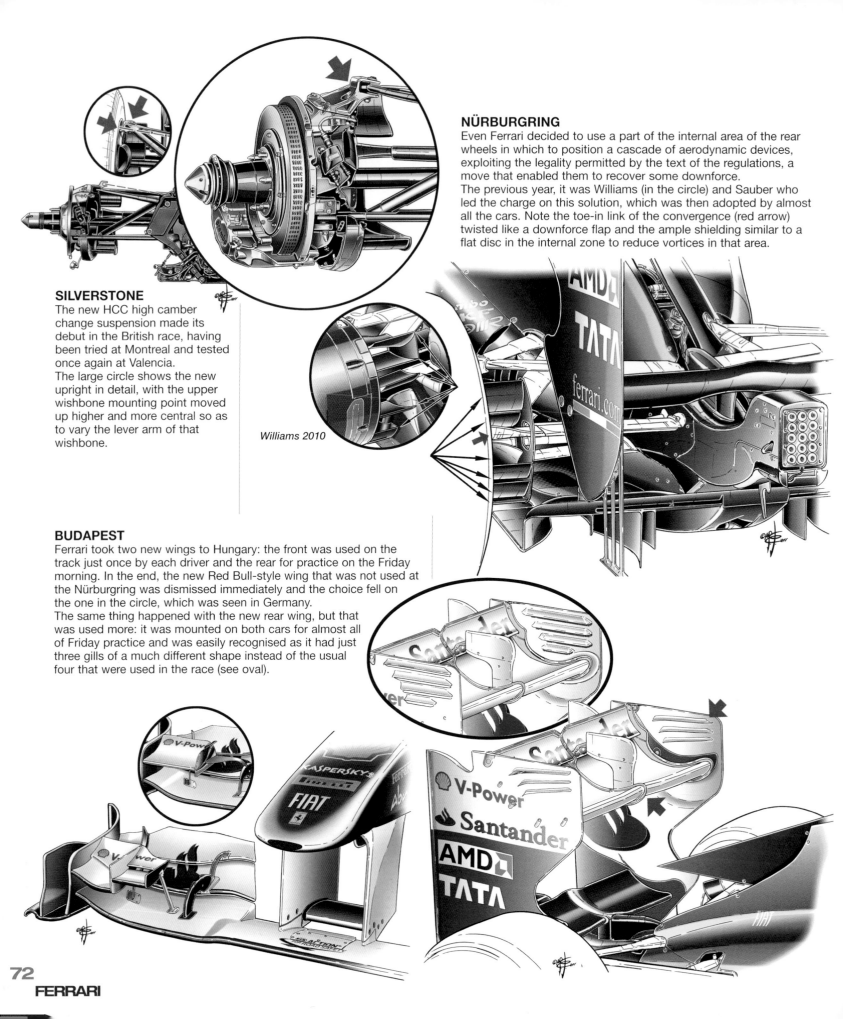

## NÜRBURGRING

Even Ferrari decided to use a part of the internal area of the rear wheels in which to position a cascade of aerodynamic devices, exploiting the legality permitted by the text of the regulations, a move that enabled them to recover some downforce.

The previous year, it was Williams (in the circle) and Sauber who led the charge on this solution, which was then adopted by almost all the cars. Note the toe-in link of the convergence (red arrow) twisted like a downforce flap and the ample shielding similar to a flat disc in the internal zone to reduce vortices in that area.

## SILVERSTONE

The new HCC high camber change suspension made its debut in the British race, having been tried at Montreal and tested once again at Valencia.

The large circle shows the new upright in detail, with the upper wishbone mounting point moved up higher and more central so as to vary the lever arm of that wishbone.

*Williams 2010*

## BUDAPEST

Ferrari took two new wings to Hungary: the front was used on the track just once by each driver and the rear for practice on the Friday morning. In the end, the new Red Bull-style wing that was not used at the Nürburgring was dismissed immediately and the choice fell on the one in the circle, which was seen in Germany.

The same thing happened with the new rear wing, but that was used more: it was mounted on both cars for almost all of Friday practice and was easily recognised as it had just three gills of a much different shape instead of the usual four that were used in the race (see oval).

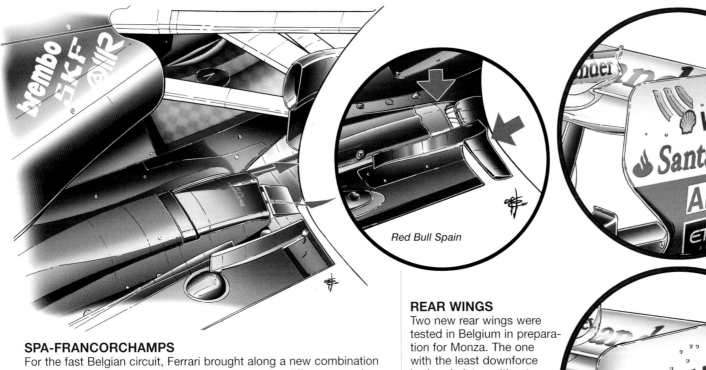

Red Bull Spain

## SPA-FRANCORCHAMPS

For the fast Belgian circuit, Ferrari brought along a new combination between the terminal part of the exhausts and the diffuser zone. In practice the feature, which was tested and then dropped by Red Bull at the Spanish GP, was picked up by Maranello. The exhaust manifold terminated with an almost divided section, while the bottom had a sort of fin/turning vane that divided the hot air released by the exhausts so that the internal part (higher, to create a kind of small step) blew above the diffuser's side channels, while the external one performed a similar function in the lower part.

## REAR WINGS

Two new rear wings were tested in Belgium in preparation for Monza. The one with the least downforce had end plates without oblique apertures, which were also new in relation to the Ferrari tradition.

## SPA FRONT WING

Fernando Alonso and Felipe Massa qualified in Belgium with two different front wings. The Brazilian retained the one used in Canada and the Spaniard had a new unit with double small raised flaps of the Red Bull school. Each had a large single flap, although in Hungary this new wing was combined with doubles.

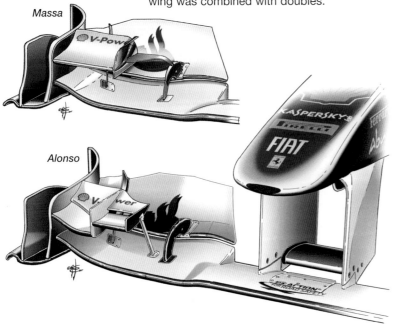

Massa

Alonso

## SPA REAR WINGS

In Belgium, Ferrari also had two rear wings available, both of them with new end plates and just three apertures, which had already been seen in Budapest. Obviously, the principal plane and flap had reduced chord. Two different positions were tested during practice before selecting the one with less downforce (see small circle) for the race; its planes were fitted with less incidence, as can be seen from the different position in relation to the coupling mask.

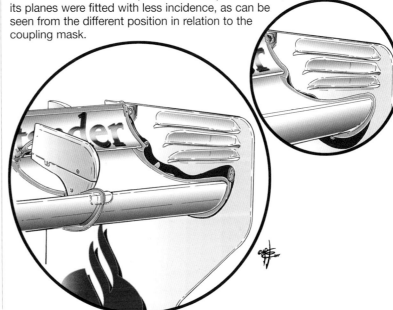

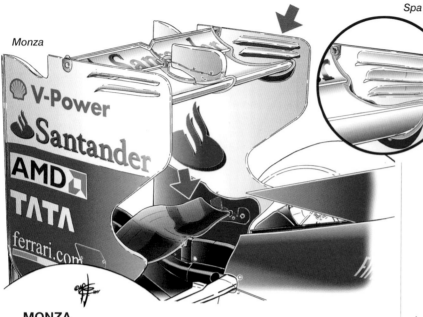

*Monza*

*Spa*

## DOUBLE BLOW

The double blow that debuted at Spa made no appearance at Monza. Both the double section of the exhaust terminal and the kind of horizontal mini-turning vane enabled the air flow to be directed above as well as below the lateral channels. The system was tested only once more at Suzuka, but without being used in the race.

## MONZA

There were ad hoc wings for Ferrari at Monza, based on those introduced at Spa but with new end plates that had one less aperture (two instead of three), because the planes were fitted in a position of less downforce to ensure higher top speed and less drag. A little downforce was recovered by the beam wing that was much twisted and had different chord between the central and peripheral zones. But the two different end plates tested at Spa were not used.

## SUZUKA

At the end of Friday morning practice in Japan, Alonso tested exhausts with the stepped terminal area introduced and used only at Spa, which were then dropped in favour of those seen in Singapore with their oval, slightly narrower terminal area.

## SINGAPORE

A new exhaust blow was used by Ferrari at Singapore, but without the stepped part of the terminals, with the divided blow first seen in Belgium. The exhaust terminals blew right next to the rear wheels to create a sort of thermal mini-skirt, all to the advantage of the rake set-up.

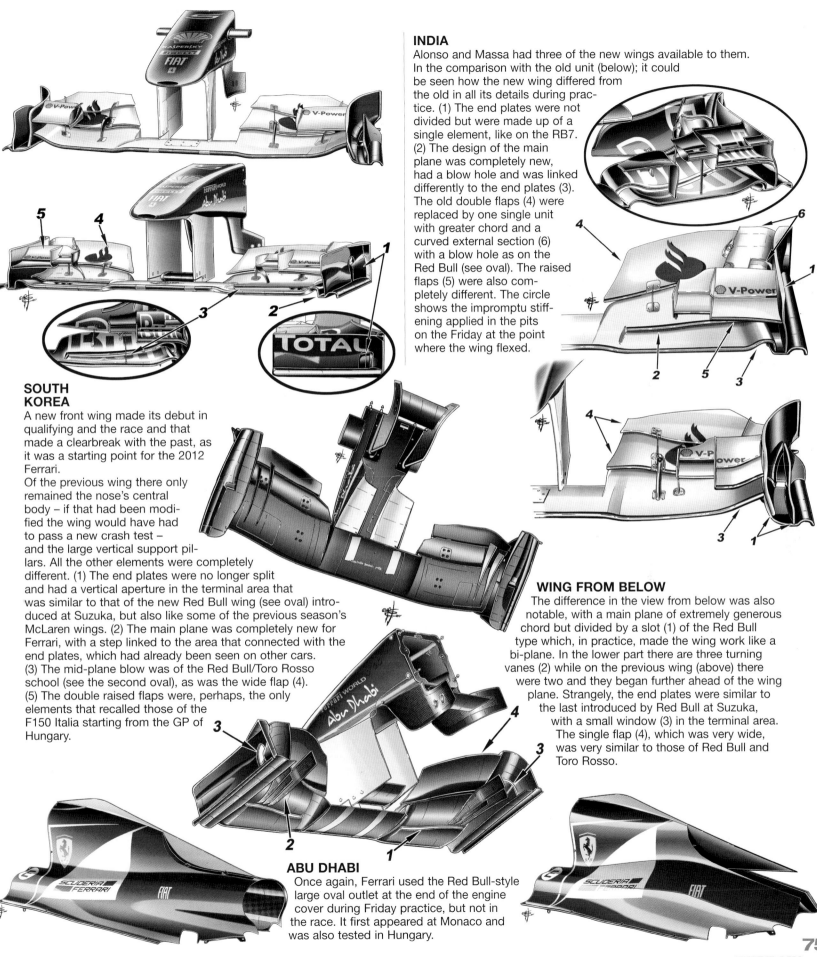

## INDIA

Alonso and Massa had three of the new wings available to them. In the comparison with the old unit (below); it could be seen how the new wing differed from the old in all its details during practice. (1) The end plates were not divided but were made up of a single element, like on the RB7. (2) The design of the main plane was completely new, had a blow hole and was linked differently to the end plates (3). The old double flaps (4) were replaced by one single unit with greater chord and a curved external section (6) with a blow hole as on the Red Bull (see oval). The raised flaps (5) were also completely different. The circle shows the impromptu stiffening applied in the pits on the Friday at the point where the wing flexed.

## SOUTH KOREA

A new front wing made its debut in qualifying and the race and that made a clearbreak with the past, as it was a starting point for the 2012 Ferrari.

Of the previous wing there only remained the nose's central body – if that had been modified the wing would have had to pass a new crash test – and the large vertical support pillars. All the other elements were completely different. (1) The end plates were no longer split and had a vertical aperture in the terminal area that was similar to that of the new Red Bull wing (see oval) introduced at Suzuka, but also like some of the previous season's McLaren wings. (2) The main plane was completely new for Ferrari, with a step linked to the area that connected with the end plates, which had already been seen on other cars. (3) The mid-plane blow was of the Red Bull/Toro Rosso school (see the second oval), as was the wide flap (4). (5) The double raised flaps were, perhaps, the only elements that recalled those of the F150 Italia starting from the GP of Hungary.

## WING FROM BELOW

The difference in the view from below was also notable, with a main plane of extremely generous chord but divided by a slot (1) of the Red Bull type which, in practice, made the wing work like a bi-plane. In the lower part there are three turning vanes (2) while on the previous wing (above) there were two and they began further ahead of the wing plane. Strangely, the end plates were similar to the last introduced by Red Bull at Suzuka, with a small window (3) in the terminal area. The single flap (4), which was very wide, was very similar to those of Red Bull and Toro Rosso.

## ABU DHABI

Once again, Ferrari used the Red Bull-style large oval outlet at the end of the engine cover during Friday practice, but not in the race. It first appeared at Monaco and was also tested in Hungary.

## EXHAUSTS

The vertical exhausts with their sort of chimney first seen in Belgium were not used for the race but were tested at Abu Dhabi on both cars, although only Massa tried them in India.
These completely closed vertical 'lungs' were applied, as shown, at the point where the four exhaust manifolds merge into the end terminal. It is for this reason that they were only discovered many races afterwards, because they were applied after the bottom had been fitted, just before the car was closed. It is called a compensator and in theory it should have limited the slight loss of power due to the narrowing necessary to achieve the blown diffuser effect with the long, flat terminal. Sophisticated fluidynamic simulation programmes were necessary to define the geometrical position (length, diameter). The compensator recovered some of the horse power lost by suitably working on the counter pressure at the exhaust. But it could also ensure hot blow during the release stage independently of the retarded ignition, which the regulations prohibited for 2012.

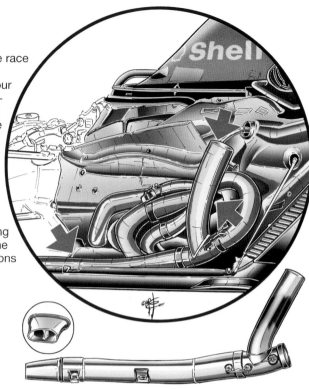

F10

## REAR SUSPENSION

In this comparison between the rear suspension of the F150 Italia and the F10 it can be easily seen how Aldo Costa's men were able to free much more space on the upper part of the gearbox while conserving the pushrod layout by compacting all the elements forward. Just note the considerable inclination of the pushrod (red arrow). While the F60 had no fewer than four dampers, the F150 Italia had three. We will start with the F10's suspension: as well as the two traditional dampers (4), there was a third transverse unit (2) as used during many seasons and moved back on the F10. Both had cup springs and one can see the inertial damper (3) with a rotating mass of high inertia. The layout was completed by the torsion bars (1) set into the rockers, and the roll bars (5).

The design of the F10 's suspension (1) indicated the inclination of the pushrod, which is almost parallel with the transverse axis, while on the F150 Itlaia was substantially inclined forward (1). The torsion bars (2) were set inside the rockers, which were also fairly inclined.

The transverse inertial damper (3) was also compact. In the centre was the group of two dampers and the separate gas cylinders (4). Note how the zone at the height of the rear axle is really clean, low and narrow.

F150

4  2  3  5

1

## FRONT VIEW

As the front view also confirms, the F150 boasted no major new developments compared to the old F10. The biggest difference was the steering arms, which were no longer aligned with the interior of the upper wishbones.

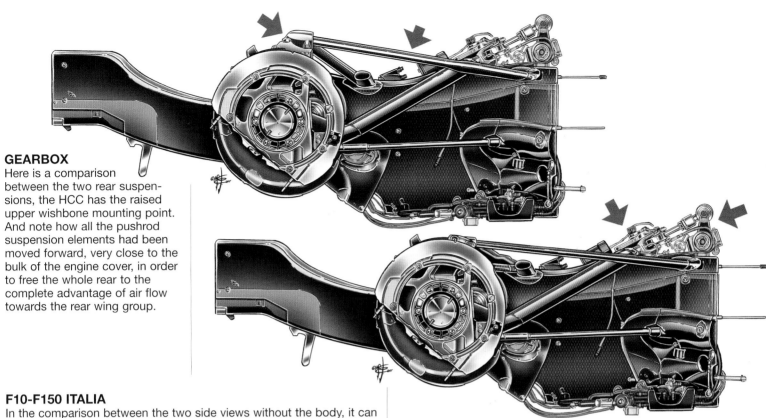

## GEARBOX

Here is a comparison between the two rear suspensions, the HCC has the raised upper wishbone mounting point. And note how all the pushrod suspension elements had been moved forward, very close to the bulk of the engine cover, in order to free the whole rear to the complete advantage of air flow towards the rear wing group.

## F10-F150 ITALIA

In the comparison between the two side views without the body, it can be clearly seen how the F150 Italia retained the general layout of the F10 while also introducing important new developments. (1) The shape of the chassis was very similar, including the monocoque's height from the ground. (2) The entry mouths of the sidepods were higher and the lower part was tapered. (3) The radiators were still at double inclination. (4) The exhausts were inclined forward to provide long, flat terminals that blew into the zone ahead of the rear wheels (5) and into the lateral channels. (6) Note the forward grouping of the suspension elements to free space in the rear wing area which, from the British GP onwards, no longer had vertical support.

### EVOLUTION OF THE SEASON

During the 2011 season Ferrari introduced no fewer than 10 different front wings (Australia, China, Spain, Germany, Hungary, Italy, Singapore, Japan, South Korea and India). There were nine rear wings (Australia, Malaysia, Turkey, Spain, Canada, Great Britain, Hungary, Belgium and Italy). Plus four different bodies (Australia, Malaysia, Turkey and Great Britain) and seven different exhaust combinations plus diffusers (Australia, Turkey, Spain, Canada, Great Britain, Hungary and Belgium).

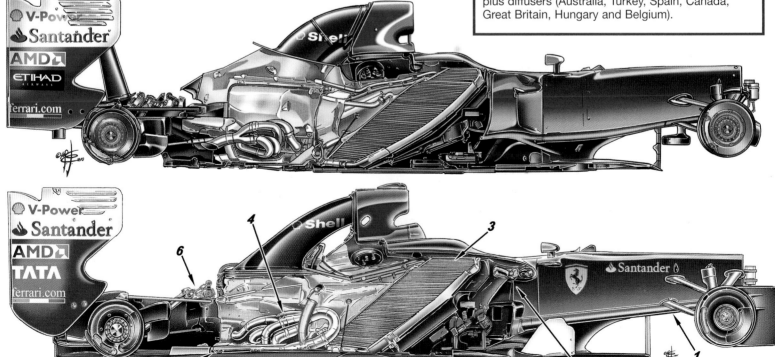

**FERRARI**

The 2011 was the second severely negative season for Mercedes-Benz, who were working with a project that was deeply flawed by the mistake of building a car with the shortest wheelbase of all: 3,208 mm, no fewer than 273 mm less than the McLaren, which was longest of the 12 competing cars.

It was a careful choice, explained Ross Brawn, linked to the fact that with the height of the single diffuser, a long wheelbase would have led to a straight area in front of the one limited for the diffusers and that, in turn, would also be too long as it would have risked stalling the lower aerodynamics.

However, they did not take into account the fact that with the hot blow, that risk would have been overcome by the thermal mini-skirt effect created by the exhausts.

Not only that, but such a short wheelbase brought with it serious compromises, with a raising of the centre of gravity; in fact, to be able to install big enough radiators , they opted for their positioning on two levels, so with a major weight up high.

That arrangement also created cooling problems that forced the team to open large gills at the rear of the sidepods, a problem that was partly resolved from the Turkish Grand Prix onwards.

The team's B car made its first appearance in Spain, the side-pods having completed their crash test, but this version also had divided radiators and a major break in the lower area to carry more air to the rear end.

First with 'traditional' exhausts, the MGP W02 appeared in Melbourne with a salami slice-type terminals that exited in an advanced position before they began to narrow in the Coca-Cola zone and these were retained until the GP of Valencia.

It was not until Silverstone that the Red Bull-type exhausts made their debut and they stayed on the car for the rest of the season, obviously with detailed refinements in line with the various tracks.

The big surprise at Suzuka happened during Friday practice, when both drivers tested a new front wing that was suitably hidden in an anomalous way during fitting and disassembly.

Mercedes MGP W01

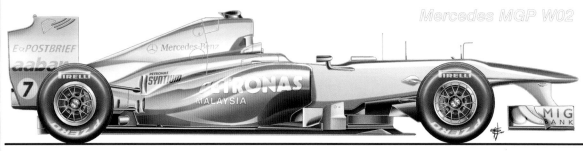

Mercedes MGP W02

Mercedes MGP W02
*Melbourne*

Mercedes MGP W02
*Barcelona*

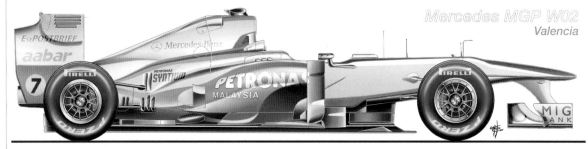

Mercedes MGP W02
*Valencia*

The reason was the wing's F-Duct, fitted so that the team could gather data to help form the basis of the 2012 car. It was a tactical decision opposed by McLaren, who decided not to use an F-Duct on its rear wing at the end of 2009 to wrong-foot its opponents with this weapon that they did use in 2010. The whole thing was Ross Brawn's able interpretation of the regulations, which did not prohibit the use of an F-Duct on the front wing. The only regulation

| CONSTRUCTORS' CLASSIFICATION | | | |
|---|---|---|---|
| | 2010 | 2011 | |
| Position | 4° | 4° | = |
| Points | 214 | 165 | -49 ▼ |

Mercedes MGP W02
*Silverstone*

Mercedes MGP W02
*Monza*

constraint said that the device was not to be operated by the driver, but had to work autonomously by air pressure at high speed. It was a feature that was negated by the specialised press when it was discovered and then became the object of discussion during the winter break.

Mercedes-Benz came fourth and a long way behind Ferrari in the constructors' championship, but worst of all the team never once scored a 2011 podium position. So that spurred them into a campaign of acquisitions that was heady stuff, with the engagement of three technical directors from other teams – Bob Bell, Aldo Costa and Geoff Willis – in the hope of a re-launch in 2012.

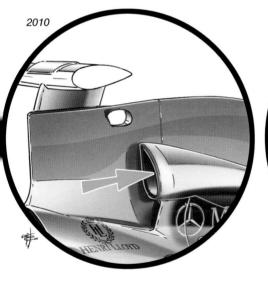

*2010*

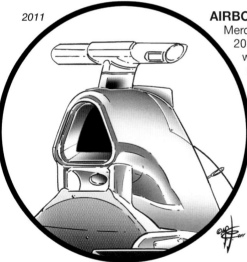

*2011*

### AIRBOX

Mercedes-Benz decided not to continue with one of the 2010 developments, the knife-edge safety roll bar with its two small airbox intakes at the sides that reduced the section at that point of the car and improved air flow towards the rear wing.
The MGP W02 went back to the classic airbox, which also acted as roll bar.

### MELBOURNE

Mercedes-Benz did not take its wing with double raised flaps to its Australian debut, with which it experimented at the last Barcelona test. Instead, the car had a new one with a blow in the principal plane and traditional flaps.

## MELBOURNE SIDE VIEWS

Mercedes-Benz arrived in Melbourne for the season's first race with a car that was somewhat modified compared to the one at its presentation. (1) The team had three different front wings available to it. (2) The turning vanes had disappeared from inside the front wheels. (3) There were various turning vanes in front of the sidepods. (4) The vertical ones were also modified. (5) The exhausts had been further advanced to just over halfway along the sidepods, while the earlier units were low and exited in the terminal area. (6) There were gills to improve cooling. (7) A new rear wing with different horizontal gills. (8) A diffuser with various middle vanes not visible in the illustration.

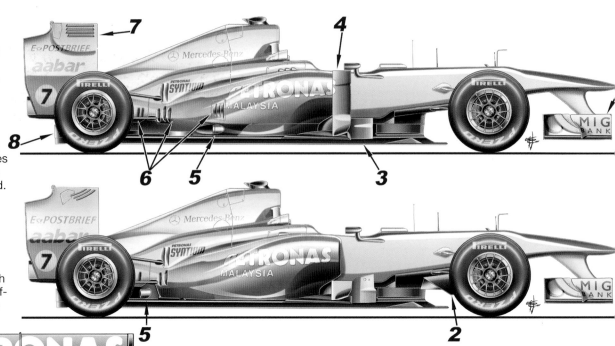

## HYDRAULIC SUSPENSION

This is nothing new, but it is still interesting and not exploited by other teams: it comprised hydraulic elements (1) to control the car's roll and pitch, connected to dampers and controlled by a vertical cylinder (2). Springing was ensured by the torsion bar set into the pull-rod suspension rockers.

## BARCELONA

Practically a B version of the Mercedes-Benz appeared in Barcelona, having completed the lateral crash test that was necessary to be able to make slight modifications to its lateral protection and increase the size of the double radiators in the sidepods. The objective was to improve cooling, the weak point of Stuttgart's car. Numerous gills were eliminated due to these changes, all to the advantage of aerodynamic efficiency.

## MONACO

To resolve its car's overheating problem, Mercedes-Benz copied the McLaren and Renault solution and applied an ear to each side of the engine air intake. That fed a separate channel with air that cooled the oil radiator, which was at the end of the engine manifold.

## UPRIGHT

The mounting point of the upper wishbone that was raised and moved to the centre to modify camber change in the rear suspension set a trend. Ferrari also adopted that technology for the F150 Italia's suspension.

## PROTECTION

As in 2010, the small brake fluid cylinders on the car were protected from blows during fast pit stops by carbon fibre fairing.

## NÜRBURGRING

The Red Bull-style wing with the double raised flap made its debut on the Stuttgart cars at the Nürburgring; it was combined with a bi-plane wing where almost all the teams had their double flap. A similar layout was seen during the last pre-championship tests, but it was never taken to a race weekend until the German event.

## SILVERSTONE

Mercedes-Benz introduced its Red Bull-type version of exhaust blow the very day such systems were banned. It did so with a decidedly short terminal and without the 5 cm lateral cut in the external channel. Note the two small vertical fins for better air flow in the upper part of the lateral channels, completely covered in insulating material.

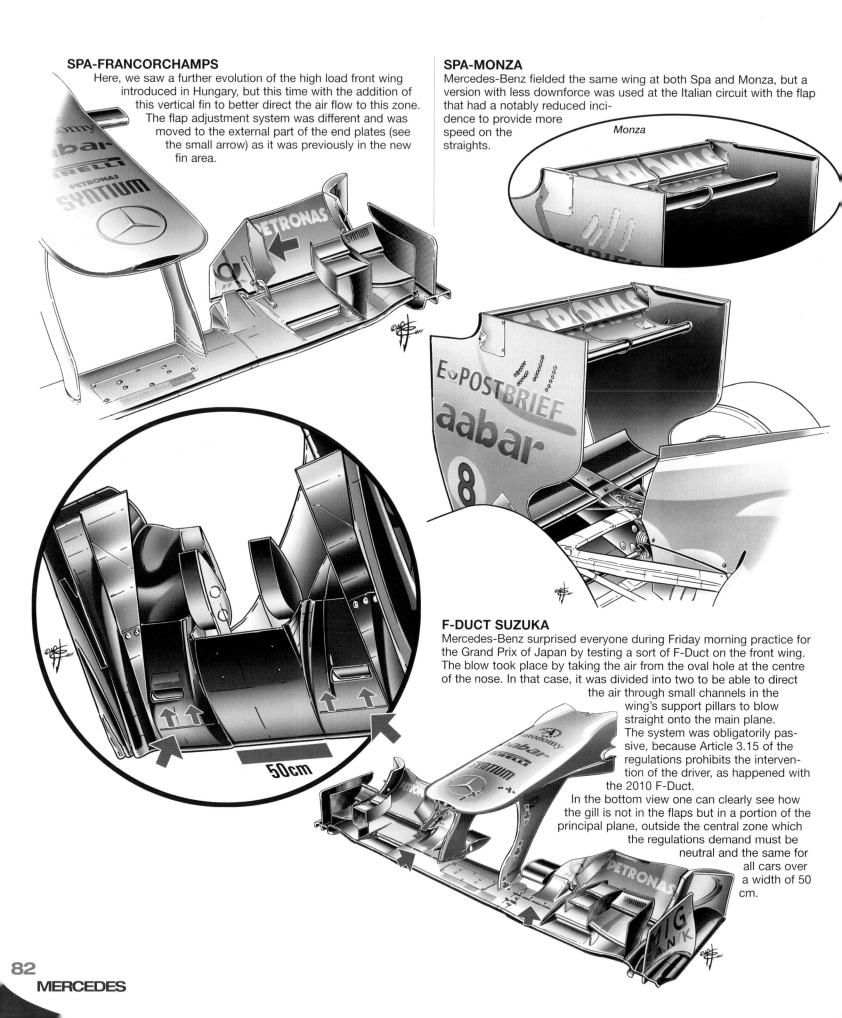

## SPA-FRANCORCHAMPS

Here, we saw a further evolution of the high load front wing introduced in Hungary, but this time with the addition of this vertical fin to better direct the air flow to this zone. The flap adjustment system was different and was moved to the external part of the end plates (see the small arrow) as it was previously in the new fin area.

## SPA-MONZA

Mercedes-Benz fielded the same wing at both Spa and Monza, but a version with less downforce was used at the Italian circuit with the flap that had a notably reduced incidence to provide more speed on the straights.

*Monza*

**50cm**

## F-DUCT SUZUKA

Mercedes-Benz surprised everyone during Friday morning practice for the Grand Prix of Japan by testing a sort of F-Duct on the front wing. The blow took place by taking the air from the oval hole at the centre of the nose. In that case, it was divided into two to be able to direct the air through small channels in the wing's support pillars to blow straight onto the main plane. The system was obligatorily passive, because Article 3.15 of the regulations prohibits the intervention of the driver, as happened with the 2010 F-Duct.

In the bottom view one can clearly see how the gill is not in the flaps but in a portion of the principal plane, outside the central zone which the regulations demand must be neutral and the same for all cars over a width of 50 cm.

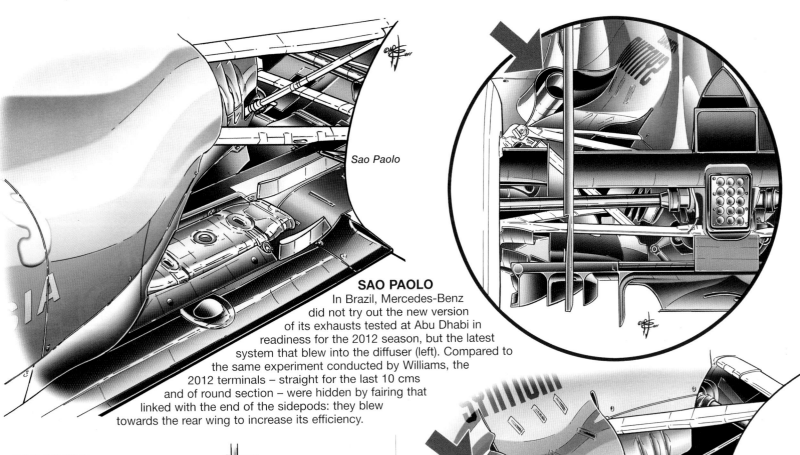

*Sao Paolo*

*Test 2012*

## SAO PAOLO

In Brazil, Mercedes-Benz did not try out the new version of its exhausts tested at Abu Dhabi in readiness for the 2012 season, but the latest system that blew into the diffuser (left). Compared to the same experiment conducted by Williams, the 2012 terminals – straight for the last 10 cms and of round section – were hidden by fairing that linked with the end of the sidepods: they blew towards the rear wing to increase its efficiency.

## SAO PAOLO

Some cars had reversed negative camber at the rear end on the Brazilian track. In general, the limits fixed by the Pirelli technicians were 4° front and 2° rear, while at Spa and Monza some decided to go beyond those values. At Saõ Paolo, the tendency was very limited and on the rear ends of the Mercedes-Benz and Red Bull cars they even used a slight positive camber of about 0.7°. The reason was an attempt to preserve the rear tyres even more by increasing their footprint on the ground. On mixed sections of the track, where there was little lateral stress and a relatively low speed with the addition of a greater tendency to oversteer, it was the right rear tyre, more than anything else, that was under stress. Result: the handling of the tyres was improved, even if there was a slight degradation on their shoulders when, generally, there is more wear on the interior.

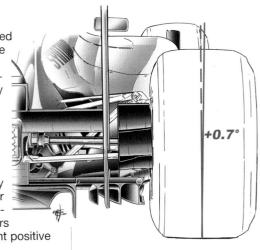

+0.7°

## WHEEL NUT

Mercedes-Benz can take the credit for having brought some new technology to F1 tyre changes. With the arrival of Pirelli and the policy of a multiplicity of pit stops to change tyres, all the teams tried to make their tools for the purpose more efficient and reduce pit time: traffic lights, hydraulic jacks and hand operated jacks were among the tools of the trade. But Mercedes-Benz integrated the tyre's fixing nut into their rim design making them as a one piece while having, obviously, a transverse movement in the central area destined to block the wheel. That way, the mechanics did not run the risk of losing the wheel nuts or fitting them incorrectly as they always stay in position during all phases of the job. It is a method that was adopted long ago in NASCAR and DTM. The result? Mercedes-Benz was often the fastest team in tyre changing, with times of less than three seconds.

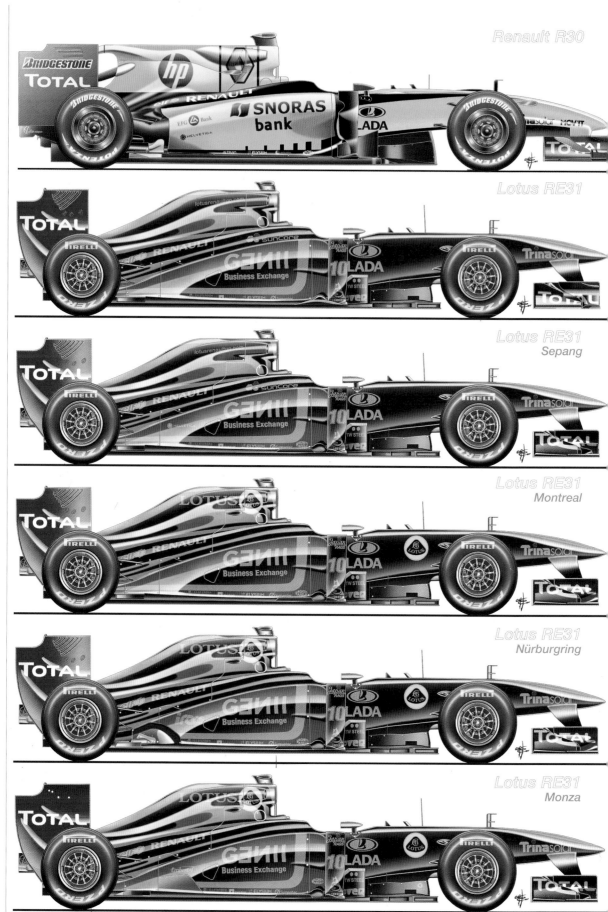

**R**enault must take the credit for fielding a car that was completely different from all the others, having attempted a real technical revolution with the advanced blow of the exhausts, a technique never before seen in Formula 1.

So it was no coincidence that the R31 was the great star of pre-championship testing and was also highly competitive in the season's first two races in Australia and Malaysia, first with Vitaly Petrov and then Robert Kubica's replacement, Nick Heidfeld: the Pole had been in a serious accident while competing in the Ronde di Andora rally in Liguria, Italy, driving a Skoda Fabia. So the loss of Kubica was a tough break for Renault as they grappled with such a project as extreme as the R31.

But the Frenchmen still amazed everyone with their bold move in the exhaust blow area, one in which they were leaders in 1983, when the RE30 entered for the GP of Monaco revealed its new feature in which the exhausts blew directly into the diffuser's lateral channels.

As expected, it is repeated every time the opposition is faced with a new development, there were protests and requests to ban Jean Claude Migeot's discovery but then, after being given the Federation's consent, everyone used that technique on their turbo cars.

The latest Lotus Renault went as far as to make its exhausts exit from the front of the sidepods to energise the air flow that passed under them and feed the diffuser, thereby increasing efficiency. The idea of this development, admitted the team's technical boss James Allison, was to obviate the car's original chronic understeer generated by the downforce guaranteed by the blow in the diffuser area with Bridgestone tyres and the Red Bull-type exhausts, designed in mid-2010. In theory, the central blow ensured better aerodynamic balance and already created downforce in the initial areas of the sidepods to proceed in a more constant manner as far as the diffuser. A bold solution which, despite the inevitable raising of the centre of gravity due to moving the very long, inclined radiators upwards making the

*Renault R30*

*Lotus RE31*

*Lotus RE31*
*Sepang*

*Lotus RE31*
*Montreal*

*Lotus RE31*
*Nürburgring*

*Lotus RE31*
*Monza*

**LOTUS-RENAULT**

| CONSTRUCTORS' CLASSIFICATION | | | |
|---|---|---|---|
| | 2010 | 2011 | |
| Position | 5° | 5° | = |
| Points | 163 | 73 | -90 ▼ |

*Lotus RE31*
*Suzuka*

sidepods bigger, showed itself to be superior to all the traditional Red Bull exhausts when tested in the wind tunnel and during CFD simulations.

The first difficulty arose from the track use on the car on the new Pirelli tyres which, to be preserved, required greater load at the rear end, but especially with the discovery that even a minimum variation of shape in the delicate exhaust exit zone created immediate and considerable aerodynamic imbalance.

As can be seen from the illustrations, the exhausts directed almost 90° towards the outside blew against the aerodynamic devices, indispensible in managing the air flow in that area of the car. To shield them from heat, numerous forms of protection in metal materials were tried, without ever achieving a fully satisfactory result.

It was also necessary to take into account the disadvantage in weight terms, which meant that a choice had to be made when opting whether or not to use metallic inserts.

So that is why the experiment lasted just one test session on the Friday morning during the GP of Germany weekend.

The laboratory car was assigned to Nick Heidfeld, with its Red Bull-type exhausts, a feature that had been tested on the Duxford circuit in the UK just before the trip to Germany.

This version of the R31 showed its shape limitations even more, linked to the original choice of the advanced exhausts, which turned out to be massive and bulky in the rear area, where the other cars ended with much

more tapered lines.

And this experiment underlined the need for a great deal of development work, because the Red Bull-style blow did not suit the R31's suspension or diffuser. In spite of an attempt to increase the rake effect when the rear end

lowered itself in fast corners, the diffuser tended to stall.

If one adds to this the fact that, after the controversial happenings of the GP of Great Britain, it became clear that the exhaust blow into the diffusers would be banned for 2012, it is easy to

## CENTRAL EXHAUSTS

After a lull of 28 years, Renault instigated a new revolution on the exhausts front. In 1983, the RE30 turned up at Monaco with the first exhausts that blew directly into the diffuser. Almost 30 years later, along came the R31 with exhausts that blew into the front part of the sidepods to energise the air flow in the lower area of the car. It was a feature that stupefied those attending the car's press launch, but one which produced reliability problems almost right away. Despite cooling specifically devoted to the exhaust blow zone and in spite of the use of metal materials, that area was still literally cooked by the heat of the exhausts. And the minimum deformation or alteration had negative effects on the R31's aerodynamics.

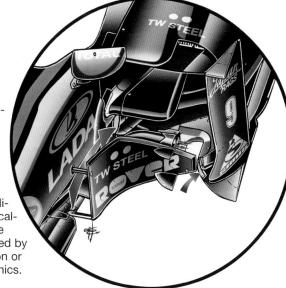

understand why the experiment was immediately dropped so that the team could concentrate on the development of the car with central blow, starting with a completely different project for the coming season.

But the new developments tried out during Friday practice often needed more test driving before being taken to the race grid. And that was partly because of the difficulty of using 60% models instead of the previous 50% units in the wind tunnel.

But development continued right through to the last race, despite the evident thumbs down for the basic solution of the R31 project which was, anyway, put out of play by the Federation banning the exhausts' hot blow for 2012. Renault still distinguished itself for the extreme care with which its front wing had been designed with its highly sophisticated end plates, and for a diffuser that exploited the external channel a lot more. The compact and rational KERS installation created in collaboration with Magneti Marelli was extremely positive, both in terms of weight and performance.

## SIDEPODS

From the outside, the R31's sidepods had an extremely voluminous shape because the low passage of the exhaust manifolds meant the radiators had to be raised compared to those of the opposition.

## SIDEPOD INSTALLATION

In this sequence, put together with the support of James Allison, we can easily see how the installation of the long exhaust terminals forced the team to raise and incline the radiators, which are also very long. Also note how the four exhausts exit the engine, obviously turned around.

## FRONT CHASSIS AND SUSPENSION

Revealed: the shape of the R31's monocoque with the front hoop and some elements of the front suspension highlighted, like the torsion bars (1), the roll bar (2) which can be screwed off laterally, and the steering column (3) set down low. The steering arms are, therefore, placed inside the wing plane faring of the lower wishbone. The lateral protection structures (4) are applied to the monocoque, while that of the protection roll bar for the head (5) is hidden by the shape of the body.

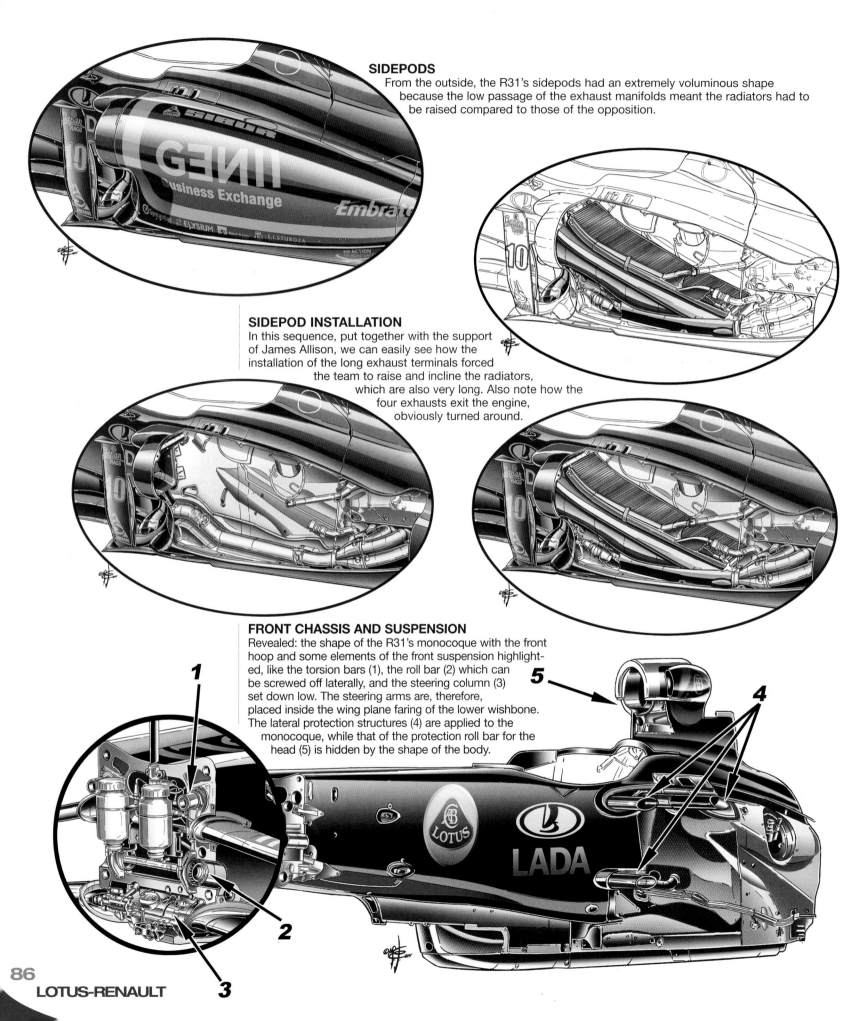

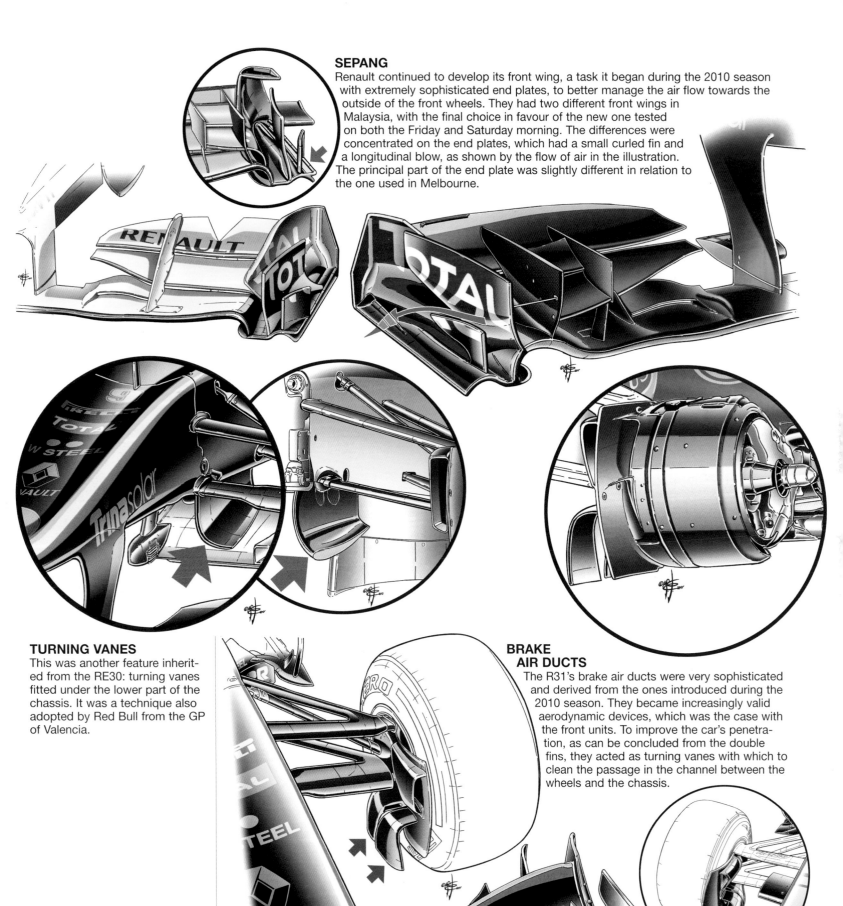

## SEPANG

Renault continued to develop its front wing, a task it began during the 2010 season with extremely sophisticated end plates, to better manage the air flow towards the outside of the front wheels. They had two different front wings in Malaysia, with the final choice in favour of the new one tested on both the Friday and Saturday morning. The differences were concentrated on the end plates, which had a small curled fin and a longitudinal blow, as shown by the flow of air in the illustration. The principal part of the end plate was slightly different in relation to the one used in Melbourne.

## TURNING VANES

This was another feature inherited from the RE30: turning vanes fitted under the lower part of the chassis. It was a technique also adopted by Red Bull from the GP of Valencia.

## BRAKE AIR DUCTS

The R31's brake air ducts were very sophisticated and derived from the ones introduced during the 2010 season. They became increasingly valid aerodynamic devices, which was the case with the front units. To improve the car's penetration, as can be concluded from the double fins, they acted as turning vanes with which to clean the passage in the channel between the wheels and the chassis.

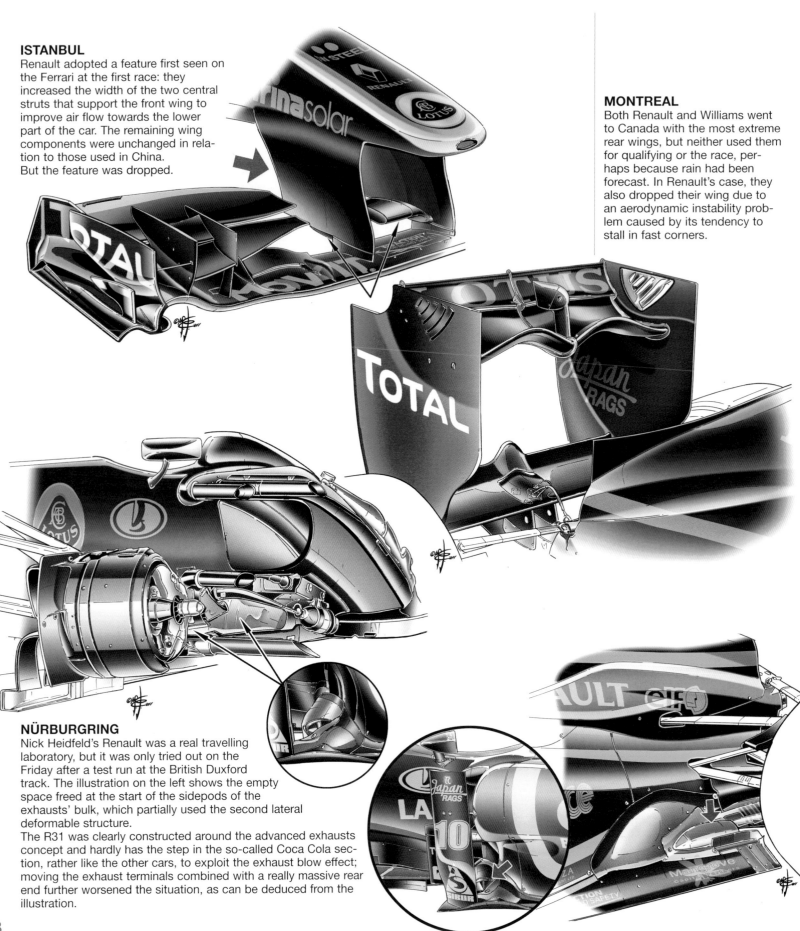

## ISTANBUL

Renault adopted a feature first seen on the Ferrari at the first race: they increased the width of the two central struts that support the front wing to improve air flow towards the lower part of the car. The remaining wing components were unchanged in relation to those used in China.
But the feature was dropped.

## MONTREAL

Both Renault and Williams went to Canada with the most extreme rear wings, but neither used them for qualifying or the race, perhaps because rain had been forecast. In Renault's case, they also dropped their wing due to an aerodynamic instability problem caused by its tendency to stall in fast corners.

## NÜRBURGRING

Nick Heidfeld's Renault was a real travelling laboratory, but it was only tried out on the Friday after a test run at the British Duxford track. The illustration on the left shows the empty space freed at the start of the sidepods of the exhausts' bulk, which partially used the second lateral deformable structure.
The R31 was clearly constructed around the advanced exhausts concept and hardly has the step in the so-called Coca Cola section, rather like the other cars, to exploit the exhaust blow effect; moving the exhaust terminals combined with a really massive rear end further worsened the situation, as can be deduced from the illustration.

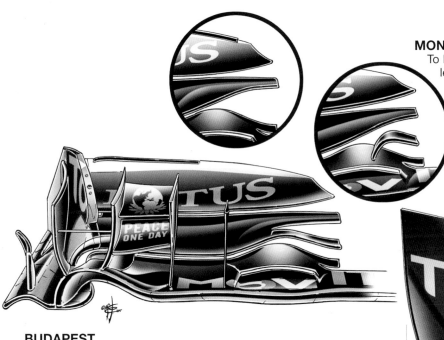

## MONZA

To Renault goes the credit for having fielded the rear wing with the least amount of chord, especially as regards the main plane. As confirmed by the R31's top speed: 347.2 kph for Bruno Senna and 344.8 kph for Vitaly Petrov, placing themselves right behind Sergio Perez in the Sauber, who clocked 349.2 kph.

## BUDAPEST

Here, Renault had three different front wings: the one from Monaco (in the circle on the left), the one used as from Valencia (circle, right) and the new one in the large illustration that first appeared at the Nürburgring, which was then selected for both qualifying and the race.

## INDIA

With hot weather forecast for India, Renault decided not to use its new body with its more accentuated (in yellow) narrow Coca-Cola zone used by Senna in Japan and Korea and which can be seen in the large illustration.

The standard version (circle) was wider in the area in front of the rear wheels. Note that the new narrower version briefly appeared at Singapore on the Friday, but it caused Petrov's car to overheat.

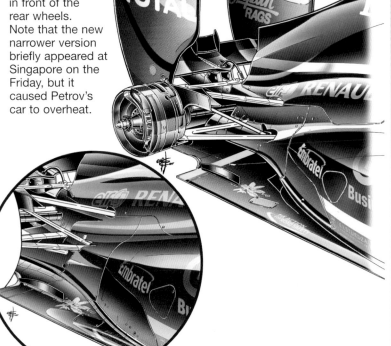

## ABU DHABI

One single example of the Red Bull-style new wing finally made its debut, it having been scheduled to appear for the first time at Suzuka: that was put off because it had not passed its fatigue test in the factory. Like the RB7, it had a main plane with less chord and one slot (1) at the point where it linked with the neutral central section and a newly curled flap (2) with notable chord.

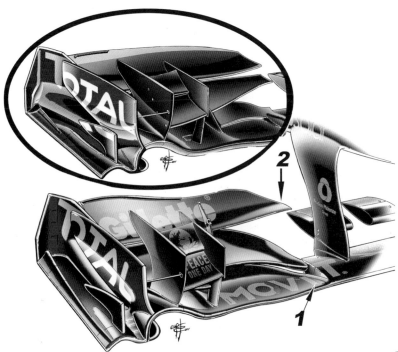

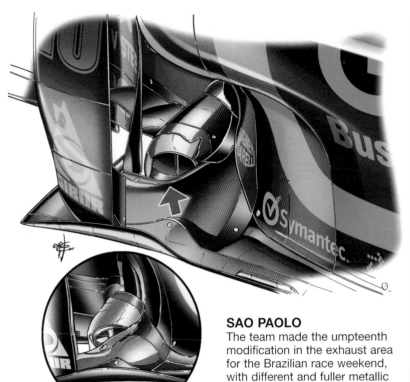

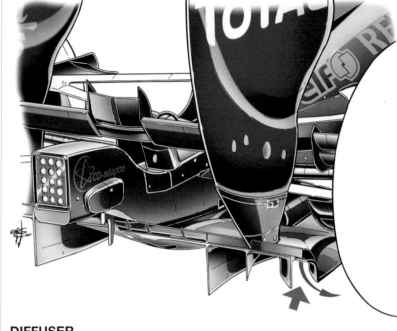

## SAO PAOLO

The team made the umpteenth modification in the exhaust area for the Brazilian race weekend, with different and fuller metallic material inserts to avoid damaging the aerodynamic appendages that caused a considerable loss of efficiency and downforce.

## DIFFUSER

Renault was the only team to fully exploit the width of the diffuser's channels, even using a portion cut to 45° to better extract air from the zone inside the rear wheels and improve the inferior aerodynamic efficiency.

## GEARBOX AND SUSPENSION

The simple rear suspension layout permitted some very fast adjustment work. The torsion bar (1) was inserted from above; in (2) we show the gearbox's radiator; the damper (3) is inside and set into the rocker arms down low (4) to which is connected the roll bar, which can be screwed off transversally. The downforce fin (5) applied to the brake air duct that had the caliper fitted vertically (6) in front of the rear axle.

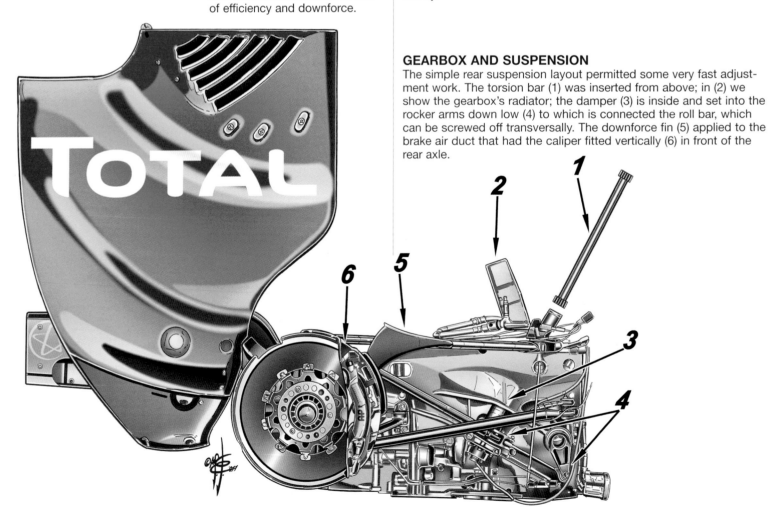

| CONSTRUCTORS' CLASSIFICATION | | | |
|---|---|---|---|
| | 2010 | 2011 | |
| Position | 7° | 6° | +1 ▲ |
| Points | 68 | 69 | +1 ▲ |

Force India's 2011 season was more than honourable, even if without the podium positions of 2009, as the VJM04 battled on equal terms with the mighty Mercedes-Benz and Renault. The team's development work was substantial, especially in the second half of the year, and their two drivers took it in turns to score points nine times in 10 races. Force India did so much work that it became a threat to its French rival, which eventually got the upper hand due to the podia it scored with the revolutionary RE31 in the earliest races.

The VJM04 was a worthy descendent of the previous year's car, of which it retained many features including the nose hump in the lower area, brake calipers in the overhanging position ahead of the front axle and the general architecture of the previous car, despite the use of KERS by this team for the first time. It should be remembered that the engine, gearbox and KERS were the same as those of McLaren, and for that reason the Force India had the second longest wheelbase after the MP4-26.

As on the McLaren, the KERS installation had elements concentrated inside the fuel tank and did not use the 2009 McLaren system of dividing them between the two sides of the car. The rear suspension was also similar to that of the MP4-26, as it was of the pull rod instead of the pushrod on the 2010 cars.

Andy Green, who succeeded James Key on his departure for Sauber in 2010, retained the architecture of the previous car but improved its general handling so that it really seemed at ease on all the tracks.

A substantial wind tunnel study also made its contribution using CFD systems. The Force India car was one of just two 2011 teams to use the knife-edge roll bar and the divided engine roll hoop inlet to improve the quality of air flow towards the rear wing,

Force India VJM03

Force India VJM04

Force India VJM04
Melbourne

Force India VJM04
Montreal

Force India VJM04
Silverstone

a factor that became even more determinate in vertical downforce after the double diffuser was banned.

The developments that appeared at the various Grands Prix were not always used in racing right away, which was the case with the new nose in Turkey, for example; its aerodynamic appendages in the lower area were dismantled to become a medium-low load unit for fast tracks.

The Red Bull-type exhaust blow first appeared on the Force India cars during Friday practice for the GP of Spain, but it did not race until Silverstone, simultaneously with fresh rear aerodynamics that included new concept sidepods, engine cover and diffuser. All of which almost made up a B version of the VJM04, which was immediately successful as it took an excellent sixth place in qualifying in Paul Di Resta's hands.

New rear suspension appeared for the first time in Hungary and that enabled the team to create a more raked set-up – with the rear end about 10 mm higher off the ground – a rear engine cover for hot tracks, complete with central hot air outlets a la Red Bull and a new diffuser.

Like their McLaren cousins, the Force India cars often used asymmetric brake air ducts at the front end to achieve different thermal dissipation values, especially in relation to the operating temperatures of their tyres.

The final part of the season included the introduction of small improvements, especially to the rear end of the car and its diffuser, as happened in both India and Abu Dhabi.

After all that development work, the team took an admirable sixth place in the constructors' championship, right behind the top teams.

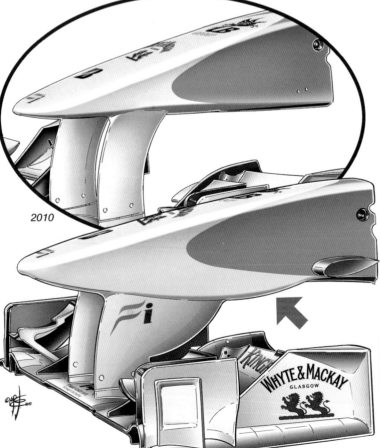

2010

## NOSE

The VJM04 retained a great similarity to its predecessor in the shape of its nose, with the characteristic hump in the lower area that distinguished the 2010 car from its debut. Like the VJM03, the 2011 car underwent the development of the central part of its nose during the season, as shown in the circle.

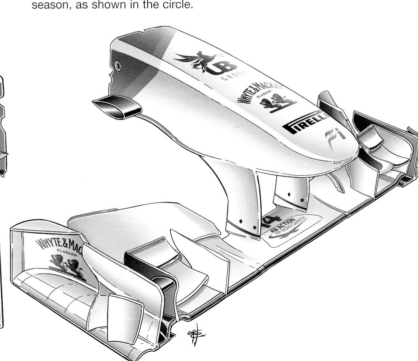

## ISTANBUL-MONTREAL

A brand new nose made its appearance at the GP of Turkey having completed a new crash test and was designed for medium load circuits like Istanbul. So it had lost the voluminous part of the lower area, where it was given a turning vane of the kind brought in by McLaren the previous year and was retained for the MP4-26. The end plates were also of the McLaren school and had two vertical gills. But that nose was never raced and lost its aerodynamic appendages in the lower area to make way for a more tapered shape first seen at the GP of Canada to become the version for fast tracks.

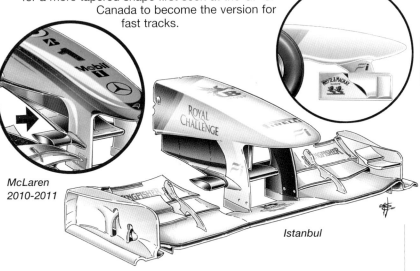

*McLaren 2010-2011*

*Istanbul*

## AIRBOX

Lotus and Force India were the only teams to use the knife-edge roll bar, an engine air box, which was low and divided, like the one that was surprisingly introduced by Mercedes-Benz in 2010 to improve the quality of the airflow towards the rear wing. Note the double manifold to cool the gearbox radiator.

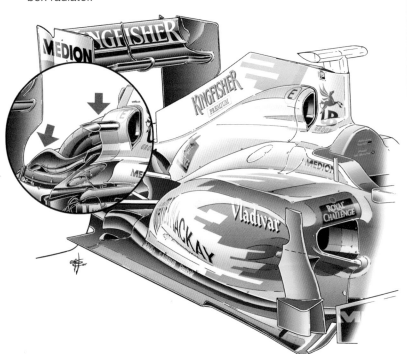

*2010*

## FRONT BRAKES

Also inherited from the VJM03 was the vertical position of the brake calipers down low near the rear axle, which was not taken up by any other team. Asymmetric drums were often tested that were more or less open, dependent on the various track demands.

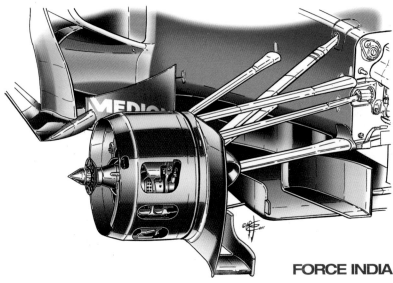

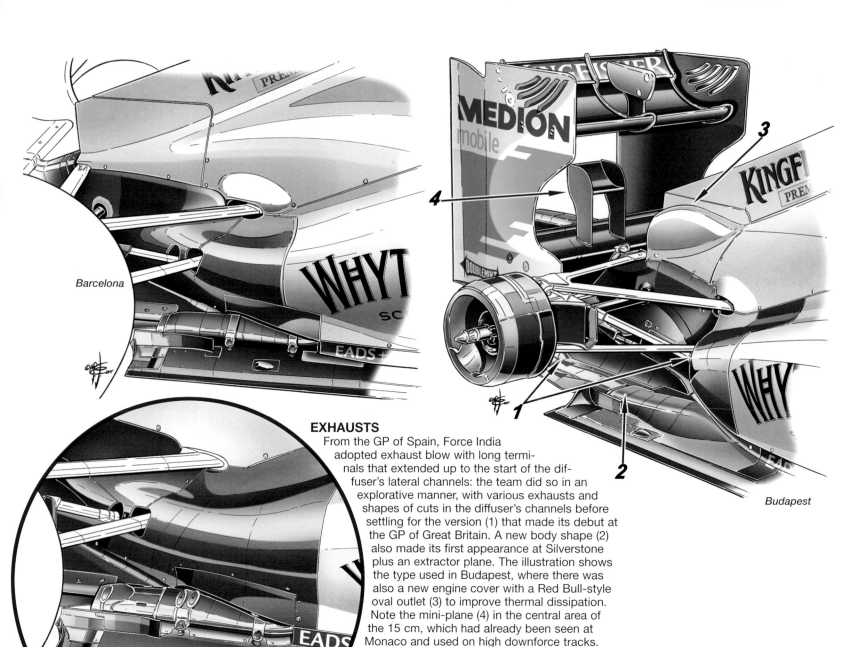

*Barcelona*

*Budapest*

*Silverstone*

## EXHAUSTS

From the GP of Spain, Force India adopted exhaust blow with long terminals that extended up to the start of the diffuser's lateral channels: the team did so in an explorative manner, with various exhausts and shapes of cuts in the diffuser's channels before settling for the version (1) that made its debut at the GP of Great Britain. A new body shape (2) also made its first appearance at Silverstone plus an extractor plane. The illustration shows the type used in Budapest, where there was also a new engine cover with a Red Bull-style oval outlet (3) to improve thermal dissipation. Note the mini-plane (4) in the central area of the 15 cm, which had already been seen at Monaco and used on high downforce tracks.

## SAO PAOLO

Force India and Toro Rosso were the teams that produced the most new developments in the last few races of 2011. That was the case with this new diffuser that had a mini-flap in the central section (1) of the Toro Rosso school and copied by most other teams. The middle vanes (2) were very low. (3) Note the two small flaps in the zone above the deformable structure. (4) The exhaust terminals had a decidedly oval section, less squashed than those of other cars.

| CONSTRUCTORS' CLASSIFICATION | | | |
|---|---|---|---|
| | 2010 | 2011 | |
| Position | 8° | 7° | +1 ▲ |
| Points | 44 | 44 | = |

The first Sauber created under the direction of ex-Force India's James Key did not digress much from the previous car, especially in aerodynamics. A number of features of the earlier cars appeared on their 2011 successor, like the shape of the nose, the sidepods, the imposition of the front wing and the turning vanes below the chassis. The wheelbase dimensions inevitably increased, given the Ferrari school return to KERS with the whole battery group enclosed inside the fuel tank. The association with Maranello was extremely close due to the Prancing Horse's supply of not only the Swiss team's engines but also its KERS and gearbox. The latter obliged the Hinwil team to opt for pushrod rear suspension, just like the F150 Italia; a choice made during the design stage when the value of exhaust blow was underestimated, but which limited the potential of the C30 during the season.

In February, when the results of the CFD study showed the advantages of the technology that Red Bull Racing embraced so enthusiastically, it was too late to slip it into Sauber's design of the new car that was to compete in the season's early races.

So the team pushed aerodynamic development in other sectors, arriving in Melbourne in extremis with new features – an effort that was later frustrated by the disqualification of both drivers, meaning they lost the well-earned total of 10 points they had scored, all for a banal small constructional error on the rear wing (see the Controversies chapter).

The race to design exhausts a la Red Bull dominated the first part of Sauber's season, with the debut of the first version taking place as early as the GP of China, but only in Friday practice. Tried again in Turkey, the Red Bull-type exhausts began to deliver their first positive results from the Spanish GP, where we also saw the first important package of developments, with two

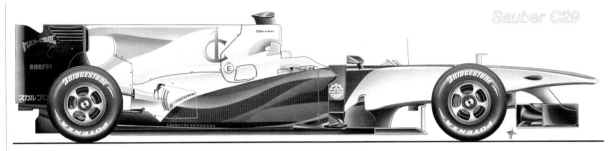

Sauber C29

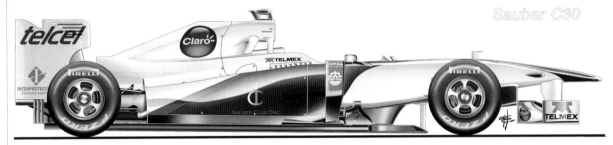

Sauber C30

Sauber C30
Barcelona

Sauber C30
Montreal

Sauber C30
Monza

new front wings, an engine cover linked to a different one at the rear and new brake air ducts front and rear.

The subsequent announcement by FIA that hot blow exhausts would be banned in 2012, which was made official at the GP of Turkey, forced the team to drop its exhausts project, partly due to installation and budgetary difficulties. It was a decision that severely conditioned the development of the C30 as the 2011 season continued, but which enabled the team to concentrate all its efforts on the design of the 2012 car.

But despite all of that, the C30 turned out to be a good car that was easy to set up and caused a very low wear rate of its Pirelli tyres, a factor that became a considerable advantage on some tracks but a handicap at those of low ambient temperatures or with less abrasive asphalt, requiring great effort to bring the tyres to their correct operating temperatures. Much work was done on the front wing while remaining loyal to the initial concept, with end plates closer to the centre of the car and, therefore, with less exploitation of the maximum width allowed for wing planes.

It was a feature that enabled the team to privilege the channelling of the air flow towards the outside of the front wheels.

Fins introduced at Monza in the shape of a saddle under the front part of the chassis were new and they were replaced from the GP of Singapore by two Renault school turning vanes, which had already been copied by Red Bull for Valencia.

Great care was taken over the efficiency of the brake ducts, in part due to increasingly close cooperation with Brembo.

The last development of the season was taken to the GP of Japan with the introduction of two new front wings, the first that privileged performance in qualifying and the second that increased top speed and aerodynamic efficiency.

## MELBOURNE DISQUALIFICATION

Both Saubers scored points in Melbourne but lost them on disqualification, because the cars did not comply with the required 10 mm minimum bend radius of the new wing's flap, which made its debut at the Australian circuit.

## EXHAUSTS

On its debut, the Sauber C30 had traditional exhausts (1) but did have other interesting new features such as the 45° lateral channel of the diffuser (2) like the Renault, and the fringes (3) in the lower area of the end plates of the rear wing, which appeared in 2009 on the Toyota but were not used by any team in 2010; a series of negative lift mini-winglets (4) are applied to the brakes ducts.

## FRONT WING

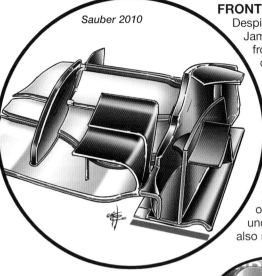

*Sauber 2010*

Despite the appointment of new technical director James Key the constructional philosophy of the front wing stayed the same, with end plates close to the centre to create an interior alignment with the tyres. The comparison with the 2010 car's end plates shows that the flat, low part (1) remained very wide and the vertical units were divided. The step (2) between the planes and the end plates was also unchanged. The new development was the use of a raised flap in the central area (see black arrow) with a shape similar to those of the 2010 McLaren that first appeared at Singapore.

The three vertical turning vanes (3) under the lower part of the nose that work together with the turning vanes under the chassis were new; the illustration of the lower area also shows the three mini-end plates (4).

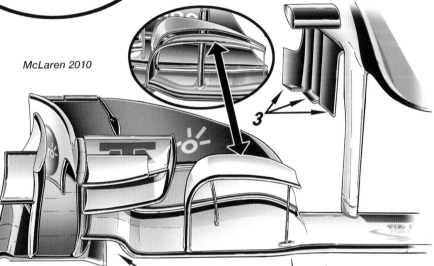

*McLaren 2010*

## SUZUKA

The last evolutionary package of the season appeared in Japan, where there were new front and rear wings. The illustration shows a comparison between the new front, which differs completely from all the previous elements.

The end plate is divided (1) rather like that of the Williams. The main plane was completely new and more curved (2) at the point where it links with the end plate and had a straighter progression, which required a different shape of the flaps (4) as their predecessors had even more pronounced curves. The raised flap was completely new, wider and with a spoon shaped element (3).

## SEPANG

The heat of Malaysia brought a modification to the sidepods' dissipation of heat with the addition of an outlet in a kind of vertical chimney at the sides of the turning vanes. It was a feature that was also used at other hot circuits.

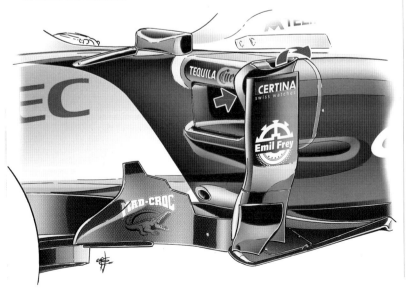

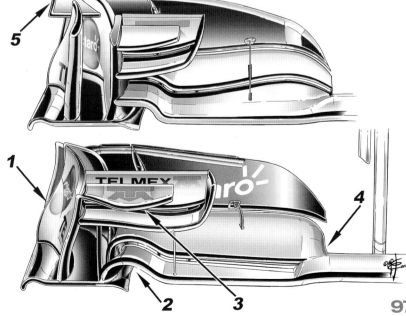

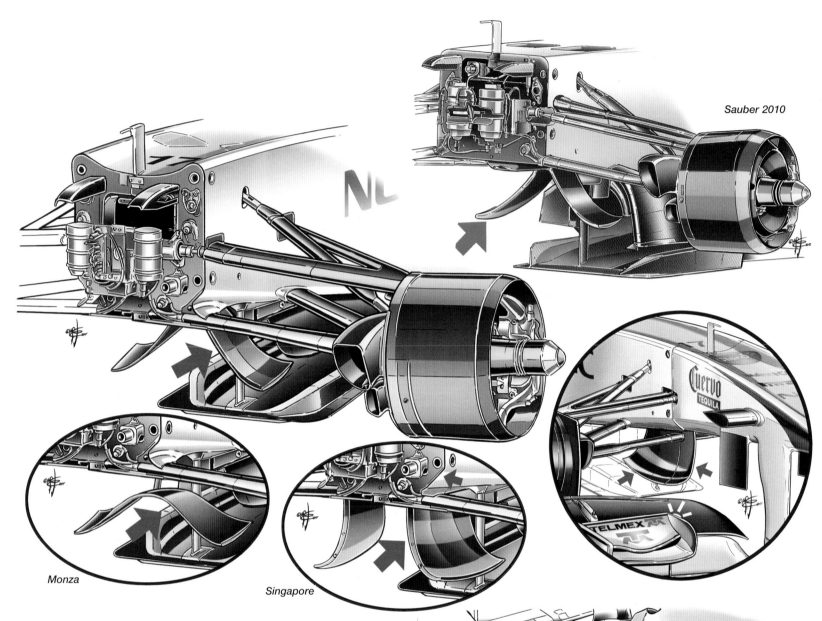

*Sauber 2010*

*Monza*

*Singapore*

## V-SHAPE TURNING VANES

Another feature inherited in its entirety from the 2010 car was the strange upside down V-shape of the turning vanes under the chassis. Until Monza they were practically identical to those of the old car, but at the Italian circuit they became arched to then switch at Singapore to the same as those of Renault, which in turn were copied by the Red Bull. In practice, they were aligned with those already on the lower area of the nose, which had been there since the start of the season to form a single element and better channel the flow of air towards the lower rear zone of the car.

## BLOWN EXHAUSTS

Despite their debut during practice for the third GP of the season in China, the Red Bull-type blown exhausts project was set aside from the GP of Turkey, when it was made known that this system was to be banned in 2012. It was a decision that enabled the team to concentrate its efforts and resources on developing the following season's car and, of course, slowed that of the C30.

| CONSTRUCTORS' CLASSIFICATION | | | |
|---|---|---|---|
| | 2010 | 2011 | |
| Position | 9° | 8° | +1 ▲ |
| Points | 13 | 41 | +28 ▲ |

Toro Rosso STR05

The 2011 season was positive for Toro Rosso, which went up one position in the constructors' championship but of greater importance, it scored 28 points more than in 2010.

With its headquarters in Faenza, Italy, the team completed its personnel structure under the direction of Giorgio Ascanelli and now numbers about 250, with an aerodynamics department headed by Ben Batler, which enabled it to design a much different car than that of its Red Bull 'cousin'. To many, the STR6 was one of the most innovative cars of the season, especially due to its aerodynamics.

Ascanelli used the double bottom layout, first brought out by Jean Claude Migeot back in 1992 on the fairly uncompetitive Ferrari F92, with the objective of creating the most energised air channel possible to feed the rear end and, therefore, the diffusers to reduce the loss of load caused by the double diffuser ban.

The STR6's sidepods were higher in relation to the bottom, with a significant passage of air.

To reduce the negative centre of gravity effect determined by the approximate 10-12 cm increase in height, the radiators were less inclined longitudinally.

The exhaust terminals were also new and flowed in a rectangular boxing effect in the area in front of the rear wheels.

In pre-season tests, this feature was compared with a practically conventional version with round exhausts that exited from the upper sidepod area.

But the original was confirmed on its debut in Australia, although that was further evolved at the third race, the Grand Prix of China, before being replaced at the Japanese GP by one very similar to that of Red Bull, which was retained for the rest of the season.

Another feature introduced since the first tests and copied by most teams, starting with Red Bull, was the blow into the trailing edge in the upper areas of

Toro Rosso STR06

Toro Rosso STR06
Melbourne

Toro Rosso STR06
Valencia

Toro Rosso STR06
Spa-Francorchamps

the diffuser channels to improve its efficiency; in effect, it was as if the incidence of the extractor planes had been increased.

Unlike Sauber, which used both a Ferrari engine and gearbox, Toro Rosso developed its own transmission and was able to retain pull rod rear suspension.

The SR6's Brembo brake calipers were prone as at the front end of the Red Bull RB6, the only teams to adopt this technique.

The advantages of the engine's hot blow effect came in at the

**99**

GP of Belgium, a little later than the opposition.

Meanwhile, there were two important stages in the evolution of the SR6, the first in Spain. At Barcelona, there was a new, more compact and light transmission with new rear suspension on Jaime Alguersuari's car, permitting greater exploitation of the rear aerodynamics.

The second phase appeared at Valencia, where the 'Red Bull's poor relation' practically fielded a B-version of its car.

After the new gearbox and rear suspension came new, completely redesigned sidepods.

To better exploit the aerodynamic concept of the 'pods, which had been raised in relation to the stepped bottom; the shape of the initial area and the inlet were modified. So the space between the lower parts of the sidepods and the bottom was increased, all to the advantage of the air flow in that zone.

All of which meant a great deal of work in installing new radiator package and all the accessories. There was another revolution concerning the original exhaust terminals introduced when the car made its debut, reviewed and corrected in China, which made room for big long terminals with oblique cuts in the area ahead of the rear wheels.

The diffuser was also modified, losing its small flap, and that move was immediately copied by Adrian Newey's Red Bull, while Sauber-type fringes were applied in the lower area of the end plates, a change that had already been made by McLaren, Red Bull and Ferrari.

The last important evolution was the adoption of long exhaust terminals a la Red Bull at Suzuka, which remained on the car for the rest of the season.

## DOUBLE FLOOR
Toro Rosso dusted off Jean Claude Migeot's double floor idea for the Ferrari F92 and applied it to the STR6 to carry more air to the rear of the car and, therefore, make the extractor planes more efficient. It was a solution dictated by aerodynamic needs, which had slightly raised the car's centre of gravity with the radiators obviously installed higher.

## EXHAUSTS
At its launch, the STR6 brandished this new exhaust solution which blew with a sort of squared megaphone, as an alternative to the more traditional type with rounded terminals that exit up high at the rear of the sidepods. The new technique was retained for the start of the season.

*Melbourne*

## DIFFUSER
To Toro Rosso goes the merit of having introduced a new development on the STR6 that was immediately copied by 'magician' Newey and was on the Red Bull from the first race of the season. It was a small flap added to the trailing edge of the diffuser to increase its efficiency. In practice, it was as if the plane in itself was of greater inclination. Another new development was the mini central tunnel overhang (within the 15 cm permitted by the regulations) in relation to the longitudinal limit of the diffuser. Note the external rounded part, which was then modified for the first race, as can be seen in the illustration on the right. Also note the mini-channel in the usually flat area inside the wheel.

*Presentation*

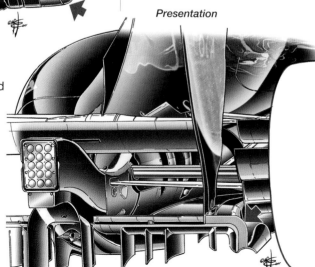

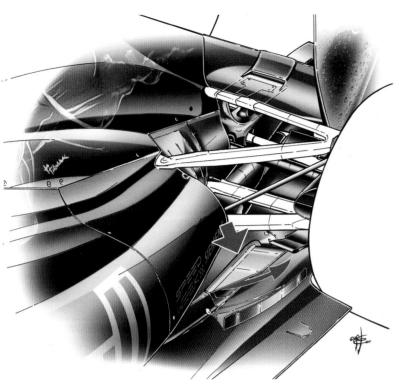

## ISTANBUL

At the Grand Prix of Turkey, Toro Rosso presented the new feature of integrating the brake discs' coupling flange into the upright, so eliminating the fixing elements.

A method that produced greater rigidity and some weight saving. The illustrations show the technique applied to the front end, but a similar method was also used at the rear.

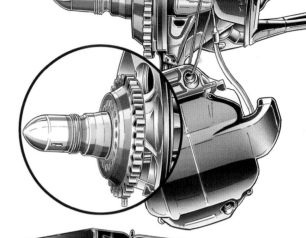

## SHANGHAI

The exhaust exits were modified on the Toro Rosso with the addition of a small horizontal fin to better direct the hot air flow towards the lateral channels of the diffuser. The shadow plate applied to the brake air intakes was also new.

## BARCELONA

Here, there was a new gearbox for the Toro Rosso, built to both gain weight and better integrate itself into the car's aerodynamics, with the lower wishbone of the suspension (1) notably raised. That meant better exploitation of the fins' position (2), connected to the brake air intakes for the purpose of better directing the exhaust blow into the special lateral channels. The intakes (3) were also different, with the calipers moved from their low horizontal position. Raising the centre of gravity was compensated for by an easier and better management of the cooling facility; also see the different drums, the new ones closed and the old semi-open versions.

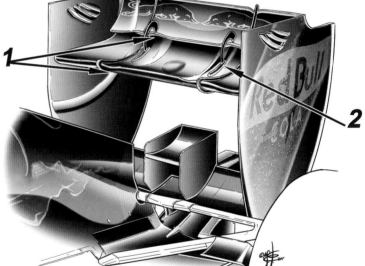

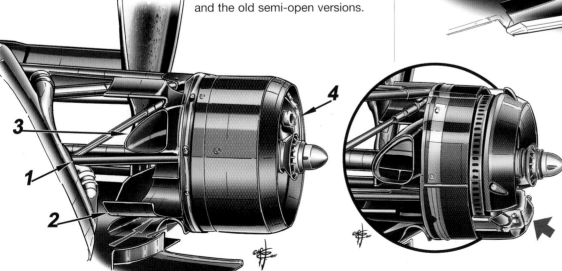

## MONACO

Toro Rosso was the only team to bring in a new rear wing of such unusual shapes, with both the main plane and the flap of sinuous progression. It was an attempt to better the firmness of downforce along the car's entire length. The actuators of the DRS (flap adjuster) system were new and split.

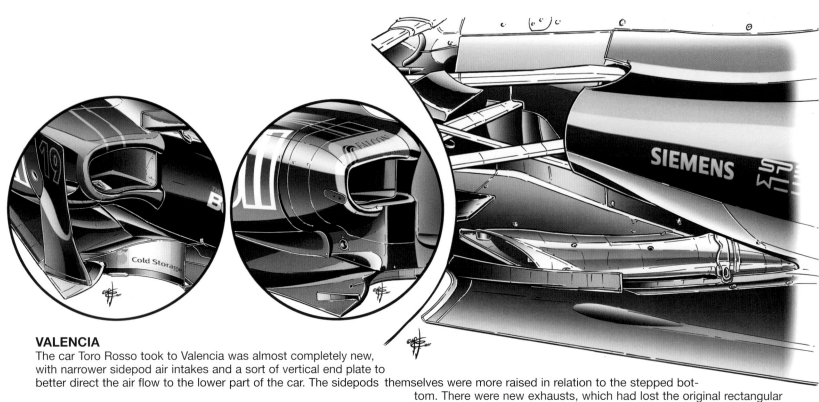

## VALENCIA

The car Toro Rosso took to Valencia was almost completely new, with narrower sidepod air intakes and a sort of vertical end plate to better direct the air flow to the lower part of the car. The sidepods themselves were more raised in relation to the stepped bottom. There were new exhausts, which had lost the original rectangular shape of the terminals that blew outwards and became those similar to the systems of the other teams with long, fairly flat and wide terminals that blew closer to the rear wheels.

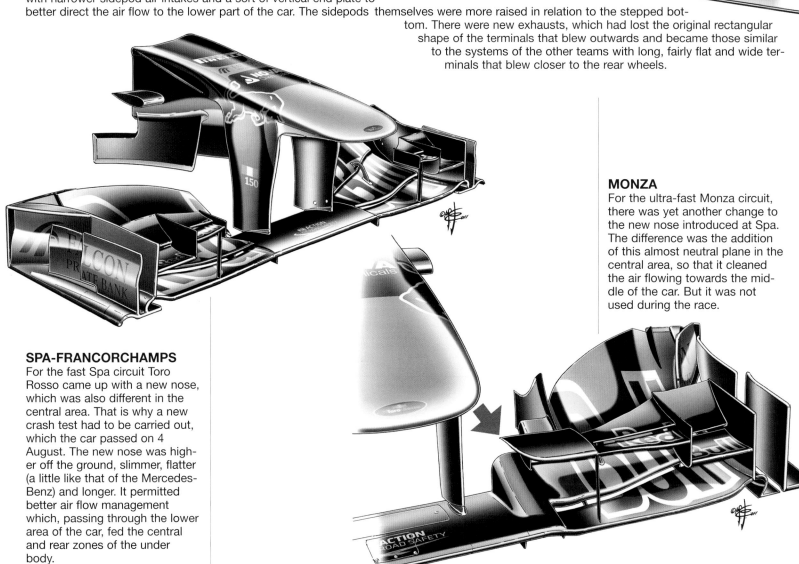

## MONZA

For the ultra-fast Monza circuit, there was yet another change to the new nose introduced at Spa. The difference was the addition of this almost neutral plane in the central area, so that it cleaned the air flowing towards the middle of the car. But it was not used during the race.

## SPA-FRANCORCHAMPS

For the fast Spa circuit Toro Rosso came up with a new nose, which was also different in the central area. That is why a new crash test had to be carried out, which the car passed on 4 August. The new nose was higher off the ground, slimmer, flatter (a little like that of the Mercedes-Benz) and longer. It permitted better air flow management which, passing through the lower area of the car, fed the central and rear zones of the under body.

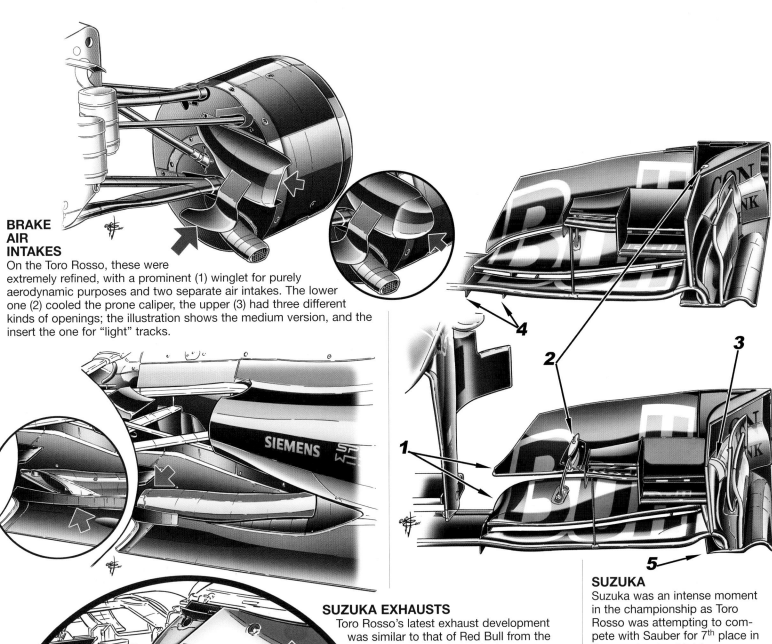

## BRAKE AIR INTAKES

On the Toro Rosso, these were extremely refined, with a prominent (1) winglet for purely aerodynamic purposes and two separate air intakes. The lower one (2) cooled the prone caliper, the upper (3) had three different kinds of openings; the illustration shows the medium version, and the insert the one for "light" tracks.

## SUZUKA EXHAUSTS

Toro Rosso's latest exhaust development was similar to that of Red Bull from the Suzuka race. Their terminals were no longer cut like 'slices of salami' as introduced at Valencia.

The small, vertical fin indicated by the arrow in the circle was also different, as it had become shorter. The detail shows how the Toro Rosso also used the closed extension of the exhausts first seen on the Ferrari at Spa. The sort of chimney plugged upwards worked as a lung to accumulate hot gases that were released downwards when the engine was decelerating.

## SUZUKA

Suzuka was an intense moment in the championship as Toro Rosso was attempting to compete with Sauber for 7th place in the constructors' table.

So the Italian-based team used a new front wing, all the elements of which were different.
(1) Both flaps were new in shape, but especially the adjustment system for the second unit, which no longer took place through the pin inside the end plates but with an element placed mid-flap (2). The end plates retained their three separate elements but with a slot (3) shown in yellow in the innermost plate. The old wing had two small middle vanes to separate the neutral zone, as required by the regulations, from the lateral one (4) but on the new unit there was only one. The small horizontal plane (5) was also different and linked the end plate with the principal plane.

The 2011 season should have been an important one for Williams. Instead the FW33, born of a radical and ambitious project, turned out to be a disaster causing the team to lose three positions in the constructors' championship.

The aerodynamics were the inspiring factor that convinced Sam Michael to launch himself into laborious and expensive programme like gearbox miniaturisation, which nobody had dared to embark on until that moment.

It took no fewer than 3,500 km of bench testing at the Toyota facility in Cologne, Germany, to bring about the new transmission, which had the differential box in a previously unseen position that drastically reduced bulk in height terms. The difficulty was created by the incredible angle that the drive sfhats ended up with: about 14°, practically double the recognised maximum limit.

The basic concept of the project originated from an analysis of the Red Bull RB5, conceived for a single diffuser in 2009.

That, too, was a car with a very low gearbox to boost good air flow towards the lower part of the wing: with the prohibition of the double diffusers for the 2011 season, the idea of being able to free the area in front of the wing as much as possible took on great importance and, without doubt, the FW33 was the car with the lowest body terminal zone of all, even lower than that of the dominant RB7.

So it was a shame that all that work clashed with the physical dimensions of the 8-cylinder Cosworth, a handicap it was not possible to limit due to the installation of the fuel feed trumpets about which nothing could be done due to the regulation freeze on engine development.

Result: the engine cover created a sort of aerodynamic block able to destroy all the advantages the boldness that the miniaturised gearbox brought about for the beam wing.

Another new feature of the FW33 was the suspension mount support strut of the beam wing.

The consequence of the gearbox project was evident, given that it would have been impossible to fix it to its fusion, which is just about non-existent at that point. Despite the reduced dimensions,

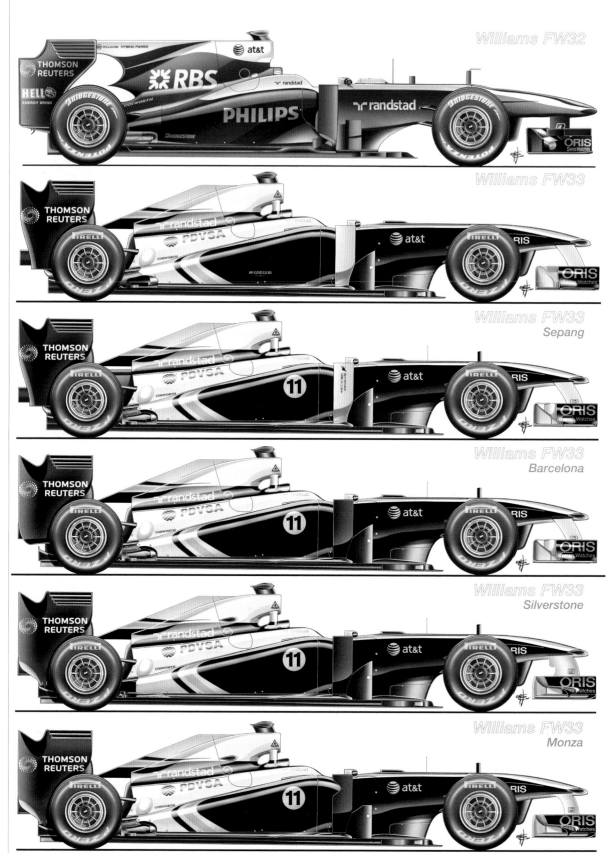

Williams FW32

Williams FW33

Williams FW33
Sepang

Williams FW33
Barcelona

Williams FW33
Silverstone

Williams FW33
Monza

| 'CONSTRUCTORS' CLASSIFICATION | | | |
|---|---|---|---|
| | 2010 | 2011 | |
| Position | 6° | 9° | -3 ▼ |
| Points | 69 | 5 | -64 ▼ |

*Williams FW33*
*Abu Dhabi*

## EXHAUSTS

Right from the first tests, the FW 33's exhausts blew in the low terminal area of the sidepods with a 'slice of salami' type section! Strange to see how the engine cover ended with such a large area, enough to partially thwart the work invested in miniaturising the gearbox.

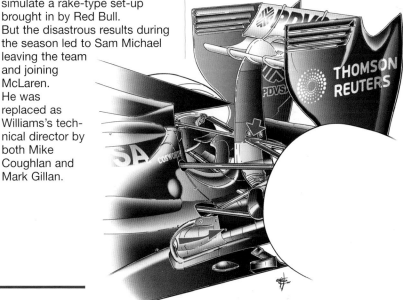

the torsional stiffness of the new transmission group was equal to that of 2010 and the loss of horsepower associated with the unusual angulation of the drive shafts was estimated at around 5 hp. Taking on the gearbox design perhaps distracted the team from research on exhaust blow, which turned out to be the season's winning weapon.

But in this field, too, the attempt to recover in relation to the opposition clashed with the inability of Cosworth to develop delayed ignition to obtain hot blowing in deceleration.

It was no coincidence that the Grand Prix in which Williams seemed the most competitive was the British, with a partial reduction in the hot blow effect that coincided with the debut of Red Bull-type exhaust terminals in the race, which weighed about 5 kg more but were necessary to ensure reliability.

Yet despite that, the 2011 season saw a great deal of development work going on at Williams, with no fewer than 11 front wings, nine diffusers, eight beam wings and five different floors making their appearance.

Completely new and interesting shapes were introduced, especially for the front wing area both in terms of planes and end plates. The objective was to be able to travel as low as possible at the front, with the rear end farther away from the ground to simulate a rake-type set-up brought in by Red Bull.

But the disastrous results during the season led to Sam Michael leaving the team and joining McLaren. He was replaced as Williams's technical director by both Mike Coughlan and Mark Gillan.

## GEARBOX

The Williams was, perhaps, the most extreme example of how aerodynamics affected mechanical decisions. To increase the amount of air that flowed towards the lower plane of the FW33's wing, an almost invisible rear end was designed, with suspension that was moved higher up so as not to interfere with the diffusers. The upper wishbone (1) was hinged to the wing support for the first time.

The pull rod layout (4) freed the whole upper zone to improve air flow in that area. The terminal part of the body (2) was the lowest of all the 2011 cars (2 cm lower than that of the RB7, for instance) as the differential box had been moved lower down. That required an unusual 14° angle in the inclination of the drive shafts (3), which normally stop at 7°.

Note the upper wishbone mount, anchored directly to the structure in titanium that supports the beam wing.

The advantages could have been greater if they had been able to reduce the bulk of the engine cover, restricted by the needs of the 8-cylinder Cosworth engine's bulk.

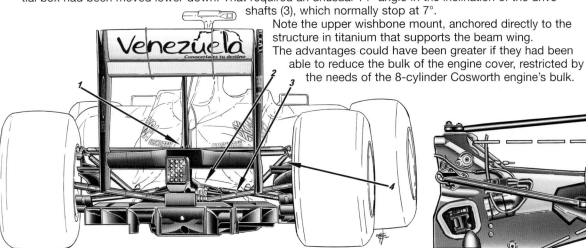

## MELBOURNE

At the season's opening race, a new front wing was used that arrived in Melbourne in the nick of time. There was only one and that was fitted to Rubens Barrichello's car. The difference was in the addition of a small external fin to the new end plates used at the last pre-season test at Barcelona.

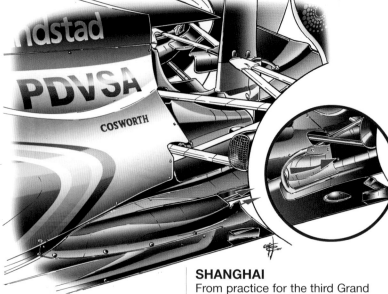

## SHANGHAI

From practice for the third Grand Prix of the season in China, Williams began to test Red Bull-type exhaust blow, but only on Barrichello's car. However, the new system was not used in either qualifying or the race at Shanghai or at the following two GPs, where it was not even tested again. Some body components continued to burst into flame, so both drivers still ran the old system shown in the circle until the GP of Monaco, where the long terminals were tested again during Friday practice.

## ENGINE AND GEARBOX

This illustration, purposely coloured in part to bring out the details better, clearly shows the incredible height reduction of the gearbox, with the suspension's upper wishbone (1) set into the structure of the beam wing support. (2) Note the inclination of the arms to achieve high anti-squat values. The exhausts face the opposite direction (3) to blow towards the low part of the sidepods.

## MONTREAL

To Williams and Renault goes the credit for having introduced two extreme features for the medium-low downforce beam wings at Montreal. The FW33's wing had a spoon shape of the BAR Honda school to provide more downforce in the central area. Renault had a V-shaped wing derived from the one that appeared last year, but it was not used for qualifying or the race, perhaps because rain was forecast.

## SILVERSTONE

For their home race, Williams came up with a new front wing with a main plane that had a larger blow in the area close to the end plates, which had been notably revised. The second main flap was divided into two key sections, with the central portion of adjustable incidence.

## SINGAPORE

The 11th new front wing for the FW33 appeared here, but it was only tested on the Friday and then set aside. The stepped section was completely new; it is indicated by the arrow and was previously more connected with the main plane. The wing supports shown by the arrow were also new and wider than their predecessors. This wing was in line with the current tendency towards a certain amount of free flexing.

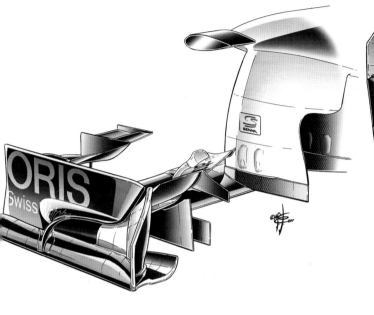

## SILVERSTONE

The race in which the Red Bull-type exhausts on the Williams worked best was the GP of Great Britain. Even if details, the modifications that had been made were important. To avoid cooking materials, the long terminals (1) were only partially in view. (2) Pyrossic protection was increased, as were the dimensions of the vertical fin. (3) The brake air intakes were new and their task was also to shield the tyres from the hot air emanating from the exhausts. In the oval is a detail of the long exhaust terminals, which had the same configuration at the beginning as the standard version.

## ABU DHABI

Mindful of the intense heat of Abu Dhabi, the FW33s had a large oval Red Bull-style air vent as did Force India, but they only used theirs in practice. The Williams vent was even larger and more squashed compared to those of other teams. Actually, this feature was introduced in Budapest, but it was never used in either qualifying or the race.

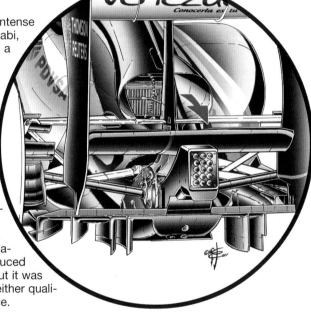

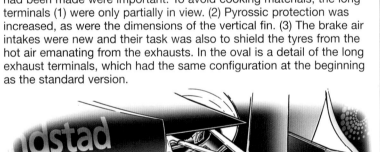

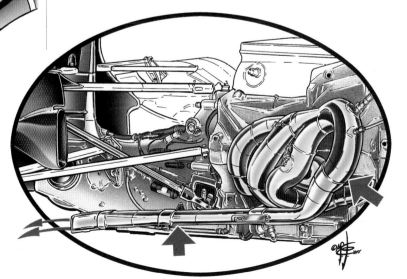

# Lotus

Even if it was not able to become part of Formula 1's A series, the Lotus T128 was a major improvement in quality over the laboratory car the team ran in 2010. All of this as result of a number of important technical agreements, like the switch from Cosworth to Renault engines, the use of Red Bull's gearbox instead of the X-Trac and the Aerolab wind tunnel directed by Jean Claude Migeot; factors that strengthened the work of the group directed by Mike Gascoyne.
The T128 boasted an interesting aerodynamic body with highly concave sidepods and a divided, low engine roll hoop inlet like that of the 2010 Mercedes-Benz, but also a new pullrod suspension – the only one among the three B Series cars – and prone front brake calipers with ducts clearly of the Renault school. And it was precisely because of the French V8 engine that Lotus was the only one of the three smaller teams to use Red Bull-type exhaust blow. But the car's Achilles heel was its power steering, which often sabotaged its performance, especially when Jarno Trulli was driving. Compared to the other three minor teams, Lotus also carried out a sterling development programme that was divided into three phases: those of its Melbourne debut, Turkey and Singapore. Two 13th places enabled them to prevail over HRT and Virgin.

*Lotus T127*

*Lotus T128*

*Lotus T128*
*Sao Paolo*

| CONSTRUCTORS' CLASSIFICATION | | | |
|---|---|---|---|
| | 2010 | 2011 | |
| Position | 10° | 10° | = |
| Points | 0 | 0 | = |

## TWIN ENGINE ROLL HOOP INLET

Lotus and Force India were the only teams to adopt divided engine air inlets – first used by Mercedes-Benz in 2010 – which were obviously within the limits of the thickness of the central structure, as imposed by the Federation. Note the divided manifold with two intakes down low to cool the gearbox's radiator.

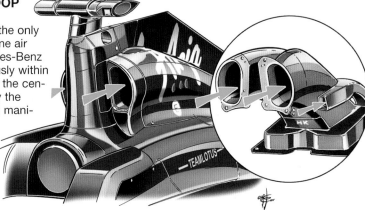

*HRT F110*

# HRT

The objective of the Spanish team was to finish the season and it did so, as in 2010, beating last placed Virgin. It was a result which, in theory, should have encouraged the team to lay the foundations for a better performance in 2012. Geoff Willis was taken on to direct the work, but when he got there he found the same Dallara chassis of the 2010 car that was to be adapted to the new regulations. The only small advance was the replacement of the X-Trac gearbox for a Williams, but still of the 2010 variety. The rear suspension was still pushrod as was that of Virgin.
Financial difficulties forced Willis to leave the team which, compared with 2010, did put

*HRT F111*

Virgin VR01

Virgin MVR02

Virgin MVR02
Sao Paolo

## Virgin

For the second season, Virgin was the worst of the 'B series' teams and finished behind HRT in the constructors' championship despite the Spanish squad's more limited budget. The divorce from Nick Wirth was not much of an advantage, being replaced in extremis by Pat Symmonds as external consultant as he was unable to follow the team at the circuits. Powered by Cosworth, Virgin also kept the X-Trac gearbox and its rear suspension was pushrod.

There was a minimum development programme with the first stage making itself known in Turkey, where we saw a different diffuser, a new front wing and an attempt at exhaust blow that was not used in the race. The most important new feature was the nose cone, which was higher from the ground and led to another crash test.

From Singapore, a new version of their exhaust made its debut, exiting down low at the end of the sidepods with their salami slice sections. The design and evolution of the car, which was only based on CFD simulations, was finally tried out in McLaren's wind tunnel from October after reaching an agreement to do so with the Woking team.

### EXHAUSTS

After useless attempts to reproduce the blow effect with techniques similar to those of Red Bull, Virgin brought out these exhausts at Singapore, exiting down low in the narrowing area of the sidepods.

| CONSTRUCTORS' CLASSIFICATION | | | |
|---|---|---|---|
| | 2010 | 2011 | |
| Position | 12° | 12° | = |
| Points | 0 | 0 | = |

| CONSTRUCTORS' CLASSIFICATION | | | |
|---|---|---|---|
| | 2010 | 2011 | |
| Position | 11° | 11° | = |
| Points | 0 | 0 | = |

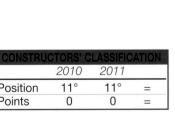

together a minimal development programme resulting in the exit of the exhausts midway along the sidepods, rather like Mercedes-Benz had at the beginning of the season. A 13th place enabled HRT to overtake Virgin in the constructors' championship table.

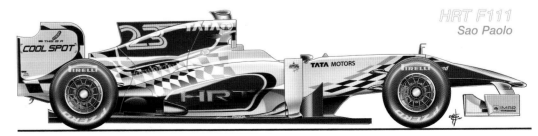

HRT F111
Sao Paolo

The 2012 season began under the banner of new technical developments.
As often happens when new technical regulation limitations come in, the designers' reaction has the effect of seeing new features proliferate to recover lost efficiency that result in major advances being made in the cars' technical development.

The prohibition of exhaust blow straight into the diffusers was practically outflanked by the introduction of new sidepod shapes and maniacal research into the aerodynamic development of the cars' rear ends in an effort to return to downforce values that were not far off those of 2011.

The biggest surprise was that it was not just the usual top three teams that came up with new, trend setting developments, but also some of the others that usually play a secondary role in Formula 1.

Especially Sauber, which changed the shape of the terminal area of its sidepods; and Williams with their new features, cleverly combined with those of their 2011 miniaturised gearbox plus, of course, Mercedes-Benz with its front F-Duct.

Two top teams disappointed, especially at the start of the season. Red Bull was forced to renounce its original development of the RB8, which was rejected by FIA.

That forced design guru Adrian Newey to retreat to an improvised solution, which cost the team the world championship in an experimental phase on the track, but had two positive outlets: in Bahrain and Valencia with the introduction of the D version of the car.

The other team was Ferrari, battling with a project that burnt its bridges with past experience and seemed a long way from being competitive, yet surprisingly it underwent constant and carefully conceived developments that put the F2012 up there with the best of them.

McLaren started the season so well in Australia, but seemed to become less effective even in the exploitation of their tyres, particularly with Jenson Button, who was the best interpreter of the Italian tyres in 2011. Among other things, the MP4-27 was the

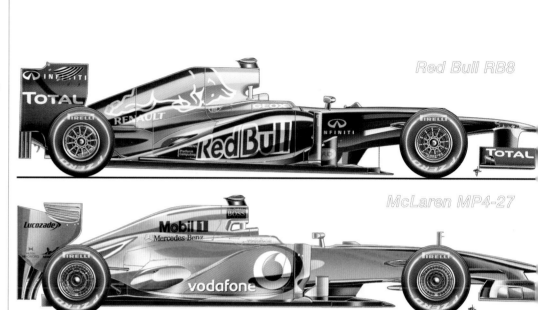

Red Bull RB8

McLaren MP4-27

Ferrari F2012

Mercedes W03

Lotus RE20

Force India VJM05

# The 2012 SEASON

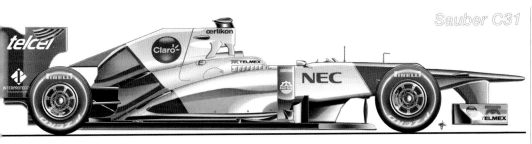

*Sauber C31*

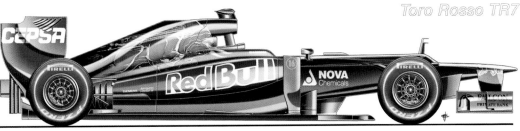

*Toro Rosso TR7*

*Williams FW34*

*HRT F112*

*Caterham*

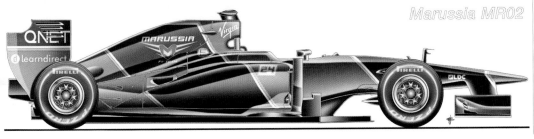

*Marussia MR02*

only car – together with the Marussia – not to have a stepped nose; not even in the evolution of the car that made its debut at the GP of Spain, as mentioned in the 2012 New Regulations chapter. And now we come to the tyre factor: for the 2012 season, Pirelli became even more of a key player in the world championship and a more determinate factor in all drivers' success.

Just consider that there were no fewer than seven different winners of the first seven races, and that reshuffled all the previous statistics. In chronological order, they were Button (McLaren), Alonso (Ferrari), Rosberg (Mercedes-Benz), Vettel (Red Bull), Maldonado (Williams), Webber (Red Bull) and Hamilton (McLaren). So seven different drivers in four different cars, including Mercedes-Benz' first victory and the return of Williams to success not having won a Grand Prix since 2004 in Brazil.

And all in their first season without the long-standing technical guidance of Patrick Head, who is well considered and appreciated in the sport as a leader of the British school.

The number of winners could not have been even more varied either, and both Lotus and Sauber came close to victory on two occasions.

It is difficult to make a technical assessment of the real values in the field, because tyres were the preponderant factor, so much so that they caused controversy that was more or less vehement among protagonists like Michael Schumacher, team principal of Red Bull Chris Horner and Ferrari president Luca Cordero di Montezemolo. On the other hand, one has to admit the tyres' made their contribution to creating a more spectacular Formula 1. Never have the last 10 laps of each race been so packed with uncertainty and dramatic incidents than in the 2012 season.

The Federation banned exhausts that blow into the diffuser for 2012 and introduced a nose height limit for safety reasons. That meant that one of the weapons that made Red Bull invincible in 2011 had been abolished. And in addition, hot blow of the engines was prohibited, limiting the power unit's electronic management and precise restrictions were imposed on the position of the exhaust terminals in an attempt to drastically reduce their blow effect in relation to the diffusers. A limitation that was given a sort of preview at the GP of Great Britain, the only race won by Ferrari. In that difficult situation, the thinking was to return to the technology of 1998 and exhausts that exited from the upper part of the body, but then the final text of the new regulation gave up of that thought. In practice, the Federation had ban-ished the exhausts from the diffuser zone and, therefore, from the rear axle, and imposed a sort of 'box' in which the exhausts had to be contained. Their limits were dictated in articles 5.6.1, 2 and 3 of the tech regs. They must be between 500 mm and 1200 mm from the rear axle, raised between 250 mm and 600 mm from the reference plane – the lowest part of the car, which is used for all height measurements – and between 200 mm and 500 mm from the centre line of the car transversally. Those measurements lead to the definition of a 'container' 700 mm long, 300 mm wide and 350 mm high to the inside of which the exhausts had to be located.

As can be seen from the top view, the 2012 solution shows the exhausts a long way from the rear wheels and the extractor planes, so as not to influence the car's lower aerodynamics as happened in 2011 with terminals that blew low, a few millimetres from the lateral channels of the diffuser, increasing the downforce effect. To further limit the imagination of the designers, the Federation also dictated that the last 100 mm of the exhaust terminals had to be completely straight and with an obligatory round section of with an inner diameter of 75 mm. It conceded a freedom of upwards angulation of between 10° and 30° in relation to the longitudinal axis and 10° transversally. That gave rise to quite a variety of solutions to the problem to direct the engine blow in draught more or less towards the upper part of the beam wing group or towards the lower one, especially on the debut of the new cars. But despite these limitations the various technical offices worked out how to get around those regulations, creating shapes that still helped the air flow – or at least a good percentage of blow – recover the lost downforce. Exploiting the Coanda effect, they introduced new shapes of the terminal area of the side-pods, which worked as a 'slide' for the exhaust blow, readdressing it down low as described in the 'New Solutions' section. The second technical rule concerned safety in the case of a side impact between cars. It was no coincidence that the crash test of the protection structure at the sides of the chassis was made more severe, with an upwards compression test and – a more evident matter – a brusque decrement in nose height was brought in and that led a number of cars to brandishing a step that was as unusual as it was in some cases ugly. As in 2011 the chassis' front hoop stayed at 625 mm from the reference plane but within just 150 mm it had to go to 550 mm. The large step was adopted by all the top teams' cars with the exception of McLaren.

## EXHAUST COMPARISON

When the intention of banning exhaust blow into the diffusers was made official at Silverstone, some thought of a return to technology introduced by Ferrari in 1998 by the then technical boss, Rory Byrne. Then the Federation imposed a highly detailed norm shown in a quick comparative illustration, using the outline of the Ferrari 150 Italia. The two different exhaust positions are synthesised: the one imposed in 2011 with the low blow directed to the diffusers' lateral channels, and the new version demanded by the 2012 regs with the exit a long way from the diffuser zone.

## NOSE

To limit danger in the case of lateral impact between two cars, the Federation made the side crash test more severe, especially bringing in a height reduction of the front of the car. The height of the first chassis hoop stayed at 625 mm from the reference plane as in 2011, but in just 150 mm it had to descend to 550 mm. That produced a kind of sharp step in the high point of the nose. It should be said, though, that not all the 2011 season cars exploited the maximum 625 mm to the limit. That was the case with McLaren, which already had a fairly low nose that season and was the only team – apart from Marussia – to not boast the step.

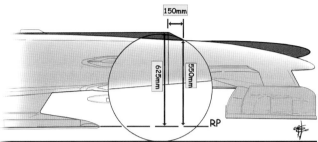

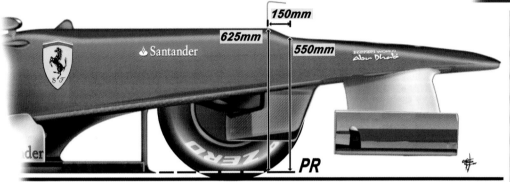

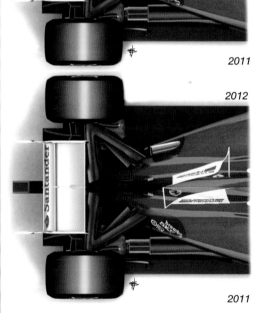

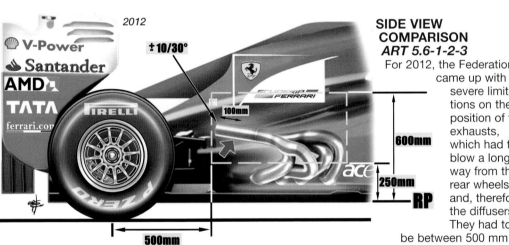

## SIDE VIEW COMPARISON
### ART 5.6-1-2-3

For 2012, the Federation came up with severe limitations on the position of the exhausts, which had to blow a long way from the rear wheels and, therefore, the diffusers. They had to be between 500 mm and 1200 mm from the rear axle and their height had to be between 250 mm and 600 mm from the reference plane and between 200 mm and 500 mm from the car's centre line in a transversal sense. The result was a 'box' to contain the exhausts that were 700 mm long, 300 mm wide and 350 mm high.

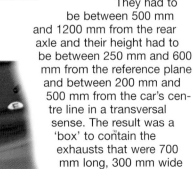

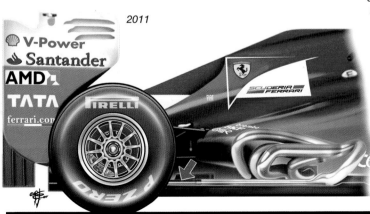

## TOP VIEW

In this comparison between the 2011 interpretation (above) and 2012 (below), the position of the exhaust terminals can be clearly seen, having been physically moved away from the diffuser area. In addition, the last 100 mm of the terminals had to be perfectly straight and positioned a long way from the rear axle, with a well determined inclination of their terminal portion of between 10° and 30° upwards in relation to the longitudinal axis and 10° in respect of the transverse one. Their shape was also fixed, with a round 75 mm diameter section.

## PROHIBITED FEATURES

The Federation not only prohibited exhaust blow directly into the diffusers, as can be seen in the first illustration, but it also brought in severe limitations on the shape of their terminals.

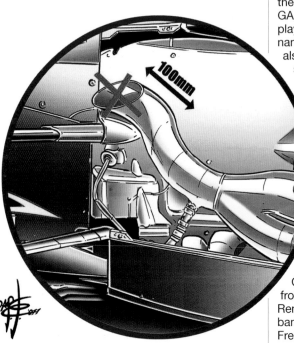

### FERRARI F2003-GA

There were no more oval shapes, like on the Ferrari F2003-GA, which clearly played an aerodynamic role as is also shown by the shape of the chimney around the exhaust and the extension in the lower area to switch the air flow to the beam wing.

## MERCEDES-BENZ

The Federation considered banning the sinuous progression of the exhaust terminals like those on the 2010 Mercedes-Benz, for example. The regulations said they had to be perfectly straight for the last 100 mm and with a freedom of angulation of between 10° and 30° in respect of the longitudinal and only 10° in relation to the transverse.

### RENAULT

Obviously, the front blow of the Renault was banned, even if the French manufacturer would certainly not have used this feature - because it turned out to be a failure. As well as the location of the exhausts in a precise position, the Federation also prohibited the oval section of the terminal part that had to be round and have a maximum 75 mm diameter.

### VIRGIN

And there was no room for this solution to the exhaust problem, with 'sliced salami' cuts as on the Virgin in the final stages of the 2011 season. In addition, exhausts had to be raised in relation to this positioning, inside the 'box' imposed by the Federation.

Only two regulations came into effect for the 2012 season: the prohibition of exhaust blow straight into the diffusers and the limitation of nose height, amply described in the New Regulations chapter. But despite that, the designers' imagination indulged itself by bringing to life numerous new developments, even if some of them were a return of those of the past. The former had been studied since the start of the 2011 season and tried out in secret during subsequent tests at the Abu Dhabi GP, but it was unable to get past the experimental stage on the track and did not even feature in the 2012 car projects. The device was the set-up corrector, developed by Renault and blocked after clarification had been requested of the Federation just before Christmas. The return of the front suspension tie rod layout was a subject of discussion during the winter

**2**

**1** **LOTUS**

Without the drum fairing that contained the braking system, one can see the upright with the lower wishbone hinged very high and underneath it; bottom right there is a small hydraulic cylinder and little piston (1) that do not appear on other F1 cars. The most important and determinate element of the pushrod suspension (2) which is not fixed directly to the upright mount but has some play (in yellow in the circular enlargement) due to a second small hydraulic power lift shown in blue at the pushrod's base  both operated by the brake pedal. That way, front end dive end under braking is opposed; this development was considered illegal by the Federation on the request for clarification by other teams in its function as a set-up corrector and mobile aerodynamic device.

break and then it actually appeared on the new Ferrari but only on that car, somewhat as happened in 2009 with the same item on the rear end of Adrian Newey's Red Bull.
Another return from the past was the aperture in the upper part of the chassis, which was banned by the Federation for the first time after Ferrari had introduced its version on the F2008. At the time, it was a winning device designed by engineer Aldo Costa, the car battling for the world title until the very last corner of the last GP; that was the last new development seen on the cars of the Prancing Horse before the current front suspension that made its debut in 2012.
It was an intelligent feature that meant improved aerodynamics in the front and would have spread the following season, if the Federation had not prohibited the passage of air between the lower and upper parts of the nose. Both Sauber and Red Bull took the same path with their cars' noses,

### FERRARI PULL-ROD

The possibility of also having a pull rod layout at the front end on the part of Ferrari was much discussed during the winter break with designers opinions divided, but in the end the great new development of the F2012 was really this return to the past, bringing back the pullrod suspension layout at the front. It was a system last used by Minardi during the 2001 season – 11 years earlier.
That decision was partly dictated by aerodynamic need to better manage air flow in the area between the wheel and the chassis. The advantage of being able to lower the centre of gravity was notable, with the suspension elements moved lower. In the illustration, the disposition was simply turned upside down, but the real layout envisaged a more complex location, with the elements prone down low, as they were on the Minardi.

with the Swiss team duplicating the development introduced by Ferrari as the great new feature of 2008, but with an aperture limited by the regulations of the period. The aperture in the stepped part of the Red Bull's nose worked differently, and was the brainchild of Adrian Newey for the RB7.
The development that set the trend and surprised everybody was certainly the shape of the terminal area of the Sauber's body and the partial return of exhaust blow due to a knowledgeable management of the Coandă effect; even if in a less effective manner than in 2011, exhaust blow went back to feeding the diffuser's lateral channels. Brake air intakes, the aerodynamic function of which has become basic to both the cars' front and rear ends, made an important contribution to air flow management in those zones.
The rear intakes brought in by Mercedes-Benz and Williams are worth mentioning as well as the fronts on the German car, as they moved the cooling task from the inside to the outside of the 'housings' in the small space between the latter and the tyre, notably improving aerodynamic efficiency in the channel between the wheel and the chassis; it was a design that soon set a trend.
And in the brake air intake area we saw another two unique developments: the opportunity of mechanics managing heat dissipation during a tyre change in such a way as to influence tyre temperatures, first used by McLaren, and the sophisticated creation of hubs and rims seen on the Red Bull RB7 project that were banned by the Federation after six races. It was a system that managed the flow of hot air through special apertures to improve aerodynamics in the outer area of the front wheels.

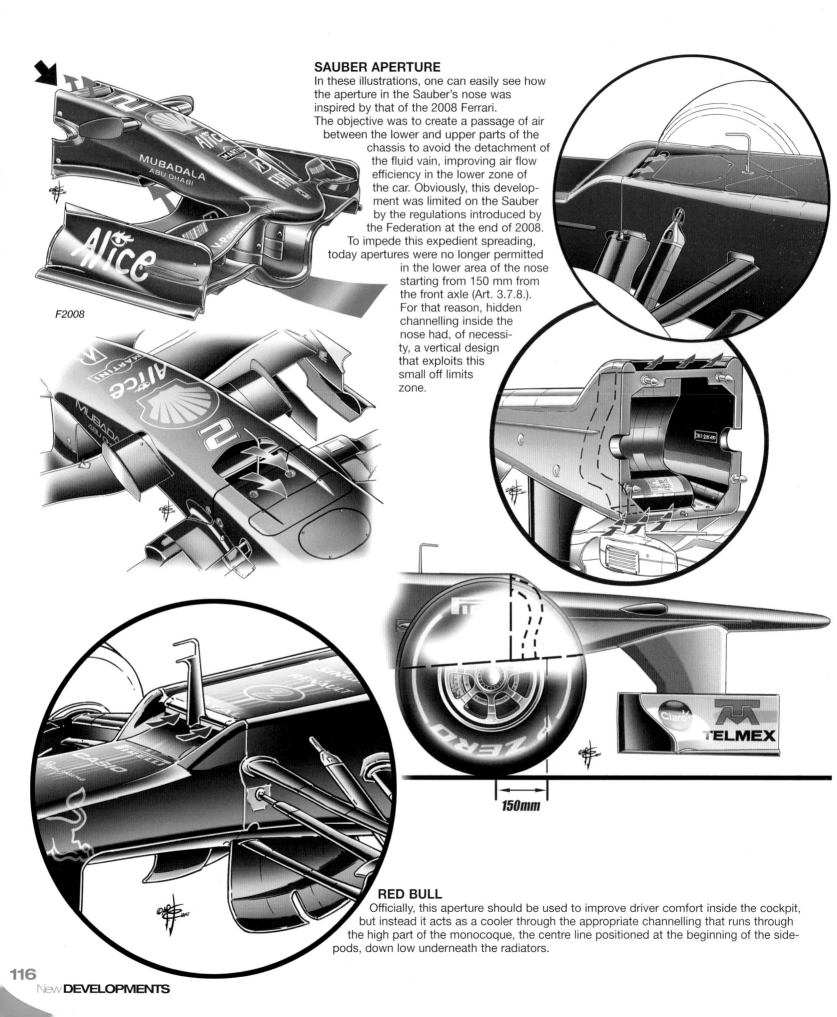

### SAUBER APERTURE

In these illustrations, one can easily see how the aperture in the Sauber's nose was inspired by that of the 2008 Ferrari. The objective was to create a passage of air between the lower and upper parts of the chassis to avoid the detachment of the fluid vain, improving air flow efficiency in the lower zone of the car. Obviously, this development was limited on the Sauber by the regulations introduced by the Federation at the end of 2008. To impede this expedient spreading, today apertures were no longer permitted in the lower area of the nose starting from 150 mm from the front axle (Art. 3.7.8.). For that reason, hidden channelling inside the nose had, of necessity, a vertical design that exploits this small off limits zone.

F2008

150mm

### RED BULL

Officially, this aperture should be used to improve driver comfort inside the cockpit, but instead it acts as a cooler through the appropriate channelling that runs through the high part of the monocoque, the centre line positioned at the beginning of the side-pods, down low underneath the radiators.

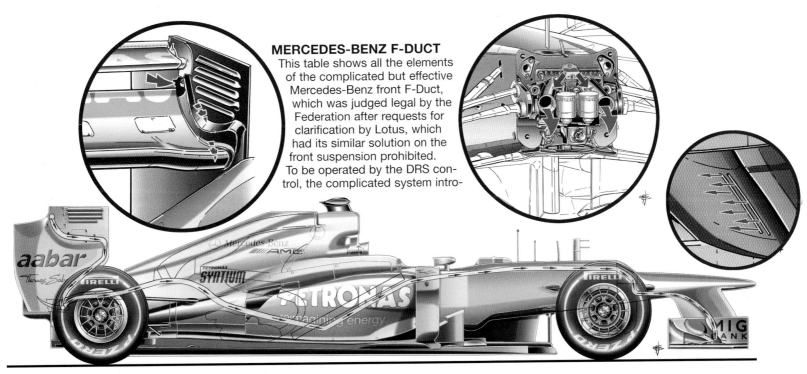

## MERCEDES-BENZ F-DUCT

This table shows all the elements of the complicated but effective Mercedes-Benz front F-Duct, which was judged legal by the Federation after requests for clarification by Lotus, which had its similar solution on the front suspension prohibited. To be operated by the DRS control, the complicated system intro-

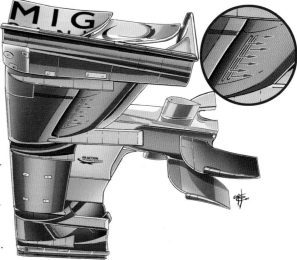

duced by Mercedes-Benz envisaged the entry of air from the end plates of the rear wing through a special aperture visible in the circle. The flow then passed through the end plates, the beam wing and then flowed along the whole car with a channelling of about ¾ cm diameter. It then exited from the front of the chassis (second circle) to blow through the front wing support pillars and into the lower part of the flap (last detail). In the illustration of the wing seen from below, we can clearly see the two apertures that stall the front wing at the same time as the DRS is operated.

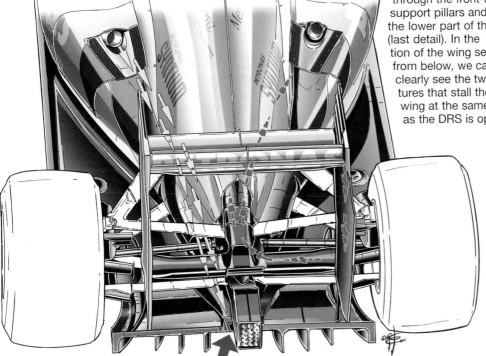

## MERCEDES-BENZ

The front F-Duct fed through a special aperture at the adjustable flap movement point (see the blue arrows) was not the only new Mercedes-Benz development. Another was the exploitation of the off limits zone of the central 15 cm in order to create a sort of double diffuser also partially fed by exhaust blow, which digresses from the feature used by almost all the cars of McLaren and Sauber.

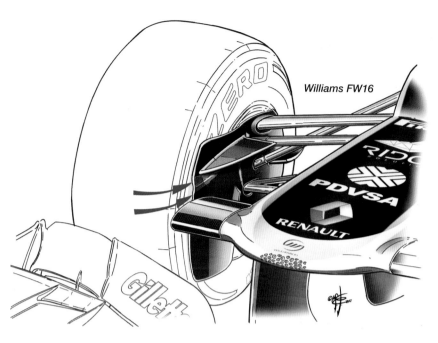
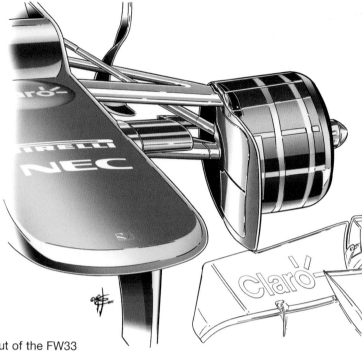

*Williams FW16*

## WILLIAMS-SAUBER

Williams must take the credit for having introduced brake air intakes on the debut of the FW33 without 'ears' inside them. They took their air from the small space between the carbon fibre housing and the rim, with obvious benefits for the quality of the flow inside the channel between the wheel and chassis. There was no longer the harmful turbulence generated by the old intakes with their 'ears' and in their place there were just deflectors to straighten the flow towards the centre of the car. And that was a feature copied immediately by Sauber (side illustration) from pre-season testing and by Ferrari from the GP of Canada.

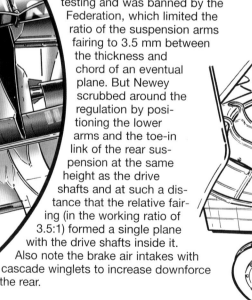
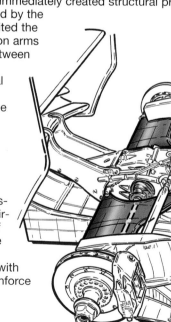

## RED BULL

Adrian Newey brought back faired drive shafts first seen on the unfortunate Williams FW16 in 1994. At the time, the ingenious technician placed a large wing plane that incorporated the upper wishbone and the drive shafts. It was a technique that immediately created structural problems during testing and was banned by the Federation, which limited the ratio of the suspension arms fairing to 3.5 mm between the thickness and chord of an eventual plane. But Newey scrubbed around the regulation by positioning the lower arms and the toe-in link of the rear suspension at the same height as the drive shafts and at such a distance that the relative fairing (in the working ratio of 3.5:1) formed a single plane with the drive shafts inside it. Also note the brake air intakes with cascade winglets to increase downforce at the rear.

## FERRARI

The pre-season tests saw many different Ferrari exhaust developments for the F2012.

Initially, the terminals were faired inside the body (see large illustration) that acted as a conveyor to direct the hot air flow towards the lower area and brush the internal part of the rear wheels. It was a feature also adopted by McLaren and that came to light due to the position of the thermo tape and protection applied at Jerez to the lower part of the wing's end plates (circle below, right); from the early laps, the upper part of the body was cut and that 'cooked' due to the high temperature (detail, left). And during the first test session, longer terminals that were more inclined inwards were tried and it seemed they gave good results (centre circle).

In the subsequent test at Barcelona there was an even more similar version to the one with the blow towards the central area of the Red Bull, with a further vent of the body and the terminals moved more to the interior (large circle, above), which used the development for the Red Bull's debut. It was a version that was retained for the early races.

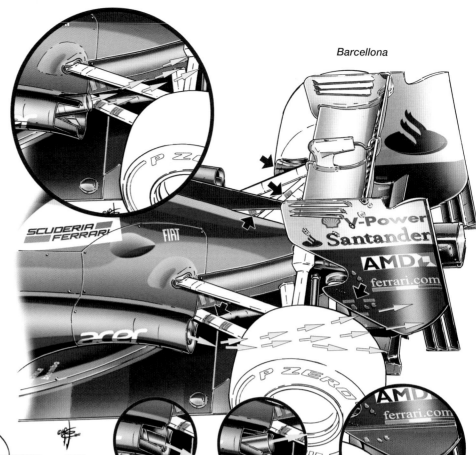

*Barcellona*

*Jerez*

## SAUBER

The major new pre-season development came from Sauber, which had dropped the classic Coca-Cola shape in the terminal part of the body in favour of sidepods that ended as far as the raised plane, as on some F3 cars. In practice, it had a sort of slide, which, due to the Coandă effect, conveyed the hot air flow from the exhaust to the bottom of the rear wheels and, therefore, towards the lateral channels of the diffuser.

## McLAREN

To McLaren goes the credit for being the first to hit on the idea of positioning the exhausts and the shape of the body in this zone. In practice, it brought to life a kind of tunnel/slide which, as always due to the Coandă effect, carried the air flow towards the diffuser's lateral channels. A development that was then copied by many teams, Red Bull, Sauber, Force India, Williams, Toro Rosso and Ferrari in chronological order.

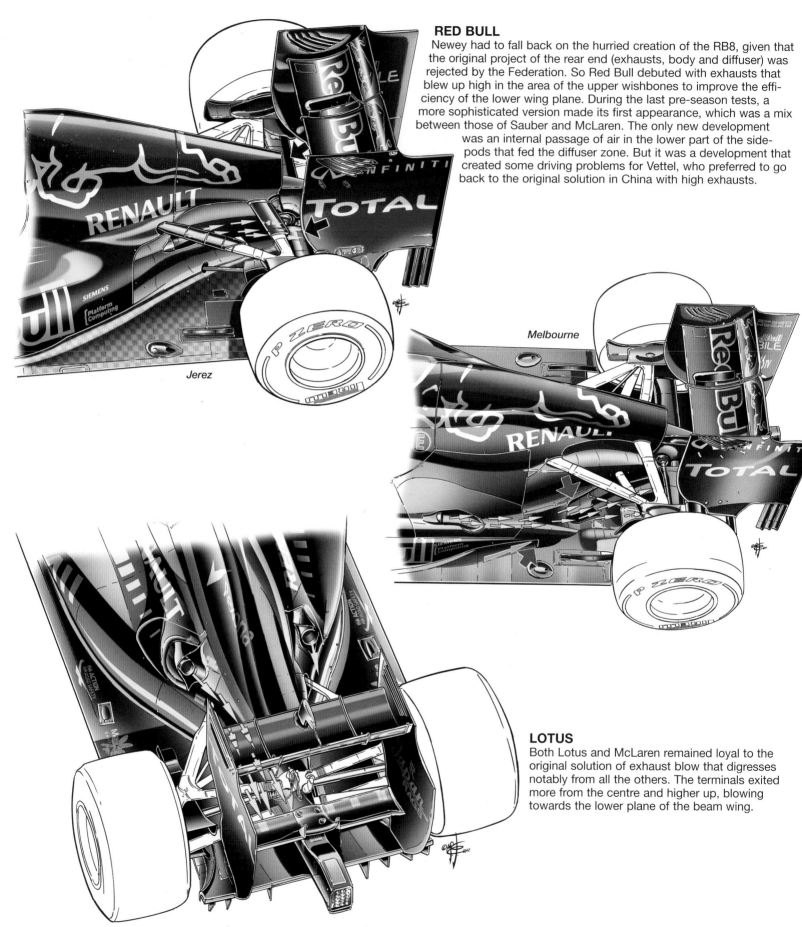

## RED BULL

Newey had to fall back on the hurried creation of the RB8, given that the original project of the rear end (exhausts, body and diffuser) was rejected by the Federation. So Red Bull debuted with exhausts that blew up high in the area of the upper wishbones to improve the efficiency of the lower wing plane. During the last pre-season tests, a more sophisticated version made its first appearance, which was a mix between those of Sauber and McLaren. The only new development was an internal passage of air in the lower part of the sidepods that fed the diffuser zone. But it was a development that created some driving problems for Vettel, who preferred to go back to the original solution in China with high exhausts.

*Jerez*

*Melbourne*

## LOTUS

Both Lotus and McLaren remained loyal to the original solution of exhaust blow that digresses notably from all the others. The terminals exited more from the centre and higher up, blowing towards the lower plane of the beam wing.

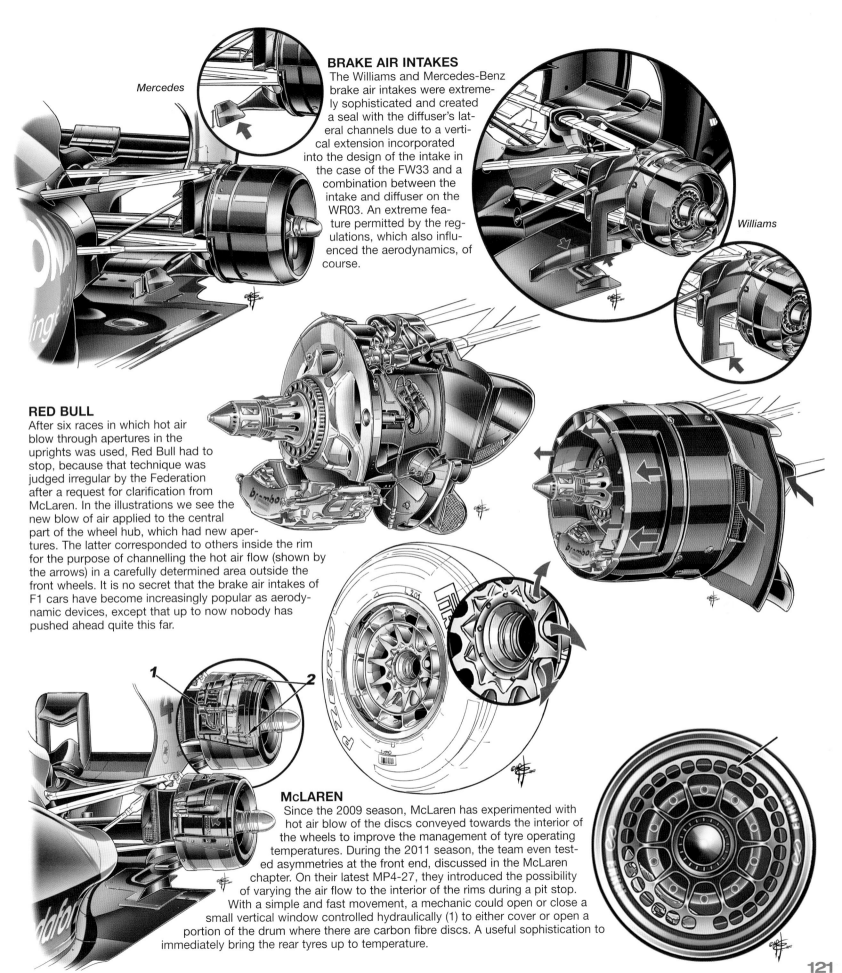

*Mercedes*

## BRAKE AIR INTAKES

The Williams and Mercedes-Benz brake air intakes were extremely sophisticated and created a seal with the diffuser's lateral channels due to a vertical extension incorporated into the design of the intake in the case of the FW33 and a combination between the intake and diffuser on the WR03. An extreme feature permitted by the regulations, which also influenced the aerodynamics, of course.

*Williams*

## RED BULL

After six races in which hot air blow through apertures in the uprights was used, Red Bull had to stop, because that technique was judged irregular by the Federation after a request for clarification from McLaren. In the illustrations we see the new blow of air applied to the central part of the wheel hub, which had new apertures. The latter corresponded to others inside the rim for the purpose of channelling the hot air flow (shown by the arrows) in a carefully determined area outside the front wheels. It is no secret that the brake air intakes of F1 cars have become increasingly popular as aerodynamic devices, except that up to now nobody has pushed ahead quite this far.

## McLAREN

Since the 2009 season, McLaren has experimented with hot air blow of the discs conveyed towards the interior of the wheels to improve the management of tyre operating temperatures. During the 2011 season, the team even tested asymmetries at the front end, discussed in the McLaren chapter. On their latest MP4-27, they introduced the possibility of varying the air flow to the interior of the rims during a pit stop. With a simple and fast movement, a mechanic could open or close a small vertical window controlled hydraulically (1) to either cover or open a portion of the drum where there are carbon fibre discs. A useful sophistication to immediately bring the rear tyres up to temperature.

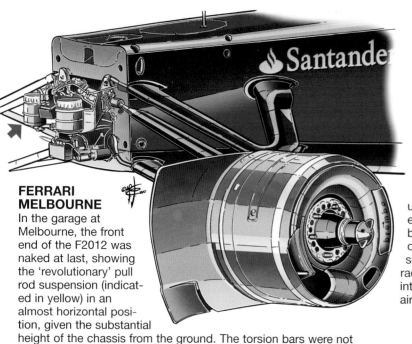

## FERRARI MELBOURNE

In the garage at Melbourne, the front end of the F2012 was naked at last, showing the 'revolutionary' pull rod suspension (indicated in yellow) in an almost horizontal position, given the substantial height of the chassis from the ground. The torsion bars were not in a long line from the front anymore: there were only fixing holes for the nose, but set much lower and almost vertically in the suspension's rockers, the elements of which have been moved down. The brake air duct was derived from the last version to have been introduced the previous season.

## FERRARI

As well as its vertical radiators, there was for the first time a connection between the gearbox and the chassis on the F2012, as on the Renault. It provided greater overall stiffness , much appreciated by Fernando Alonso when he won his world championships with the French constructor. This feature was introduced to make up for the lesser rigidity of the then new 111° V engine in 2001, but from that moment it became an integral part of all the subsequent French cars. The illustration shows the faring that hides the oil radiator, cooled by the ear-type intake behind the main air box.

## SAUBER SEPANG

Perhaps it was the Swiss team that set most trends right from the car's debut, especially for the position of its exhausts and the hot air outlet of the sidepods (indicated by the red arrow). At the second round at Sepang, clarification of the cut (shown in yellow) in front of the rear wheels was requested: it allowed part of the flow from the exhausts to pass through the lower area of the lateral channels. The technique was pronounced legal because it had no closed perimeter, which is prohibited by the regulations.

## SEPANG RED BULL

Red Bull brought in a new nose in Malaysia and experimented with two bodies in the exhaust area. Webber began testing a feature introduced in Australia, which is in the circle. Vettel went back to the debut version on the track during the last pre-season test session at Barcelona. In the end, both raced with this second solution which, among other things, provided a more aggressive outward blow.

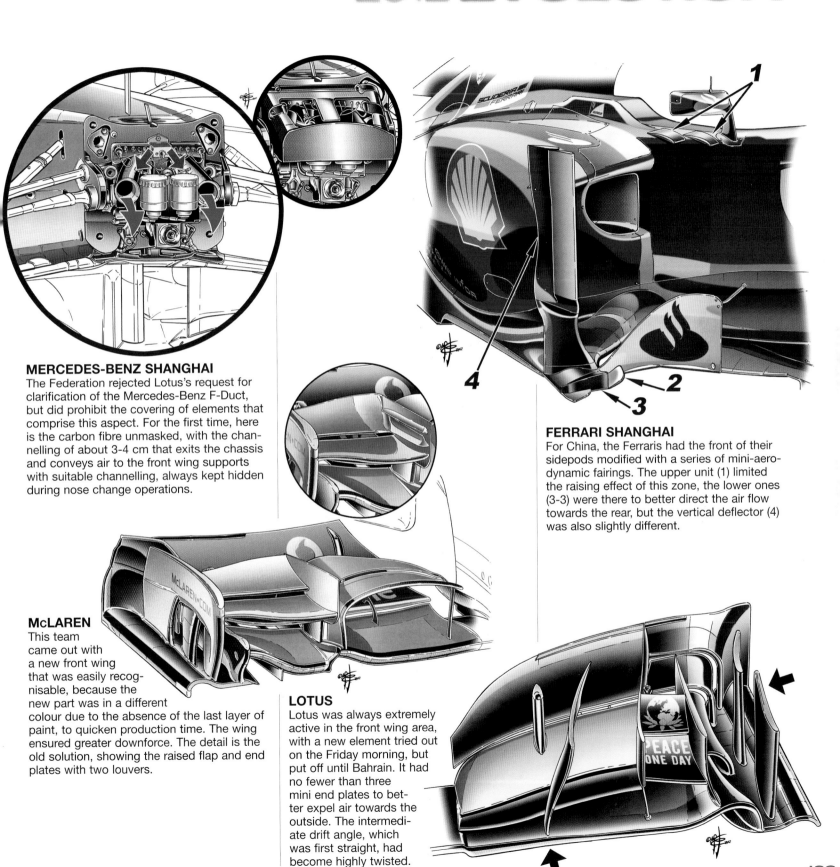

## MERCEDES-BENZ SHANGHAI

The Federation rejected Lotus's request for clarification of the Mercedes-Benz F-Duct, but did prohibit the covering of elements that comprise this aspect. For the first time, here is the carbon fibre unmasked, with the channelling of about 3-4 cm that exits the chassis and conveys air to the front wing supports with suitable channelling, always kept hidden during nose change operations.

## FERRARI SHANGHAI

For China, the Ferraris had the front of their sidepods modified with a series of mini-aerodynamic fairings. The upper unit (1) limited the raising effect of this zone, the lower ones (3-3) were there to better direct the air flow towards the rear, but the vertical deflector (4) was also slightly different.

## McLAREN

This team came out with a new front wing that was easily recognisable, because the new part was in a different colour due to the absence of the last layer of paint, to quicken production time. The wing ensured greater downforce. The detail is the old solution, showing the raised flap and end plates with two louvers.

## LOTUS

Lotus was always extremely active in the front wing area, with a new element tried out on the Friday morning, but put off until Bahrain. It had no fewer than three mini end plates to better expel air towards the outside. The intermediate drift angle, which was first straight, had become highly twisted.

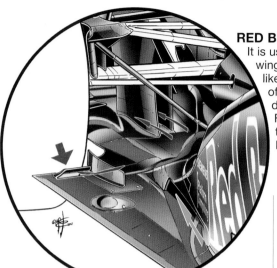

## RED BULL

It is useless trying to keep count of Red Bull's wings: refinements are always being made, like this small appendage in the area ahead of the rear wheels, which was stuck on during Friday afternoon practice.

First, one appeared on Webber's car and then on Vettel's, despite the more central higher blow preferred by the German.

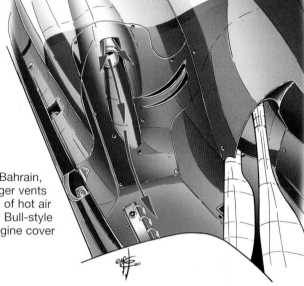

## SAUBER

In readiness for the tremendous heat of Bahrain, Sauber prepared new sidepods with bigger vents in the exhaust area for better evacuation of hot air from the radiators. But in the end, a Red Bull-style bigger oval aperture at the end of the engine cover was preferred.

## RED BULL

There was surprise that Adrian Newey had relinquished one of the new features of the RB8 project that seemed to be in difficulty in the early races of the season. In Saturday morning practice a new aerodynamic rear end appeared, in which the two entry intakes and outlets at the end of the sidepods were closed, as shown in the illustration below. That should have brought important aerodynamic benefits, but instead their abolition improved the car's handling. The two drivers only used the two extreme exhaust versions, and then both of them opted for the type used by Webber in China.

## FERRARI SAKHIR

There was a new front wing for Ferrari in Bahrain, which had a different end plate linkage (1) of the raised flaps to improve plane efficiency and reduce negative vortices in that zone. The part of the flap near the end plates (2) was also different to improve air flow towards the outside of the wheel.

## PROTEST AGAINST RED BULL

The protest began in Bahrain in 2011 and then it was happened officially in Monaco against the Red Bull hole in the area in front of the rear wheels. The discussion revolved around the fact that the regulations prohibited complete holes, while they allowed apertures provided they had no closed perimeter. That was the case with the Sauber and Ferrari, each of which had a small cut in the perimeter of the hole.

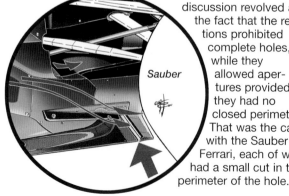

*Red Bull*

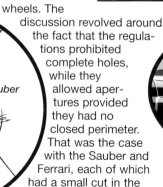

*Sauber*

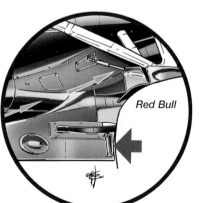

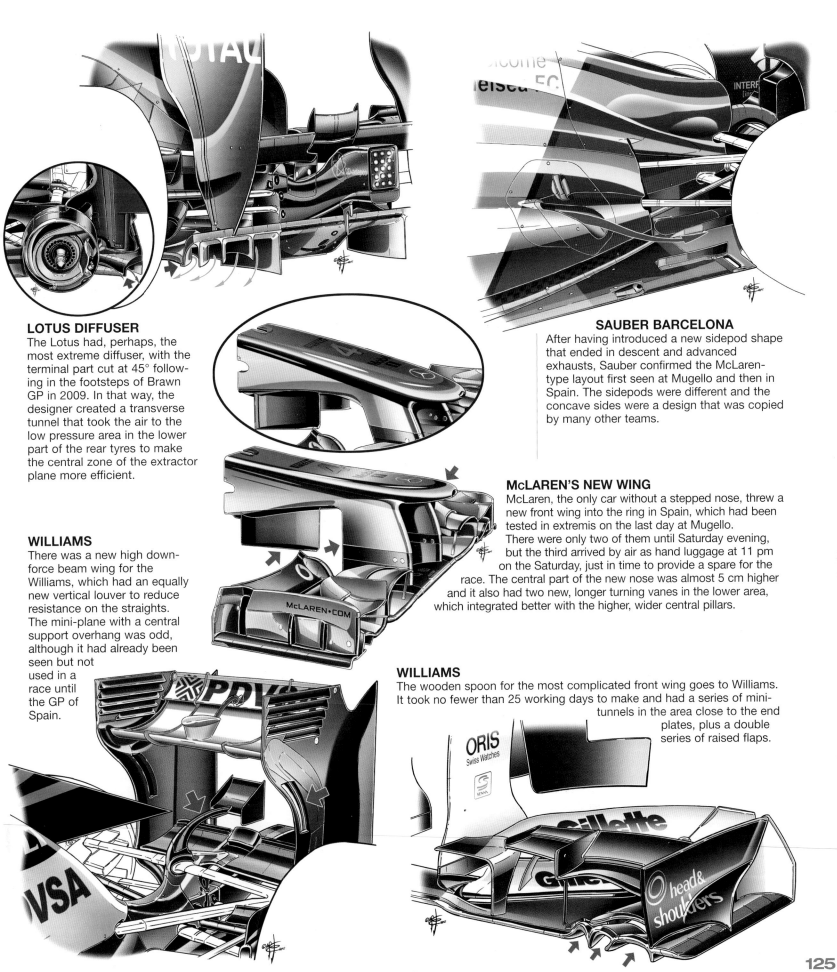

## LOTUS DIFFUSER

The Lotus had, perhaps, the most extreme diffuser, with the terminal part cut at 45° following in the footsteps of Brawn GP in 2009. In that way, the designer created a transverse tunnel that took the air to the low pressure area in the lower part of the rear tyres to make the central zone of the extractor plane more efficient.

## WILLIAMS

There was a new high down-force beam wing for the Williams, which had an equally new vertical louver to reduce resistance on the straights. The mini-plane with a central support overhang was odd, although it had already been seen but not used in a race until the GP of Spain.

## SAUBER BARCELONA

After having introduced a new sidepod shape that ended in descent and advanced exhausts, Sauber confirmed the McLaren-type layout first seen at Mugello and then in Spain. The sidepods were different and the concave sides were a design that was copied by many other teams.

## McLAREN'S NEW WING

McLaren, the only car without a stepped nose, threw a new front wing into the ring in Spain, which had been tested in extremis on the last day at Mugello. There were only two of them until Saturday evening, but the third arrived by air as hand luggage at 11 pm on the Saturday, just in time to provide a spare for the race. The central part of the new nose was almost 5 cm higher and it also had two new, longer turning vanes in the lower area, which integrated better with the higher, wider central pillars.

## WILLIAMS

The wooden spoon for the most complicated front wing goes to Williams. It took no fewer than 25 working days to make and had a series of mini-tunnels in the area close to the end plates, plus a double series of raised flaps.

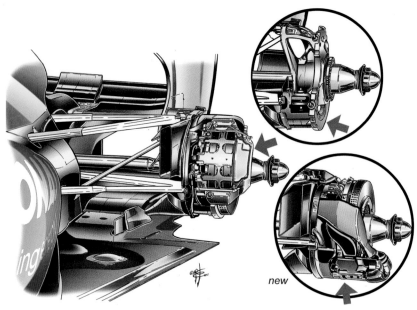

## FERRARI MONACO

Fernando Alonso and Felipe Massa raced with various front turning vanes: the Brazilian used an oval one under the chassis a la Red Bull, while the Spaniard the usual ones under the nose. The brake air ducts with the modified Red Bull-style turning vanes were new and fed more air to the ear intake. They then introduced faring in the area of the small brake cylinders to protect them from knocks when changing the nose, like Mercedes-Benz.

*new*

*Massa*

## MERCEDES-BENZ BARCELONA

The Mercedes-Benz that appeared at Barcelona was almost a 'B' version, with the new wider nose tested at Mugello, a new carbon fibre gearbox and different rear suspension down low. The brake calipers were positioned differently and were no longer vertical in front of the rear axle but horizontal and the suspension geometry was also new. New sidepods bowed in at Monaco, so Mercedes had to do all the crash tests – front, side and rear – again.

## FERRARI EXHAUSTS

Ferrari went back to the original low blow to the bottom of the rear wheel, but they did so by joining the group of cars that took up the technique pioneered by McLaren at the beginning of the season and, obviously, with a similar design to the one on the Sauber since Mugello testing. In the comparison, we can

*Monaco*

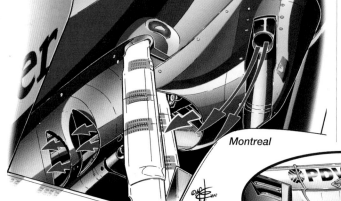

*Montreal*

## WILLIAMS

For the fast Canadian track, Williams came out with a much different rear wing than the other teams, among other things with an upturned spoon shape, which in practice was the opposite of the one they used for the 2011 GP there. But this time, the new wing was used for both qualifying and the race.

2

easily see how the blow of the old system retained for Monaco was mainly internal. Note the new Williams-type brake air ducts (1) with the long vertical seal. One of the many winglets applied to the brake ducts already there for Monaco is also visible and was there to create downforce. At Montreal, they added two longitudinal finlets to better direct the air flow to the inside of the rear wheels.

1

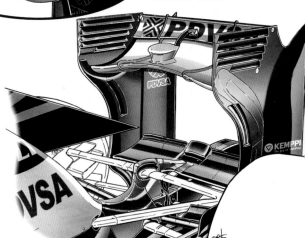

## RED BULL RB8 D

An almost completely new version of the RB8 was taken to Valencia. Adrian Newey once again brought back the blow that travelled to the inside of the terminal area of the sidepods but in a more sophisticated manner, with its aerodynamics completely revised. This revision had a certain similarity to the shape of the first of the kind by Sauber, with a body that did not narrow like a Coca-Cola bottle, but almost widened to end at the level of the raised plane.

The entry mouth of the internal channel was notably enlarged to then divide itself into two separate channels: the first to flow in the starter hole area and the second blew to lap against the side channels of the diffuser. The hot air outlet was also different, as it was in the zone in front of the drive shafts but almost at the end of the gearbox.

## McLAREN

This team's experiments continued at Valencia, with the new rear suspension first seen in Canada on Lewis Hamilton's car, but it was only tested by Jenson Button on the Saturday in Spain. It had a different front arm mount of the upper wishbone to modify its anti-dive characteristics.

## RENAULT

Romain Grosjean qualified and raced with a new front wing, while Kimi Raikkonen used the one from Montreal. The differences are numerous: the connection of the raised flaps with the end plates (1) was round to improve efficiency. And a small vertical slot (2) was added as well as a new curled 2 cm high Gurney flap (3) in the last flap, which ended with an inwards blow (4) that was not on the Canadian version. This latest modification was also fitted to Raikkonen's car for both qualifying and the race.

## FERRARI VALENCIA

The Valencia win came at the culmination of a development phase of the new aerodynamic package, centred on new McLaren-style exhausts first seen in Canada. The package also included a new front wing; two different kinds of turning vanes at the front, with Alonso loyal to those applied underneath the nose (see the large illustration) and Massa the new, oval Red-Bull-style ones; new brake ducts a la Williams; different aerodynamic appendages in the sidepods area; new exhausts; new engine cover; an evolution of the diffuser and rear wing assembly.

**Giorgio Nada Editore Srl**

*Editorial manager*
Leonardo Acerbi

*Editorial coordination*
Giorgio Nada Editore

*Graphic design and cover*
Aimone Bolliger

*Contributors*
Franco Nugnes (engines)
Ing. Giancarlo Bruno (suspensions and tyres)

*Computer graphic*
Alessia Bardino
Camillo Morande
Elena Cerro
Gisella Nicosia
Marco Verna

*3D animations*
Camillo Morande
Generoso Annunziata

Printed in Italy by
Grafiche Flaminia Srl
Foligno (PG)
September 2012

© 2012 Giorgio Nada Editore, Vimodrone (Milan, Italy)

*The catalogue of Giorgio Nada Editore publications is available on request at the address below.*

Giorgio Nada Editore
Via Claudio Treves,15/17
I - 20090 VIMODRONE MI
Tel. +39 02 27301126
Fax +39 02 27301454
e-mail: info@giorgionadaeditore.it
www.giorgionadaeditore.it

*Distribution*
**Giunti Editore Spa**
via Bolognese 165
I - 50139 FIRENZE
www.giunti.it

Formula 1 2011-2012. Technical analysis
ISBN 978-88-7911-553-7